C0-ARR-814

Inside Washington

Government Resources For International Business

William A. Delphos

THOMSON

Australia · Canada · Mexico · Singapore · Spain · United Kingdom · United States

THOMSON
SOUTH-WESTERN

Inside Washington
William A. Delphos

Vice President/ Editorial Director
Jack Calhoun

Vice President/ Editor-in-Chief
Dave Shaut

Acquisitions Editor
Steve Momper

Channel Manager, Retail
Chris McNamee

Channel Manager, Professional
Mark Linton

Production Manager
Patricia Matthews Boies

Production Editor
Darrell E. Frye

Manufacturing Coordinator
Charlene Taylor

Senior Designer
Mike Stratton

Compositor
Navta Associates, Inc.

Printer
Phoenix Book Technology
Hagerstown, MD

International Division List

ASIA (Including India):
Thomson Learning
60 Albert Street, #15-01
Albert Complex
Singapore 189969
Tel 65 336-6411
Fax 65 336-7411

AUSTRALIA/ NEW ZEALAND:
Nelson
102 Dodds Street
South Melbourne
Victoria 3205
Australia
Tel 61 (0)3 9685-4111
Fax 61 (0)3 9685-4199

LATIN AMERICA:
Thomson Learning
Seneca 53
Colonia Polanco
11560 Mexico, D.F. Mexico
Tel (525) 281-2906
Fax (525) 281-2656

CANADA:
Nelson
1120 Birchmount Road
Toronto, Ontario
Canada M1K 5G4
Tel (416) 752-9100
Fax (416) 752-8102

UK/EUROPE/MIDDLE EAST/AFRICA:
Thomson Learning
Berkshire House
168-173 High Holborn
London WC1V 7AA
United Kingdom
Tel 44 (0)20 497-1422
Fax 44 (0)20 497-1426

SPAIN (includes Portugal):
Paraninfo
Calle Magallanes 25
28015 Madrid
España
Tel 34 (0)91 446-3350
Fax 34 (0)91 445-6218

TABLE OF CONTENTS

Appendices

Acknowledgments

The publication of this book would not have been possible without the dedication and cooperation of a significant number of people, both within our organization as well as in the government and other various organizations. We would like to express our gratitude for their contributions.

The diligent and dedicated research team at Delphos International spent many hours working with government agencies and multilateral development organizations to provide the most up-to-date, comprehensive information possible. Once the information was obtained, it was synthesized and rewritten for the business audience based on our practical use of many of the programs.

We would especially like to thank Jennifer Daines and the following individuals for their diligence and dedication to this new edition: Svetoslav Gatchev, Linda Habgood, Dominic Miller, Mark Mondik, Todd Morath, Tsewang Namgyal, Ksenia Serebryanikova, Suzi Sidek, and Sinan Yircali.

William A. Delphos
March 2004
Washington, D.C.

Preface

Imagine walking into the neighborhood grocery store to buy a jar of chunky peanut butter. As you enter the store, you are stunned to discover that the aisles have been rearranged. Instead of familiar product groups, the displays are organized by manufacturer—Procter & Gamble, General Mills, Del Monte, Kraft, and so forth. What should have been a simple shopping excursion has now become a bizarre hunting expedition, where success rests on a combination of dogged determination and hours spent watching CNBC. Who manufactures peanut butter? Which company makes chunky peanut butter? And who makes chunky peanut butter in a recyclable plastic tub?

Several U.S. government agencies, development finance institutions, and Washington, D.C.-based offices of foreign government agencies provide services for U.S. businesses seeking to enter the international marketplace. The purpose of this book is to make information about U.S. government assistance and resources more accessible to the international business community. The book is designed to unscramble the scores of government programs available for American and international firms seeking to do business globally—taking them off the shelves now marked U.S. Department of Commerce, Export-Import Bank of the United States (Ex-Im Bank), United States Small Business Administration (SBA), Overseas Private Investment Corporation (OPIC), International Finance Corporation (IFC) and putting them on more logical shelves such as financing, regulations, and market information.

When I first arrived in Washington in 1981 to take an appointment at OPIC, I was amazed at the range and scope of government resources available to help companies expand overseas. I realized that I could have used many of the programs in my previous position as managing director of international operations at a large multinational corporation. My research and experience confirmed that the vast majority of business executives also were unaware of these "well-kept secrets."

Since that time, Washington's approach to supporting the overseas expansion of U.S. companies has changed significantly. Government agencies work more closely with each other to assist the business community. Ex-Im Bank, OPIC, and the U.S. Trade and Development Agency (USTDA) now take a more proactive approach. The Department of Commerce (DOC) and Department of State now advocate U.S. business positions abroad, and U.S. agencies are more sensitive to overseas competition and are more willing to neutralize the effects of subsidized financing from competitors. Recognizing the shortage of investment capital in the developing world (or "emerging markets" in today's parlance), the U.S. government has taken the lead to support a number of private equity funds that can shore up good overseas projects where existing lending programs and private capital are insufficient. Export assistance has become more accessible to businesses looking to broaden their operations.

While U.S. government agencies have "reinvented" themselves, development finance institutions such as the World Bank have recognized the critical role of private industry in emerging markets and have adjusted their lending programs accordingly. Development banks now actively work with OECD-based and local private businesses to spur growth and technology transfer to developing countries. On the public sector side, technical assistance, training, and improved procurement procedures make projects funded by these organizations multi-billion-dollar opportunities few companies can afford to pass up.

While it would be an exaggeration to suggest that this publication is all-inclusive, every effort has been made to include detailed descriptions of the major government programs available for U.S. businesses considering overseas operations. It is my hope that this book will make a significant contribution to strengthening the working partnership between the private sector and the government—a partnership that is critical for U.S. competitiveness and growth and for reducing poverty in the developing world.

William A. Delphos
March 2004
Washington, D.C.

Overview

Delphos International is proud to introduce the newly updated 2004 edition of *Inside Washington*. Since 1998, many changes have occurred in the policies, programs, and resources available to American businesses looking for opportunities abroad. Some government programs have been augmented or reinvented, while others have been discontinued. Many of the services and publications are now available online, making them easily accessible and affordable. Financial innovation continues as many agencies have rolled out new small business, corporate finance, and capital markets products and services. Development finance institutions (DFIs) and export credit agencies (ECAs) have grown substantially. Delphos International recently published two separate books on these organizations, *Inside the World's Development Finance Institutions* and *Inside the World's Export Credit Agencies*. Readers should consult those publications for in-depth coverage of DFIs and ECAs. *Inside Washington 2004* continues to cover Ex-Im Bank, the World Bank, IDB, and the other Washington D.C.-based ECAs and multilaterals.

With advances in technology, improved communication capabilities, and increased cooperation between governments, the importance of having access to the most accurate and up-to-date information has become critical for success in the international marketplace. While it would be impossible to include every new program or service available, the 2004 edition of *Inside Washington* is an up-to-the-minute, user-friendly guide to the broad array of resources available to businesses looking to expand into foreign markets. No batteries or Internet connection required!

WINNING GLOBALLY

The world is getting smaller. Global business opportunities have never been more abundant, and the importance of possessing the right information at the right time has never been clearer. In an era when global markets and worldwide business practices can be changed in one day by a single company such as Enron and when even the smallest companies are looking to capitalize on the benefits of overseas exports and imports, successful companies are the ones availing themselves of the right resources at the right time.

The Potential

Most executives in the United States are already aware of the potential for growth and new opportunities located beyond U.S. borders. Multinational corporations have long recognized the value of international expansion, and their investments have made enormous contributions to the acceleration of trade and economic growth in many areas of the world. However, if the United States is to maintain a competitive position in global commerce, more small- and medium-sized firms must be encouraged to enter international markets, especially those in the developing world, which are some of the fastest-growing customers for U.S. goods and services.

Advances in technology and transportation, combined with an increasingly supportive international business environment, have made the possibilities for growing companies immeasurable. Capitalizing on these opportunities, however, often proves a formidable challenge to even the most savvy of business executives. The maze of services, organizations, programs, and processes available seem to have no end, and as for finding the right officer in the right agency . . .

The Impact

To a great extent, the success or failure of these enterprises depends on their ability to cooperate and connect with the right resources and programs. Currently the stage is set to host a new era of international growth for small- and medium-sized U.S. firms as long as companies are able to access the financial and technical assistance required for expansion. Most of the government financing options available are offered at a much lower cost than other funding sources, providing a very appealing option to companies looking for assistance. The security, stability, financial backing, vast resources, and technical support available to projects funded in part by these agencies are unparalleled.

In addition to facilitating investment projects, financial institutions are beginning to emulate the World Bank and require added levels of social and environmental responsibility from borrowers interested in their services. In June of 2003, a group of ten commercial and investment banks became the first signatories to the Equator Principles. Institutions following these voluntary standards require that the development projects they support adhere to environmentally and socially sound policies. These policies are primarily defined by the International Finance Corporation (IFC) of the World Bank and ensure that basic levels of health and safety, pollution control, land acquisition, and natural resource preservation are maintained. Guaranteeing compliance with host country laws and regulations is of primary concern. This type of "corporate responsibility" is just one of the many recent trends in international business practice that is influenced by the leadership of the global development community.

About the Book

Until now, businesses seeking government assistance for international projects were often forced to wander through the bureaucratic labyrinth of Washington in search of answers. With this reference guide, however, the maze of agency authority lines has been erased. The book is a compilation of the scores of U.S. government-supported business assistance programs, many of which are still well-kept secrets that can connect businesspeople with the right programs and services. To minimize confusion while maximizing results, information in this book is arranged according to the type of assistance available rather than by agency. Readers unfamiliar with the international marketplace should notice that the chapters flow logically from "getting started" information to the nuts and bolts of putting together a business deal. The first three chapters focus on targeting and locating the appropriate service. Many of these products and services are now available online or outside the Beltway through a network of regional offices. The last four chapters, however, focus specifically on the products directly available to businesses and the organizations providing them. The organizations found in these chapters are exclusive to the Washington, D.C. area.

Most of the trade and investment incentive programs which help U.S. businesses compete internationally are administered by the federal government and multilateral organizations located in Washington, D.C. Organizations that provide this type of assistance include the Departments of Agriculture and Commerce, Office of the U.S. Trade Representative, U.S. Agency for International Development, Export-Import Bank of the United States, Overseas Private Investment Corporation, U.S. Small Business Administration, U.S. Environmental Protection Agency, U.S.

Trade and Development Agency, World Bank, International Finance Corporation, and the Inter-American Development Bank. Brief descriptions of these organizations and how they relate to promoting international business development can be found at the end of this chapter.

Chapter One: Obtaining Information

This chapter outlines the wide array of information available to U.S. firms considering international operations, including market background reports, statistical profiles, country economic analyses, and international demographic data. Organizations and services that assist business in finding this information are also included.

Chapter Two: Targeting Opportunities

This chapter contains information on specific programs—publications, databases, search services, and contract bid notifications—as well as information resources and services that are designed to help businesses identify specific international trade and investment opportunities.

Chapter Three: Regulations and Requirements

This chapter explores the regulations and requirements of doing international business. It covers information on international taxation issues, including foreign sales corporations and profit repatriation, as well as information on international agreements and treaties, rules and regulations, export license assistance, and host country incentives.

Chapter Four: Technical Assistance

This chapter provides detailed descriptions of the programs and services that help jump-start projects and provide project life cycle assistance. It includes feasibility study funding, training, advice, and assistance.

Chapter Five: Trade Assistance

This chapter describes financing and insurance programs, as well as other services that are available to support the exporting efforts of U.S. businesses. These services often improve and equalize competition for U.S. goods and provide the means needed to conduct international transactions that might not otherwise be possible.

Chapter Six: Project Finance

This chapter provides information on programs and products in support of foreign direct investment in emerging markets. Products described in this section include loans, guarantees, and equity, which are typically provided on an off-balance sheet, limited recourse basis.

Chapter Seven: Insurance

This chapter details the various types of political risk insurance and other forms of protection that are available for international ventures.

In addition to the contact information noted throughout the book, the appendices include relevant contact information for international, state, and regional offices of many government agencies.

No single volume can fully describe the scope and diversity of the hundreds of government programs that have been used to help companies expand internationally. Nevertheless, every effort has been made to present as much information as possible in an easy-to-understand format that can help business decision making to be more effective and productive.

Overview of Government Agencies

EXPORT-IMPORT BANK OF THE UNITED STATES (EX-IM BANK) The Export-Import Bank of the United States (Ex-Im Bank) provides financing support to facilitate exports of U.S. goods and services in order to create more U.S. jobs. Products include loans, guarantees, and credit insurance for U.S. exporters and their lenders that remove or mitigate the risk of default by the foreign buyer. Ex-Im Bank also provides working capital guarantees that allow small- and mid-sized U.S. businesses to expand their export programs by investing in inventory and providing terms to their overseas buyers. The agency also has a number of specialized products such as project and structured finance, aircraft finance, leasing, environmental technologies, and so forth.

INTER-AMERICAN DEVELOPMENT BANK (IDB) The Inter-American Development Bank (IDB), headquartered in Washington, D.C., is currently the primary lender to member countries in the Latin American and Caribbean region. IDB has become more involved in recent years in promoting private sector development. The Inter-American Investment Corporation (IIC), an affiliate of IDB, provides financing for private sector investment projects in Latin America and the Caribbean. IIC was capitalized in 1986 with $200 million with the primary objective of promoting the development of private enterprise in IDB's regional member countries. Additionally, IDB also has increased efforts within its own Private Sector Department to handle larger loans than those typically handled by IIC.

OVERSEAS PRIVATE INVESTMENT CORPORATION (OPIC) The Overseas Private Investment Corporation (OPIC) is a U.S. government agency that promotes private investment in developing countries through financing, political risk insurance, and private equity funds. These programs are available for development projects that involve U.S. investment and that have strong, positive benefits for the host country. Projects must not have an adverse impact on the U.S. economy, employment, or the environment. OPIC operates its programs in more than 140 developing countries.

UNITES STATES AGENCY FOR INTERNATIONAL DEVELOPMENT (USAID) The U.S. Agency for International Development (USAID) supports assistance projects to further economic and social development in developing countries. This is done through specific development projects, debt-for-equity swaps, loans, and grants given on concessional terms to less developed countries. Areas of assistance include agriculture, health, population control, education, human resources, and housing, as well as support for private voluntary organizations. USAID also provides funding for population assistance, economic reform, and stabilization and for other poverty alleviation programs. USAID maintains posts at dozens of U.S. embassies abroad. (See Appendix A for a list of USAID contacts.)

UNITED STATES DEPARTMENT OF AGRICULTURE (USDA) Through its Commodity Credit Corporation, the Department of Agriculture

(USDA) administers export sales and donations for foreign use through other agencies and provides export guarantees to foreign buyers. Its Foreign Agricultural Service gathers worldwide information through representatives stationed in 70 U.S. embassies, develops data to support trade, and works to reduce trade barriers. Its Office of International Cooperation and Development is responsible for international and technical cooperation for development assistance programs. (See Appendix D for a listing of USDA trade offices.)

UNITED STATES DEPARTMENT OF COMMERCE (DOC) The Department of Commerce (DOC) promotes domestic job creation, economic growth, sustainable development, and improved living standards by working in partnership with businesses, universities, communities, and workers. Primarily domestic-oriented financing mechanisms are made available through various DOC departments (see Appendix B). The International Trade Administration (ITA) department coordinates issues relating to trade programs and export policies, along with providing assistance and information for U.S. exporters. ITA units (see Appendix C) are staffed by trade specialists in 48 district offices and 19 branch offices in industrial and commercial centers nationwide and include domestic and overseas commercial officers, country and industry experts that promote products and offer services and programs for the U.S. exporting community.

Through commercial sections located in U.S. embassies and consulates, the U.S. Commercial Service operates in 220 cities in 78 countries. It is composed of 1,400 U.S. officers and nationals of the various host countries. The Commercial Service also operates 92 Export Assistance Centers. It is principally charged with assisting U.S. businesses through one-on-one counseling, collecting and disseminating market insight information, and representing U.S. commercial interests to host-country governments and at an array of international trade shows and missions, as well as supporting other U.S. agencies' international programs.

UNITED STATES DEPARTMENT OF ENERGY (DOE) The U.S. Department of Energy (DOE) is a valuable source of technical, market, and financial assistance for U.S. firms specializing in energy-related industries, especially those with a positive environmental impact. The DOE chairs the Committee on Renewable Energy Commerce and Trade (CORECT), an interagency working group of 14 federal agencies formed in 1984 to advance commerce and trade in renewable energy technologies by bringing together potential users, funding sources, and U.S. industry members to ensure that U.S. renewable energy applications are considered for viable applications throughout the world. The DOE also provides information, statistics, and reports on international trends and issues and provides resources for the energy industry.

UNITED STATES DEPARTMENT OF STATE Several offices of the U.S. Department of State offer assistance for exporters and valuable information resources. The Bureau of Economic, Business, and Agricultural Affairs provides export assistance to U.S. businesses about market conditions and export regulations for other countries and assists U.S. companies with protecting patents, trademarks, and copyrights against infringement while working in a foreign marketplace. Country desk officers (see Appendix A) can provide information on the current state of political, economic, and social affairs in a specific country, as well as provide contact information and advice for people visiting a foreign country for the first time.

UNITED STATES ENVIRONMENTAL PROTECTION AGENCY (EPA) While known domestically as a federal regulatory agency, the U.S. Environmental Protection Agency (EPA) is a leading advocate of the U.S. environmental industry's interests in the world market. EPA is also a primary source of manuals, directories, clearinghouses, and databases, as well as other information on environmentally sound technologies. EPA sponsors and participates in technology cooperation programs, many of which involve international development projects. Through the EPA, companies can obtain information on the implementation of environmental regulations in developing countries, learn about EPA's technology transfer and technical assistance programs, and access computerized information on environmental technologies and regional environmental development projects.

UNITED STATES SMALL BUSINESS ADMINISTRATION (SBA) In addition to its domestic support programs, the U.S. Small Business Administration (SBA) offers financial assistance, counseling, export workshops, and training to help small- and medium-sized U.S. firms enter international markets. It provides loans and loan guarantees to U.S. companies for equipment, facilities, materials, and working capital and business development support for selected export market development activities. Export counseling services (see Appendix L) and marketing information are available at no cost from the agency's Service Corps of Retired Executives (SCORE) and by university students who participate in the Small Business Institute Program. In addition, Small Business Development Centers (SBDC) (see Appendix H) based at universities offer business counseling and assistance. Contact information for SBA District Offices can be found in Appendix G.

UNITED STATES TRADE AND DEVELOPMENT AGENCY (USTDA)
The U.S. Trade and Development Agency (USTDA) funds project identification missions, feasibility studies, orientation visits and reverse trade missions, technical symposia, training, information dissemination, and procurement promotion for major development projects in developing and middle-income countries. USTDA funding is geared toward introducing foreign government officials and private companies to U.S. companies and technology in the hope that these resources would be used during project implementation.

UNITED STATES TRADE REPRESENTATIVE (USTR) The Office of the
U.S. Trade Representative (USTR) is a cabinet-level agency that is responsible for the direction of trade negotiations, formulation of overall trade policy, and bilateral and multilateral negotiations pertaining to international environmental trade. USTR represents the United States in meetings with the World Trade Organization (WTO) and the Organization for Economic Cooperation and Development (OECD), as well as conducts negotiations with the United Nations Conference on Trade and Development (UNCTAD). USTR is also responsible for administering trade cases that provide relief from unfair trade practices.

WORLD BANK/INTERNATIONAL BANK FOR RECONSTRUCTION AND DEVELOPMENT (IBRD) The International Bank for Reconstruction and Development (IBRD), or World Bank, headquartered in Washington, D.C., is responsible for providing financial and technical assistance to developing countries to stimulate economic development. Owned by more than 140 member governments, the Bank makes structural adjustment loans to help developing countries effect policy changes and lends funds to creditworthy countries or their agencies, generally for specific development

projects. Through its procurement program, contract opportunities for suppliers of goods and services are available through international competitive bidding. The Bank maintains representative offices in 57 foreign countries.

INTERNATIONAL FINANCE CORPORATION (IFC) The International Finance Corporation (IFC), a member of the World Bank Group, is a multilateral development institution that promotes productive private investment that contributes to the economic growth of developing member countries. Its principal objective is to provide the financing, technical assistance, and management needed to develop productive investment opportunities. The IFC encourages the flow of private capital, both domestically and internationally, through the establishment or expansion of local capital markets and financial institutions.

MULTILATERAL INVESTMENT GUARANTEE AGENCY (MIGA) This arm of the World Bank Group offers political risk insurance and guarantees to investors and lenders in order to promote and facilitate foreign direct investment in emerging markets. MIGA products and services encourage and foster the growth of local businesses and investments in order to provide countries with the resources necessary for reducing poverty.

Other Recent Titles by William A. Delphos

Inside the World's Development Finance Institutions, 2004
Inside the World's Export Credit Agencies, 2003
Inside the World Bank Group: The Practical Guide for International Business Executives, 1998

For more information about these publications or additional titles, contact Delphos International at +1-202-337-6300 or visit its web site at *www.delphosinternational.com.*

Obtaining Information

Before expanding into the international marketplace, business executives should learn as much as possible about the opportunities and obstacles they are most likely to encounter. To successfully penetrate lucrative markets, targeted research is essential. Many executives are unaware of the numerous publications and services offered by the government and other sources to assist in collecting specific market information. The proper use of these resources can help businesses avoid costly mistakes and discover new opportunities. Due in large part to the Internet, most of these services, including newsletters, publications, and even magazines, are available free of charge or at a minimal cost. Most of the organizations and services provide detailed information through their web sites.

This chapter details many of the services that provide critical information to businesses seeking not only to survive, but also to succeed in foreign markets. This chapter outlines the publications, databases, organizations, and services available to assist businesses in obtaining information.

The following is a brief list of the key topics described in Chapter One:

- Country information and statistics
- Geographic and regional information
- Trade information
- Current affairs and opportunities
- Industry information
- Export information

PUBLICATIONS

United Nations

INTERNATIONAL TRADE STATISTICS YEARBOOK This yearbook is a publication of the United Nations and is useful for analyzing trade by country or commodity, performing trend analysis and projections, and developing marketing strategies. It provides basic information on an individual country's external trade performance by current value, volume, and price. It also highlights the importance of trading partners and the significance of imported and exported commodities. Statistical information on approximately 170 countries is available. The yearbook costs $135.

United Nations Publications
Two United Nations Plaza, Room DC 2-853
New York, NY 10017
Tel: 800-253-9646
            212-963-8302
Fax: 212-963-3489
E-mail: publications@un.org
Web: www.un.org/publications

U.S. Department of Agriculture (USDA)

FOREIGN AGRICULTURAL SERVICE (FAS) PUBLICATIONS The FAS provides extensive industry, country and topical market research to help pinpoint the best export markets, assess how particular markets adapt to local cultures and customs, and develop effective market entry strategies.

- AGRIBiz Markets and Analysis
- FAS Attaché Reports
- FAS Commodity Pages
- FAS World Market and Trade Short Reports
- FAS Hot Country Pages
- Market-Specific Reports provide country-specific descriptions of overseas markets for high-value agricultural products. Information presented includes product briefs, market overviews, import regulations, sector reports, and labeling requirements. These reports are available online at the following address or through the Trade Assistance and Promotion Office.

Foreign Agricultural Service
MS - 1060 (Room 4965-S)
Washington, DC 20250
Tel: 202-720-6713
Fax: 202-720-7138
E-mail: info@fas.usda.gov
Web: www.fas.usda.gov

U.S. Department of Commerce (DOC)

BASIC GUIDE TO EXPORTING This guide outlines the steps involved in exporting and provides practical information and sources of government assistance to exporters. It covers topics that range from identifying markets and developing an export strategy to conducting market research, traveling overseas, finding buyers, shipping, and financing. This guide is available domestically for $19/U.S. or $26.60/foreign.

Superintendent of Documents
U.S. Government Printing Office
Tel: 202-512-1800
Fax: 202-512-2250
Web: www.access.gpo.gov

COUNTRY COMMERCIAL GUIDES This series is prepared by the DOC's International Economic Policy Division to provide helpful background data for evaluating export markets. It discusses marketing factors in individual countries; presents economic and commercial profiles of countries and regions; issues semiannual outlooks for U.S. trade; analyzes each country's investment climate; and publishes selected statistical reports on the direction, volume, and nature of U.S. foreign trade. A complete listing of available guides by country can be found on several agencies' web sites, but the most convenient is the State Department, as listed below. These guides also can be ordered in hard copy.

National Technical Information Service
U.S. Department of Commerce
1401 Constitution Avenue, NW
Washington, DC 20230
Tel: 800-872-8723
Web: www1.usatrade.gov/website/ccg.nsf

EXPORT AMERICA This publication is the official magazine of the ITA and offers practical export advice and serves as a valuable resource for small- and medium-sized exporters. Each month Export America draws on the resources of ITA and other government agencies to feature regional developments, country- and industry-specific opportunities, trade event listings, technical advice, online marketing tips, and export statistics. Each article specifically focuses on the needs of small- and medium-sized firms and includes information on technical topics such as export doc-

3

umentation and market research. This combination of feature stories and hands-on exporting advice makes Export America an essential resource for any exporter looking to enter or expand in the global marketplace. Annual subscriptions are available for $58/U.S. or $81.20/foreign; single issues are $6/U.S. or $8.40/foreign.

Superintendent of Documents
U.S. Government Printing Office
Tel: 202-512-1800
Fax: 202-512-2250
E-mail: Export_America@ita.doc.gov
Web: www.trade.gov/exportamerica

U.S. Department of State

GUIDE TO DOING BUSINESS WITH THE DEPARTMENT OF STATE This publication assists small, minority, or female-owned businesses competing with other companies doing business with the U.S. Department of State. The guide summarizes procurement programs and opportunities available to disadvantaged groups. It includes descriptions and contact information for major categories of products and services, as well as a list of subcontracting opportunities. Furthermore, it lists federal offices that supply guidance on procurement procedures and contacts for trade and investment-related issues. It is available online at the following web address.

Superintendent of Documents
U.S. Government Printing Office
Tel: 202-512-1800
Fax: 202-512-2250
Web: www.state.gov/m/a/sdbu/pubs/c6543.htm

World Bank

GLOBAL DEVELOPMENT FINANCE The World Bank's authoritative annual review of developing countries' external debt and financial flows is an indispensable reference guide for economists, bankers, country risk analysts, financial consultants, and others involved in capital projects worldwide. Print and CD-ROM versions are priced at $400 for single users, and an Analysis and Summary version is available for $55.

World Bank Bookstore
701 18th Street, NW
Washington, DC 20433
Tel: 202-458-4500
Fax: 202-522-1500
E-mail: infoshop@worldbank.org
Web: www.worldbankinfoshop.org

WORLD BANK BOOKSTORE This bookstore offers many of the newest and most popular World Bank titles, catalogs, and brochures. Offerings cover topics such as project finance, globalization, emerging markets, development issues, and more. Complimentary copies of World Bank, IFC, and MIGA Annual Reports, as well as a comprehensive listing of publications may be found here.

World Bank Bookstore
701 18th Street, NW
Washington, DC 20433
Tel: 202-458-4500
Fax: 202-522-1500
E-mail: infoshop@worldbank.org
Web: www.worldbankinfoshop.org

WORLD DEVELOPMENT INDICATORS The World Bank has been publishing this resource for nearly two decades as the statistical appendix to the World Development Report. World Development Indicators is a freestanding publication, expanded to include more than 80 data tables and 800 indicators for single-year observations. It has become an invaluable source to those who analyze business opportunities in developing countries and emerging markets. Sections include World View, People, Environment, Economy, States and Markets, and Global Links. Online subscriptions are available for $100. A hard copy is $60; a CD ROM, $275.

World Bank Bookstore
701 18th Street, NW
Washington, DC 20433
Tel: 202-458-4500
Fax: 202-522-1500
E-mail: infoshop@worldbank.org
Web: www.worldbankinfoshop.org

Other

AMBER WAVES This publication from the Economic Research Service (ERS) offers a window into the broad range of ERS research and analysis. Published five times a year, Amber Waves covers topics on farming, natural resources, and rural America. Online and print editions are available. The print edition price is $39.95/U.S. or $79.90/foreign if you subscribe prior to the spring deadline and $49.95/U.S. or $99.90/foreign after that date.

Economic Research Service
1800 M Street, NW
Washington, DC 20036
Tel: 800-999-6779
            703-605-6060
Fax: 703-605-6880

GLOBAL TRADE OUTLOOK This comprehensive information source contains current information on the ten largest emerging markets. A detailed forecast of 27 major industries is included. It also gives projections of economic growth and trade and includes an appendix of economic and trade data by country. This publication is available online at the following web address.

Superintendent of Documents
U.S. Government Printing Office
Tel: 202-512-1800
Fax: 202-512-2250
Web: www.access.gpo.gov

GLOBAL TRADE TALK This bimonthly journal provides up-to-date information on customs rules and regulations, as well as the latest foreign government actions affecting U.S. companies. The cost is $12/year or $3/copy in the U.S. and $15/year or $3.75/copy outside the U.S.

Superintendent of Documents
U.S. Government Printing Office
Tel: 202-512-1800
Fax: 202-512-2250
Web: www.access.gpo.gov

WORLD FACTBOOK This annual publication produced by the Central Intelligence Agency (CIA) includes accurate, up-to-date information on countries and geographic areas of the world, including maps for each entry and color maps of major regions. Entries for each country cover geography, demography, governments, economy, communications, and defense forces. The most recent editions are available free online at the following web address, or you may purchase a hard copy using the following contact information.

Superintendent of Documents
U.S. Government Printing Office
Tel: 202-512-1800
Fax: 202-512-2250
Web: www.cia.gov/cia/publications/factbook

DATABASES

U.S. Department of Agriculture (USDA)

FOREIGN AGRICULTURAL TRADE OF THE UNITED STATES (FATUS)
FATUS is a database of U.S. agricultural exports and imports, by commodity, that includes all countries and regions of the world. FATUS is a standard aggregation of the original U.S. trade data found in the Harmonized Tariff Schedule (HTS) of the United States. The Census Bureau of the DOC disseminates original HTS data. FATUS consists of 211 trade groups created by USDA for the purpose of summarizing U.S. agricultural trade in a form most usable by the public.

Economic Research Service
1800 M Street, NW
Washington, DC 20036
Tel: 800-999-6779
         703-605-6060
Fax: 703-605-6880
Web: www.ers.usda.gov/db/FATUS

Other

EMERGING MARKETS DATABASE (EMDB) This database, provided by Standard & Poor's, covers 53 markets and more than 2,200 stocks. Drawing a sample of stocks in each EMDB market, Standard & Poor's calculates indices designed to serve as benchmarks that are consistent across national boundaries. The database also provides extensive statistics on emerging equity markets and incorporates information on performance, valuations, and country and regional index movements. The database has gained recognition as the world's primary source for reliable and comprehensive information and statistics on stock markets in developing countries. Pricing for this service is based on the scope of usage required.

Standard & Poor's
55 Water Street
New York, NY 10041
Tel: 212-438-2046
Web: www.spglobal.com

RELATIONAL WORLD DATA BANK II (RWDB2) This regularly updated data file is a global digital representation of cartographic features of the world for use in automated mapping systems. The cost for a three 9-track computer tape set is $240. Additionally, the Cartographic Automatic Mapping Program can be used in conjunction with the RWDB2 and performs a wide variety of cartographic functions.

U.S. Department of the Interior
Geological Survey—EROS Data Center
Sioux Falls, SD 57198
Tel: 605-594-6151

ORGANIZATIONS AND SERVICES

Department of Energy (DOE)

ENERGY INFORMATION ADMINISTRATION (EIA) Created in 1977 by Congress, EIA is the department responsible for gathering and maintaining information, statistics, forecasts, and other data related to the issues surrounding worldwide energy policies and trends. Services include a listing of publications, statistics for businesses, guides to energy resources, and key contacts. Most of the information is free of charge and available online.

Energy Information Administration
1000 Independence Avenue, SW
Washington, DC 20585
Tel: 202-586-8800
E-mail: infoctr@eia.doe.gov
Web: www.eia.doe.gov

OFFICE OF POLICY AND INTERNATIONAL AFFAIRS This office within the DOE is charged with providing accurate and unbiased information to the DOE as it relates to international energy policies, including emergency management, national security, and science and technology. The office provides reports on energy activity, links to other valuable web sites, and a library of articles and publications.

> Office of Policy and International Affairs
> Department of Energy
> 1000 Independence Avenue, SW
> Washington, DC 20585
> Tel: 202-586-8660
> Web: www.pi.energy.gov

Environmental Protection Agency (EPA)

INDUSTRY SECTOR-BASED ENVIRONMENTAL STRATEGIES, TOOLS AND RESOURCES (SECTORSTAR) This in-depth environmental performance information resource is available online to help businesses, states, and communities find useful, targeted information on environmental innovation and excellence. SectorSTAR is a free service backed by the experience and technical expertise of the Global Environment and Technology Foundation in partnership with the EPA. The site contains links to many other business-oriented environmental information networks, including Greenbiz Network and EPA's compliance assistance sites. SectorSTAR also provides online information on industry- and business-oriented environmental programs in all 50 states.

> Environmental Protection Agency
> OPEI/Sector Strategies Division
> 1200 Pennsylvania Avenue, NW
> Mail Code 1808T
> Washington, DC 20460
> Tel: 202-566-2992
> Fax: 202-566-2994
> Web: www.epa.gov

Overseas Private Investment Corporation (OPIC)

INFOLINE & FACTSLINE OPIC is an independent government agency that encourages American private businesses to invest in developing countries, newly emerging democracies, and free market economies. Through OPIC's InfoLine and FactsLine, callers can request information on programs, special reports, registration, application forms, and other publications.

Overseas Private Investment Corporation
1100 New York Avenue, NW
Washington, DC 20527
InfoLine
Tel: 202-336-8799
FactsLine
Tel: 202-336-8700
E-mail: info@opic.gov
Web: www.opic.gov

Small Business Administration (SBA)

SBA ONLINE The SBA offers exporters access to application information, services, and other export assistance information. For a nominal fee, this service allows greater access to SBA's programs and data resources, including research data banks, news groups, and other program information.

Small Business Administration
409 Third Street, SW
Washington, DC 20416
Tel: 202-401-9600
Web: www.sba.gov

SERVICE CORPS OF RETIRED EXECUTIVES (SCORE) For small companies who are new to the export market, SCORE provides one-on-one counseling and training seminars by individuals who have had years of practical experience in international trade. Volunteers assist small firms in evaluating export potential and in strengthening domestic operations by identifying financial, managerial, or technical problems. Each SCORE office offers a series of presentations on international business for the local business community.

SCORE Association
Small Business Administration
409 Third Street, SW, Sixth Floor
Washington, DC 20024
Tel: 800-634-0245
Fax: 202-205-7636
Web: www.score.org

United Nations

INFOTERRA INFOTERRA is the global environmental information exchange network of the United Nations Environment Program. The network operates through a system of government-designated national focal points that are essentially national environmental information centers located in the ministry or agency responsible for environmental protection. The primary function of each center is to provide a national environmental information service.

> United Nations Environment Program
> United Nations Avenue, Gigiri
> P.O. Box 30552
> Nairobi, Kenya
> Tel: (254-2) 621234
> Fax: (254-2) 624489/90
> E-mail: eisinfo@unep.org
> Web: www.unep.org/infoterra

U.S. Department of Agriculture (USDA)

ECONOMIC RESEARCH SERVICE (ERS) This service of USDA provides economic data, models, and research information about the agricultural economies and policies of foreign countries. ERS's program encompasses research, analyses of food and commodity markets, policy studies, and development of economic and statistical indicators. The information and analyses are produced for the private sector and to help the executive and legislative branches of the federal government develop, administer, and evaluate farm, food, rural, and resource policies and programs.

> Economic Research Service
> 1800 M Street, NW
> Washington, DC 20036
> Tel: 800-999-6779
>   703-605-6060
> Fax: 703-605-6880
> E-mail: ers.nass@ntis.fedworld.gov
> Web: www.ers.usda.gov

FAS ONLINE The USDA's Foreign Agricultural Service (FAS) was created to support and expand U.S. agricultural exports. Through FAS Online, agricultural exporters obtain in-depth and up-to-date statistics on agricultural commodities, including reports on export sales, global supply and demand numbers, trade trends, and emerging market opportunities. FAS Online provides detailed country background information through its market-specific reports and attaché reports. This site also offers assistance to agricultural exporters in the form of embassy contacts and other sources of exporting information.

Foreign Agricultural Service
MS - 1060 (Room 4965-S)
Washington, DC 20250
Tel: 202-720-6713
Fax: 202-720-7138
E-mail: info@fas.usda.gov
Web: www.fas.usda.gov

U.S. Department of Commerce (DOC)

BUSINESS INFORMATION SERVICE FOR THE NEWLY INDEPENDENT STATES (BISNIS) This service of the ITA offers many services, including an e-mail service providing information on opportunities in the Newly Independent States of the former Soviet Union. Thousands of documents also are available online through the BISNIS home page.

Department of Commerce
USA Trade Center
1401 Constitution Avenue, NW
Washington, DC 20230
Tel: 800-872-8732
            202-482-4655
Fax: 202-482-2293
E-mail: bisnis@ita.doc.gov
Web: www.bisnis.doc.gov

CENTRAL & EASTERN EUROPE BUSINESS INFORMATION CENTER (CEEBIC) CEEBIC offers a wide array of services, business counseling, and information on countries in Central and Eastern Europe. Free publications are available, such as the Central and Eastern Europe Commercial Update, a monthly newsletter that highlights current economic, financial, and commercial trends; marketing; partnership opportunities; and regulatory changes in the region. CEEBIC also issues a series entitled *Poland Looks for Partners,* which alerts companies to specific Polish opportunities in energy, environment, and telecommunications.

U.S. Department of Commerce
USA Trade Center—CEEBIC
1401 Constitution Avenue, NW
Washington, DC 20230
Tel: 202-482-2645
Fax: 202-482-3898
E-mail: ceebic@ita.doc.gov
Web: www.mac.doc.gov/ceebic

INTERNATIONAL COMPANY PROFILE This service provides U.S. companies with information on foreign businesses. Reports contain information such as organization type, year established, relative size, number of employees, general reputation, territory covered, product lines handled, principal owners, and financial and trade references. Each report also contains a general comment on the firm's reliability as assessed by the U.S. Commercial Officer who conducted the investigation. Profiles are not available in countries where posts believe that adequate commercial and financial reporting is available at a reasonable cost through the private sector. Requests usually take 30–45 days, and the cost is $500 per report.

U.S. Department of Commerce
1401 Constitution Avenue, NW
Washington, DC 20230
Tel: 800-872-8723
Web: www.commerce.gov

MARKET ACCESS AND COMPLIANCE (MAC) OFFICERS Officers from ITA work to open foreign markets for U.S. goods and services by focusing on current market issues as well as developing strategies to overcome obstacles faced by U.S. businesses. MAC officers work closely with U.S. businesses, trade associations, and other government agencies to develop information related to trade negotiations, foreign country compliance, and trade agreements in order to disseminate information to U.S. companies to support their international ventures.

U.S. Department of Commerce
1401 Constitution Avenue, NW
Washington, DC 20230
Web: www.mac.doc.gov

MAC desk officers are organized into five regional areas:
Africa and the Middle East
Tel: 202-482-4651

Asia and the Pacific
Tel: 202-482-4527

Europe
Tel: 202-482-5638

Western Hemisphere
Tel: 202-482-5324

Office of Agreements and Compliance
Tel: 202-482-5767

MINORITY BUSINESS DEVELOPMENT AGENCY (MBDA) The MBDA of the DOC provides management and technical assistance, as well as access to domestic and international markets. MBDA's mission is to promote the establishment and growth of minority-owned business enterprises in the United States. Consequently, it is constantly seeking to create new and innovative ways to engage U.S. minority firms in the international business arena. MBDA assists minority firms in gaining international access in many ways, including trade missions, matchmaker programs, one-on-one client counseling, seminars, and special international program events.
MBDA International Trade Office
Department of Commerce
1401 Constitution Avenue, NW
Washington, DC 20230
Tel: 202-482-5061
Fax: 202-501-4698
Web: www.mbda.gov

NATIONAL MARINE FISHERIES SERVICE (NMFS) The NMFS is a division of the DOC and is affiliated with the National Oceanic and Atmospheric Administration (NOAA). The NMFS administers programs sponsored by NOAA that support domestic and international conservation and management of living marine resources. It offers a wide range of services to assist U.S. fishing industry businesses involved in the export of fish and fishery products. In addition, it advises seafood marketers about foreign regulations and maintains contacts with foreign government regulatory agencies to resolve sanitary and hygienic issues.

National Oceanic and Atmospheric Administration
Fisheries Headquarters
1315 East-West Highway, SSMC3
Silver Spring, MD 20910
Tel: 301-713-2355
Fax: 301-713-1081
Web: www.noaa.gov

NATIONAL TECHNICAL INFORMATION SERVICE (NTIS) This organization disseminates the results of U.S. and foreign government-sponsored research, development, and engineering activities. NTIS manages software, data files, and databases produced by federal agencies. It allows U.S. firms to access the results of over 15,000 U.S. government-sponsored research and engineering programs. NTIS presents findings in the form of newsletters, computer searches, and data files. Selected publications and services of NTIS include these:

- Newsletter Abstracts
- NTIS Published Searches
- Federal Research in Progress (FEDRIP) Database
- NTIS Bibliographic Database
- Foreign Technology Newsletter Abstracts

National Technical Information Service
5285 Port Royal Road
Springfield, VA 22161
Tel: 800-553-6847
          703-605-6000
Fax: 703-605-6900
E-mail: info@ntis.gov
Web: www.ntis.gov

OFFICE OF MULTILATERAL TRADE AFFAIRS (OMA) This division of the DOC serves as a contact point for U.S. multilateral trade policy issues related to the General Agreement on Tariffs and Trade (GATT), the Organization for Economic Cooperation and Development (OECD), the United Nations, and other international organizations.
Office of Multilateral Trade Affairs
Department of Commerce
1401 Constitution Avenue, NW
Washington, DC 20230

Tel: 202-482-0603
Fax: 202-482-5939
Web: www.state.gov/e/eb/cip/c621.htm

STAT-USA This service is a valuable source of information for current business, economic, and international trade-related information produced by the federal government. Annual subscriptions are $175, and quarterly subscriptions cost $75.

STAT-USA
Department of Commerce
HCHB Room 4885
1401 Constitution Avenue, NW
Washington, DC 20230
Tel: 800-782-8872
            202-482-1986
Fax: 202-482-2164
E-mail: statmail@doc.gov
Web: www.stat-usa.gov

TRADE DEVELOPMENT INDUSTRY OFFICERS These officers operate within the DOC as industry specialists who work with manufacturing and service industry associations and firms to identify trade opportunities and obstacles. To assist U.S. businesses in their export efforts, industry experts conduct executive trade missions, trade fairs, product literature centers, marketing seminars, and business counseling. These industry officers are organized into the following sectors: technology and aerospace; basic industries; textiles, apparel, and consumer goods; service; environmental technology exports; and tourism. Trade Development also offers valuable trade statistics that can be accessed online.

Department of Commerce
1401 Constitution Avenue, NW
Washington, DC 20230
Tel: 202-482-0543
Fax: 202-482-4473
Web: www.ita.doc.gov/tradestats

TRADE INFORMATION CENTER (TIC) This center is often the first point of contact for U.S. exporters. A hotline directs business executives to the appropriate offices within the U.S. government agencies that assist exporters. TIC's home page provides useful information on government programs, trade education events, regulations related to exporting and importing, and so forth. Information is provided free of charge, and companies can access the center via a toll-free number or the Internet.

Trade Information Center, International Trade Administration
Department of Commerce
1401 Constitution Avenue, NW, R-71C
Washington, DC 20230
Tel: 800-872-8723
           202-482-0543
Fax: 202-482-4473
E-mail: tic@ita.doc.gov
Web: www.ita.doc.gov/tic

TRADEPORT This service is sponsored by the Economic Development Administration and is designed to offer exporters a comprehensive source of trade-related information. It provides information ranging from learning the basics of exporting and identifying overseas buyers to financing the deal and shipping the goods. TradePort also contains a useful trade Q&A service, links to other export-related sites, educational announcements, and a trade events calendar.

Department of Commerce
Economic Development Administration
1401 Constitution Avenue, NW
Washington, DC 20230
E-mail: info@tradeport.org
Web: www.tradeport.org

WORLD NEWS CONNECTION (WNC) This online service monitors foreign broadcasts, news agency transmissions, newspapers, periodicals, and government statements. The data covers socioeconomic, political, scientific, and technical issues. The information is available within 2–3 days from the time of original publication or broadcast. Information is provided for most countries in Europe, Asia, Latin America, and Africa. WNC is priced on a flat-fee basis according to the length of the subscription and can be purchased for a single user or a network. Single-user cost is $75/month or $900/year for the basic package.

National Technical Information Service
5285 Port Royal Road
Springfield, VA 22161

Tel: 800-553-6847
           703-605-6000
Fax: 703-605-6900
E-mail: into@ntis.gov
Web: www.ntis.gov

U.S. Department of State

U.S. DEPARTMENT OF STATE REGIONAL BUREAUS Regional Bureaus of the U.S. Department of State provide country-specific economic and political analysis for U.S. companies. Country desk officers in these regional bureaus maintain regular contact with overseas diplomatic missions and are a valuable source of information. The Bureaus include African, Inter-American, East Asian and Pacific, Near Eastern and South Asian, and European and Canadian Affairs. When contacting these bureaus, companies should ask to speak with commercial coordinators.

U.S. Department of State
2201 C Street, NW
Washington, DC 20520
Tel: 202-647-4000
Web: www.state.gov

African Affairs
Tel: 202-647-3503

Inter-American Affairs
Tel: 202-647-2066

East Asian and Pacific Affairs
Tel: 202-647-4835

Near Eastern and South Asian Affairs
Tel: 202-647-1552

European and Canadian Affairs
Tel: 202-647-2395

U.S. Trade Representative (USTR)

This office is responsible for developing and coordinating U.S. international trade, commodity, and direct investment policy and leading or directing negotiations with other countries on such matters. USTR provides publications to exporters challenged by foreign barriers to trade and unfair trade practices. It also is responsible for complaints against foreign unfair trade practices. Information on specific industries and sectors can be obtained through USTR's sectoral offices.

Office of the U.S. Trade Representative
600 17th Street, NW
Washington, DC 20508
Tel: 888-473-8787
Web: www.ustr.gov

World Bank

BUSINESS PARTNERSHIP CENTER (BPC) This service provides a central contact point for business inquiries about the World Bank Group's products and services and promotes cooperation and strategic partnerships with leading business organizations. The BPC acts as a referral service directing incoming business inquiries (via phone, mail, fax, e-mail, and visitors) to appropriate staff within the Bank Group for action. Information brochures and resource guides on products and services also are provided. The BPC establishes institutional linkages with business institutions, such as leading federations of industries and chambers of commerce around the world. The main aim of these partnerships is to improve information dissemination on business opportunities and to explore concrete ways to promote mutual interests, collaborate on joint initiatives, learn from the business community, and better reflect their inputs and feedback into the Bank Group's development assistance.

World Bank Group
Business Partnership Center
1818 H Street, NW
Washington, DC 20433
Tel: 202-522-4272
Fax: 202-522-1727
E-mail: Business_Partner@worldbank.org

INVESTMENT PROMOTION NETWORK (IPANET) This service was developed by the Multilateral Investment Guarantee Agency (MIGA) of the World Bank to promote international investments. IPAnet provides information on global market opportunities, operational conditions in host economies, and existing and prospective investors. IPAnet also provides a news page that contains links to international journals, newspapers, and other electronic media sources. Membership is free, but is required to gain access to online databases.

Multilateral Investment Guarantee Agency
Investment Marketing Services Department
1818 H Street, NW
Washington, DC 20433
Tel: 202-473-5431
Fax: 202-522-2650
E-mail: IPAnet@worldbank.org
Web: www.ipanet.net

THE LIBRARY NETWORK This network of 12 libraries and resource centers serves the World Bank and the International Monetary Fund. Its mandate is to provide information, products, and services to support the commitments of the two institutions. This network offers research services, consulting, procurement of information products, content organization, and document delivery while monitoring the latest information, industry trends, and business challenges. Only the following libraries admit visitors, and appointments are generally required.

- **International Finance Corporation (IFC) Library**
  The IFC maintains a collection of specialized periodicals and trade journals, as well as selected monographs and reference materials. Major subject areas include business and finance, capital markets, foreign investment, and privatization. Non-Bank visitors are welcome to use the library, but appointments are recommended. The IFC Library's card catalog and the holdings of the other libraries of the World Bank Group are accessible online.
  Tel: 202-473-9533
  Fax: 202-974-4345
  E-mail: library@ifc.org

- **Joint Bank-Fund Library (JL)**
  The Joint Bank-Fund Library (JL) is the largest library in the Network. The core collection includes materials in the areas of economics, trade, public policy, international and governmental finance, government statistics, development issues, and economic conditions of the countries of the world.
  Tel: 202-623-7054
  Fax: 202-623-6417

- **Sectoral and IT Resource Center (SITRC)**
  The Sectoral and IT Resource Center grants access to researchers in the DC area.
  Tel: 202-473-9533

  The World Bank
  1818 H Street, NW
  Washington, DC 20433
  Tel: 202-473-1000
  Fax: 202-477-6391
  Web: http://www.jolis.worldbankimflib.org

Other

INTERNATIONAL TRADE DATA NETWORK (ITDN) The ITDN is a nonprofit, data multiplier that provides the business community with timely and detailed market intelligence needed to become competitive in the global arena. The primary mission of the ITDN is to facilitate the dissemination of trade information through resource sharing as opposed to resource ownership. This has been achieved by establishing partnership arrangements with the public and private sectors and by taking advantage of technological advances in data processing, networking, and communications. The ITDN is a function of the Rhode Island Export Assistance Center (RIEAC) at Bryant College in Smithfield, Rhode Island. For unrestricted access to ITDN information and news feeds, you must become a member of the Network. The single-user corporate rate is $65/year; the personal noncompany rate is $59/year.
  RI Export Assistance Center
  Bryant College
  1150 Douglas Pike
  Smithfield, RI 02917
  Tel: 401-232-6407
  E-mail: postoffice@itdn.net

UNCTAD This organization compiles statistics for the analysis of international trade, foreign direct investment, commodities, and development. Statistics are based on existing national and international data sources. Unrestricted free access is provided in UNCTAD Statistics in brief on their web site. For users who require more detailed information or a full-time series, UNCTAD offers online databases. UNCTAD produces statistical publications such as the Handbook of Statistics, the World Investment Directory, the Handbook of World Mineral Trade Statistics, and the Commodity Price Bulletin.

UNCTAD
Palais des Nations
8-14, Avenue de la Paix
1211 Geneva 10
Switzerland
Tel: 41-22-907-1234
Fax: 41-22-907-0043
E-mail: info@unctad.org

WORLD TRADE CENTERS ASSOCIATION (WTCA) ONLINE WTCA OnLine links U.S. businesses to nearly 300 World Trade Centers in almost 100 countries. Business opportunities are posted by thousands of World Trade Center members worldwide. Companies can create their own offers, company catalog, and personalized view of e-commerce services including news, international company information, trade opportunities, catalogs, stock quotes, package tracking, worldwide weather, and more. WTCA OnLine's Business Matchmaker delivers matching business opportunities, monthly WTCA events and WTCA news directly via e-mail. The WTCA also assists international trade by bringing together exporters, importers, and those who service the business. Trade opportunities also are posted through an electronic bulletin board. Online services are free.

World Trade Centers Association
60 East 42nd Street, Suite 1901
New York, NY 10165
Tel: 212-432-2626
Fax: 212-488-0064
E-mail: wtca@wtca.org
Web: www.wtca.org

2

Targeting Opportunities

Numerous government programs and publications are available to assist business executives in marketing their products and services abroad, as well as locating opportunities for growth and expansion. Publications and database services identify everything from trade and procurement leads to potential cross-border investment opportunities. U.S. government and multilateral agency experts can provide insight into the best methods of penetrating any given market. Most of these sources of information are provided free of charge or at a nominal cost and can make a considerable difference to small businesses or companies just beginning to venture into the international marketplace.

In most countries, relationships must be well developed before business transactions take place. Laying the groundwork and establishing a network are crucial first steps to the success of any international operation. This chapter outlines the publications, databases, and organizations and services that can help U.S. firms target international opportunities and make contact with those most suited to their individual needs. Additionally, a section at the end of the chapter discusses procurement. Organizations that extend loans to governments, such as the World Bank, often open up bidding for project goods and services to the private sector. These opportunities offer excellent development opportunities to businesses qualified to secure these contracts.

The following is a list of topics included in Chapter Two:

- Business development leads
- Consulting services
- Export counseling
- Market information
- Trade services
- Project procurement information

PUBLICATIONS

Department of Commerce (DOC)

BISNIS SEARCH FOR PARTNERS This publication is produced by the Business Information Service for the Newly Independent States (BISNIS) to help U.S. companies locate investment opportunities in the expanding markets of the former Soviet Union. This publication is distributed biweekly via e-mail with a limited selection of leads published in a monthly newsletter. Investment leads are listed by country and provide information such as industry, company name, and contact, as well as a brief description of the project and goods and services sought.

Business Information Service for the Newly Independent
    States
Department of Commerce
1401 Constitution Avenue, NW
Washington, DC 20230
Tel: 202-482-4655
Fax: 202-482-2293
E-mail: bisnis@usita.gov
Web: www.bisnis.doc.gov

CENTRAL AND EASTERN EUROPE COMMERCIAL UPDATE This publication of the DOC's Central and Eastern Europe Business Information Center (CEEBIC) is produced in cooperation with USAID. This publication provides a wide range of vital information on conducting business in Central and Eastern Europe. The topics covered include finance- and marketing-related information, commercial aspects of various cities and regions, new developments in a specific industry, changing business conditions and regulations, small business concerns, and specific trade and investment opportunities. A section of this publication is devoted to partnership opportunities with firms in the region. Specific trade and investment leads also are listed here according to country, along with project descriptions and contact information.

Department of Commerce
USA Trade Center—CEEBIC
1401 Constitution Avenue, NW
Washington, DC 20230
Tel: 202-482-2645
Fax: 202-482-3898
E-mail: ceebic@ita.doc.gov
Web: www.export.gov/ceebic

COMMERCIAL NEWS USA (CNUSA) This DOC publication provides worldwide publicity for U.S. products available for immediate export. Published ten times a year and distributed outside the United States, this service enables foreign firms to identify and contact U.S. exporters of specific products, giving U.S. companies a direct indication of market interest by generating sales leads, agent contacts, and other benefits. Specific regions may be targeted in advertising.

Each edition of CNUSA contains short descriptions and photographs of 150 to 200 new products, together with the names and addresses of the exporters, and ultimately reaches over 500,000 business and government leaders worldwide. CNUSA also is sent to Chambers of Commerce abroad and to DOC district offices. The minimum cost to advertise in the publication is $495.

Associated Business Publications International
317 Madison Avenue, Suite 1900
New York, NY 10017
Tel: 212-490-3999
Fax: 212-986-7864
Web: www.cnewsusa.com

INTERNATIONAL TRADE ADMINISTRATION NEWSLETTERS The ITA publishes the CEE/NIS Telecommunications Newsletter, Latin American Telecommunications Newsletter, Satellites & Wireless Telecommunications Newsletter, and the Sub-Saharan Africa Telecommunications Newsletter, which are distributed via e-mail. Publications include highlights of telecommunication projects with potential opportunities for investment. Furthermore, the articles provide detailed descriptions of projects along with specific contact information. Contact the Office of Telecommunications at the ITA for subscription details.

Office of Telecommunications
International Trade Administration
U.S. Department of Commerce
1401 Constitution Avenue, NW
Washington, DC 20230
Tel: 202-482-2872
Fax: 202-482-5834
E-mail: tic@ita.doc.gov
Web: www.ita.doc.gov

TRADE AND TENDERS The Commercial Service of the United States, the European Bank for Reconstruction and Development

(EBRD), the World Bank, and other institutions regularly provide the Business Information Service for the Newly Independent States (BISNIS) with information on export opportunities and tenders in this region. BISNIS disseminates these leads via a biweekly electronic report known as Trade and Tenders to help U.S. companies find business opportunities in the expanding markets of the newly independent states. BISNIS may also consider other private sector-generated trade leads and tenders, but only in electronic form and dependent on available space. To post trade leads, e-mail the following address.

Business Information Service for the Newly Independent
   States
Department of Commerce
1401 Constitution Avenue, NW
Washington, DC 20230
Tel: 202-482-4655
Fax: 202-482-2293
E-mail: bisnis@usita.gov
Web: www.bisnis.doc.gov

Inter-American Development Bank (IDB)

IDB PROJECTS This publication includes a listing of project proposals, the status of projects underway, procurement notices, and business opportunities offered by IDB. The publication includes contact information for the IDB as well as an overview of IDB's operations. Subscriptions are free.

Office of External Relations
Inter-American Development Bank
1300 New York Avenue, NW
Washington, DC 20577
Tel: 202-623-1397
Fax: 202-623-1403
Web: www.iadb.org

United Nations

DEVELOPMENT BUSINESS This biweekly publication of the United Nations provides procurement information on development projects financed by the World Bank, regional development banks, and other international organizations. Information includes a Monthly Operational Summary (MOS) which lists all projects being considered for financing by the bank; General Procurement Notices (GPNs), which are issued by the borrower for projects that are subject to international competitive bidding; Specific Procurement Notices (SPNs), which are invitations to bid for specific terms or works; and Major Contract Award Notices (MCANs), which identify successful bidders on recently awarded contracts. Subscribers also receive the World Bank, Asian Development Bank, Inter-American Development Bank, and African Development Bank Monthly Operational Summaries. The cost is $495 per year. The Monthly Operational Summary (including project approvals) is available as a separate subscription for $250.

    United Nations Publications
    Development Business
    P.O. Box 5850
    Grand Central Station
    New York, NY 10163-5850
    Tel: 212-963-1516
    Fax: 212-963-1381

U.S. Department of Agriculture (USDA)

BUYER ALERT ANNOUNCEMENTS These biweekly newsletters are distributed by the USDA's overseas offices (see Appendix D) to introduce products or services to buyers from around the world. Buyer alerts reach more than 15,000 importers in over 75 countries, usually in the local language. Each alert offers product information, offer terms, and company information to potential importers. Companies may advertise up to five different products (or up to three products if completed online) in each issue, but may not advertise the same product twice. The cost to advertise is $15 per announcement.

    AgExport Connections
    Ag Box 1052
    USDA/FAS/AGX
    Washington, DC 20250-1052
    Tel: 202-690-3421
    Fax: 202-690-4374
    Web: www.fas.usda.gov/agexport/banews.html

TRADE LEADS INFORMATION SHEETS This information, published by USDA's Foreign Agricultural Service (FAS), offers U.S. exporters timely information on foreign buyers who are seeking U.S. food, agricultural, and forest products. A typical trade lead contains the buyer's contact information, specific products and quantities needed, packaging and labeling requirements, type of quotation required, as well as a bank reference. New trade leads are added to the system every Wednesday. Trade Leads also can be accessed on the FAS web page.

AgExport Connections
Ag Box 1052
USDA/FAS/AGX
Washington, DC 20250
Tel: 202-690-3416
Fax: 202-690-4374
Web: www.fas.usda.gov/agexport/tleadsinfo_old.html

U.S. Agency for International Development (USAID)

DEVELOPING PARTNERS The USAID Office of Small and Disadvantaged Business Utilization/Minority Resource Center (OSDBU/MRC) produces this quarterly publication to provide news that will help U.S. firms develop a market niche within USAID, increase the export of U.S. professional and technical assistance services and commodities, and increase the general knowledge and understanding of USAID-financed projects and programs.

U.S. Agency for International Development
OSDBU/MRC
Ronald Reagan Building, Room 7.8E
1300 Pennsylvania Avenue, NW
Washington, DC 20523
Tel: 202-712-1500
Fax: 202-216-3056
E-mail: osdbu@usaid.gov
Web: www.info.usaid.gov/procurement_bus_opp/
         osdbu/newsltr.htm

PROCUREMENT INFORMATION BULLETINS The USAID provides procurement information in the form of a mailing list. Foreign government requirements for U.S. products are advertised in these two bulletins published by USAID's Office of Small and Disadvantaged Business Utilization (OSDBU). Contact OSDBU to receive an application for the mailing list and to receive these free publications.

U.S. Agency for International Development
Ronald Reagan Building, Room 7.8E
1300 Pennsylvania Avenue, NW

Washington, DC 20523
Tel: 202-712-1500
Fax: 202-216-3056
Web: www.info.usaid.gov/procurement_bus_opp/
              procurement/announce/pib

U.S. Trade and Development Agency (USTDA)

PIPELINE REPORT This biweekly report alerts manufacturers and suppliers of upcoming projects and encourages them to contact consulting engineers and construction engineers about international project procurement. The report gives U.S. firms an opportunity to participate in the preliminary stages of large international projects. The guide details other USTDA activities, highlighting recent feasibility study grants or definitional missions completed, and also includes procurement opportunities from related agencies, including the Export-Import Bank of the U.S., the World Bank, the Inter-American Development Bank, the U.S. Agency for International Development, and the Asian Development Bank. The publication can be accessed online.

CIB Publications
U.S. Trade and Development Agency
1000 Wilson Boulevard, Suite 1600
Arlington, VA 22209
Tel: 703-875-4357
Fax: 703-875-4009
Web: www.tda.gov/pipeline/index.html

Other

NADBANK NEWS The North American Development Bank (NADB) distributes this free mailer via e-mail. It provides information about NADB's lending program, the Institutional Development Cooperation Program, and the Border Environmental Infrastructure Fund. Information includes projects under consideration for financing; project approvals; bid calls for goods, works, and consultant services; and notification of contracts awarded for goods, works, and consultant services. To subscribe to NADBank News, send an e-mail to the following address.

North American Development Bank
203 South St. Mary's, Suite 300
San Antonio, TX 78205

Tel: 210-231-8000
Fax: 210-231-6232
Web: www.nadb.org

EUROPEAN BANK FOR RECONSTRUCTION AND DEVELOPMENT PROCUREMENT OPPORTUNITIES (EBRD) This monthly newsletter is published by the EBRD and provides information on procurement opportunities at all stages of a project's development. Procurement, cofinancing notices, and contract award information are included in the publication. The newsletter can be downloaded free of charge from the following web site. EBRD also offers a facsimile service detailing procurement opportunities.

Procurement Opportunities
Subscriptions Department
European Bank for Reconstruction and Development
82-84 Peckham Rye
London SE15 4HB, United Kingdom
Tel: (44-20)-7338-7553
Fax: (44-20)-7338-6102
Web: www.ebrd.com/oppor/procure/index.htm

DATABASES

Department of Commerce (DOC)

EXPORT CONTACT LIST SERVICE This database retrieval service provides exporters with the names of prospective international customers by country or industry. The U.S. exporter specifies the SIC code, geographic area, and type of contacts desired (i.e., distributor, retailer, and so forth). The service also provides names and contact information, along with company background and product or service specialty. Names are collected and maintained by the DOC district offices and commercial officers at foreign posts. Contact list prices vary according to the format selected. The minimum fee is $10. The cost varies based on the number of countries, the product lines chosen, and the number of names retrieved.

Department of Commerce
1401 Constitution Avenue, NW
Washington, DC 20230
Tel: 202-482-3917
Web: www.commerce.gov

U.S. Agency for International Development (USAID)

AID CONSULTANT REGISTRY INFORMATION SYSTEM (ACRIS) This computerized database lists the technical service capabilities of U.S. firms and individuals. Its purpose is to assist small, medium, and disadvantaged U.S. businesses, as well as individual consultants competing for USAID technical service contracts. Maintained by the OSDBU, ACRIS brings U.S. technical service businesses and individual consultants to the attention of USAID personnel.

U.S. Agency for International Development
OSDBU
Ronald Reagan Building, Room 7.8E
1300 Pennsylvania Avenue, NW
Washington, DC 20523
Tel: 202-712-1500
Fax: 202-216-3056
E-mail: osdbu@usaid.gov
Web: www.info.usaid.gov

U.S. Department of Agriculture (USDA)

AGRICOLA AGRICOLA is a database maintained by USDA's National Agricultural Library that contains detailed publications and resources encompassing all aspects of agriculture. Topics covered include plant and animal sciences, forestry, entomology, soil and water resources, agricultural economics, agricultural engineering, agricultural products, alternative farming practices, and food and nutrition. AGRICOLA can be accessed and searched online, but also can be accessed for a fee through several commercial vendors, both online and on CD-ROM. Users can also purchase magnetic tapes containing AGRICOLA records from the National Technical Information Service (NTIS).

National Agriculture Library
10301 Baltimore Avenue, Room 304
Beltsville, MD 20705
Tel: 301-504-5755
Fax: 301-504-5675
E-mail: lending@nal.usda.gov
Web: www.nal.usda.gov

FOREIGN BUYER LISTS The USDA maintains a database of more than 20,000 foreign firms classified by their demand for certain kinds of agricultural products. Business executives can use these lists to match their products with potential customers worldwide. Lists include: company name, contact name, address, and telephone, telex, and fax numbers. This information is updated annually. The cost is $15 per list and can be ordered according to commodity and country.

AgExport Connections
FAS/USDA
Room 4939-S
1400 Independence Avenue, SW
Washington, DC 20250
Tel: 202-690-3416
Fax: 202-690-4374
Web: www.fas.usda.gov

UNITED STATES SUPPLIER LISTS These lists are maintained by USDA's Foreign Agricultural Service and are designed to meet the needs of prospective exporters and foreign purchasers of U.S. food and agricultural products. The lists are categorized by Harmonized System (HS) codes and include name, address, telephone/telex/fax numbers, Standard Industrial Classification (SIC) codes, sales information, and year the firm was established. Cost is $15 per list.

AgExport Connections
Ag Box 1052
AGX/FAS/USDA
Washington, DC 20250
Tel: 202-720-7103
Fax: 202-690-4374
Web: www.fas.usda.gov

World Bank

DATA ON CONSULTANTS (DACON) INFORMATION CENTER The World Bank's DACON Information Center maintains a computerized data bank that lists information on the qualifications of consulting firms that have participated in bank-financed projects. Registration is limited to firms with at least five full-time professionals who have at least five years of experience in their field. To register, firms should obtain an information packet and set of diskettes from the World Bank. This service is free.

DACON Information Center
The World Bank
1818 H Street, NW

Washington, DC 20433
Tel: 202-473-5067
Fax: 202-522-7479
Web: www.worldbank.org/html/opr/dacon/
            contents.html

PRIVATE PARTICIPATION IN INFRASTRUCTURE (PPI) PROJECT DATABASE The PPI Project Database tracks contract and investment information for private infrastructure projects in low- and middle-income countries in the following industries: energy, telecommunications, transport, and water. The database allows users to search and sort information using around 30 different fields. Data can be viewed and downloaded for free.

The World Bank
1818 H Street, NW
Washington, DC 20433
Tel: 202-473-5067
Fax: 202-522-7479
Web: rru.worldbank.org/PPI

Other

FEDERAL MONEY RETRIEVER (FMR) The FMR contains comprehensive and up-to-date information on all grant and loan programs (over 1,400) offered by the U. S. federal government. Multiple indexing assures fast and easy retrieval of all federal programs matching the user's needs. The database can be accessed via CD-ROM or by downloading software. Cost ranges from $39.95 to $179.95.

Federal Money Retriever
IDI Magic Technologies Corporation
P.O. Box 97655
Las Vegas, NV 89193
Tel: 800-804-5270
Web: www.fedmoney.com

SMESTAT DATABASE This database was created by the Inter-American Investment Corporation (IIC) to improve the IIC's ability to monitor and assist small- and medium-sized enterprises (SMEs) in Latin America and the Caribbean. Monitoring and offering assistance to these firms is crucial to the region's well-being as these firms account for a large portion of economic activity. Information found in the database includes statistics on country-based job creation attributable to SMEs, SME production levels, and export growth attributable to SMEs.

Inter-American Investment Corporation
1350 New York Avenue, NW
Washington, DC 20577
Tel: 202-623-3900
Fax: 202-623-2360
Web: www.iadb.org/iic

ORGANIZATIONS AND SERVICES

U.S. Department of Commerce (DOC)

AGENT/DISTRIBUTOR SERVICE This service helps U.S. companies find interested and qualified foreign agents or distributors for their products and services. U.S. foreign commercial specialists locate foreign agents, distributors, and/or representatives for U.S. company product lines. Reports provide information on up to six qualified representatives interested in representing the U.S. company and include company names, contacts, phone and fax numbers, preferred language of correspondence, interest level concerning the product, product marketability, and the specialist's assessment of each prospect's capability to distribute the product. A search usually requires 30–60 days. The cost is $250 per report.

Department of Commerce
1401 Constitution Avenue, NW
Washington, DC 20230
Tel: 202-482-4655
Fax: 202-482-2293

BALKAN RECONSTRUCTION PROGRAM This program provides detailed information regarding reconstruction and development opportunities for U.S. companies in Bosnia. The program provides information regarding Bosnia/Balkan Reconstruction, available online and via an automated fax system; as well as partnership opportunities in Bosnia, developed by on-site contractors; and customized assistance to firms that wish to invest in the area available through the Bosnia hotline. The Southeastern Europe Business Brief is an e-mail service that summarizes the latest developments in the business climate and reconstruction efforts.

CEEBIC
Department of Commerce
1401 Constitution Avenue, NW, Room 2325
Washington, DC 20230
Tel: 202-482-2645
Fax: 202-482-3898
Web: www.mac.doc.gov/ceebic/sbsfhome.html

Bosnia Hotline:
Tel: 202-482-5418

COMMERCIAL SERVICE INTERNATIONAL CONTRACTS (CSIC) The
CSIC provides contact and product information on over 70,000
foreign firms interested in U.S. products. The DOC's Country
Directories of International Contacts directs exporters to sources
that can provide directories of importers, agents, trade associa-
tions, and government agencies by country. Both services are pro-
vided through the National Trade Data Bank (NTDB). NTDB
subscription is available on CD-ROM for $59 per issue and $575
per year or online for $50 per quarter and $150 per year.
Department of Commerce
STAT-USA
HCHB, Room H 4885
Washington, DC 20230
Tel: 800-782-8872
         202-482-1986
Fax: 202-482-2164
E-mail: statmail@esa.doc.gov
Web: www.stat-usa.gov

**CONSORTIA OF AMERICAN BUSINESSES IN THE NEWLY INDEPEN-
DENT STATES (CABNIS)** This organization offers assistance to
U.S. firms wishing to enter the Russian and Newly Independent
States markets. CABNIS provides U.S. firms with on-site specialists
who help exporters identify and pursue new business opportunities. Currently CABNIS represents the commercial interest of
firms belonging to the following sectors: agribusiness and food
processing, biotechnology, coal production, utilization technologies, semiconductor production, telecommunications, and others.
ITA/OETCA
Department of Commerce
1401 Constitution Avenue, NW, Room 1800H
Washington, DC 20230

Tel: 202-482-5004
Fax: 202-482-1790
Web: www.ita.doc.gov

COUNTRY AND INDUSTRY DESK OFFICERS These DOC officers provide expert market research assistance to U.S. companies. Professional staff in the Trade Development Office focuses on an industry-specific approach to the international market, while country desk officers focus on an individual country or region. To obtain contact information for individual country desk officers (see Appendix A), contact the Trade Information Center at the DOC. To contact industry desk officers, contact the Trade Information Center.

Trade Information Center
Department of Commerce
1401 Constitution Avenue, NW
Washington, DC 20230
Tel: 800-872-8723
Fax: 202-482-4473
Web: www.ita.doc.gov

CUSTOMIZED MARKET ANALYSIS (CMA) This product offers customized product marketing information to U.S. exporters. Information is prepared by specialists who conduct interviews with local importers, distributors, end users, and manufacturers of comparable products. Analysis provides information regarding market potential, local/foreign competition, distribution channels, product pricing, market entry barriers, and licensing issues. A CMA takes approximately 60 days to prepare and costs $1,000 to $5,100 per country.

Trade Information Center
Department of Commerce
1401 Constitution Avenue, NW
Washington, DC 20230
Tel: 800-872-8723
Fax: 202-482-4473
Web: www.export.gov/comm_svc/

CUSTOMIZED SALES SERVICES (CSS) This service provides firms with key marketing and foreign representation information for specific products. Commercial sales service staff conduct interviews to obtain marketing background on the product, such as sales potential in the market, comparable products, distribution channels, going price, competitive factors and qualified purchasers. The cost varies from $500 to $2,000 depending on the country.

Trade Information Center
Department of Commerce
1401 Constitution Avenue, NW
Washington, DC 20230
Tel: 800-872-8723
Fax: 202-482-4473
Web: www.ita.doc.gov

ECONOMIC BULLETIN BOARD (EBB) The EBB is an online information system offering daily trade leads, time-sensitive market information, and the latest statistical data. The EBB is made up of two electronic bulletin boards, GLOBUS and State of the Nation. GLOBUS provides businesses with sales opportunities in foreign markets, U.S. government procurement opportunities, and in-depth market studies produced by the DOC's Commercial Service. EBB subscriptions are available online. Fees vary, ranging from $65 to $225. Free trials are available.

STAT-USA
Department of Commerce
1401 Constitution Avenue, NW, Room H 4885
Washington, DC 20230
Tel: 800-782-8872
          202-482-1986
Fax: 202-482-2164
E-mail: statmail@esa.doc.gov
Web: www.stat-usa.gov

FINANCELINK FinanceLink helps U.S. companies locate financing for the export of goods from the U.S. to the Newly Independent States of the former Soviet Union by linking U.S. exporters with U.S.-based financial service companies. A company's proposed transaction is submitted to participating financial service providers in both the private and public sectors. Finance service companies wishing to receive these regular updates of export transactions must be incorporated in, and conduct business in, the United States. Interested firms should e-mail the following address.

Business Information Service for the Newly Independent
  States
Department of Commerce
1401 Constitution Avenue, NW
Washington, DC 20230
Tel: 202-482-4655
Fax: 202-482-2293
E-mail: bisnis@ita.doc.gov
Web: www.bisnis.doc.gov/bisnis/finlin3.cfm

MATCHMAKER TRADE DELEGATIONS PROGRAM This program helps
small- and medium-sized U.S. firms establish business relationships in major international markets. Each matchmaker trade del-
egation targets major markets in two or three countries with
strong sales potential for U.S. exports. Commercial specialists
arrange appointments with prescreened business contacts as well
as interpreter services. Furthermore, these specialists also offer in-
depth country analyses and briefings. For a list of upcoming
Matchmaker Trade Delegations, contact a local Export Assistance
Center (see Appendix I).
  Trade Information Center
  Department of Commerce
  1401 Constitution Avenue, NW
  Washington, DC 20230
  Tel: 800-872-8723
  Fax: 202-482-4473
  Web: www.ita.doc.gov

MULTILATERAL DEVELOPMENT BANK OPERATIONS (MDBO) MDBO
offers information and assistance to U.S. companies interested in
supplying goods and services to overseas construction, engineering, manufacturing, and investment projects by facilitating access
to representatives from multilateral banks. It counsels and maintains a library of information on current and planned multilateral
development projects. MDBO representatives assist U.S. exporters
with business leads and provide counseling on projects. The DOC
has assigned members of the U.S. Commercial Service to each of
the major multilateral development banks.
  Multilateral Development Bank Operations
  International Trade Administration
  U.S. Department of Commerce
  The USA Trade Center

Ronald Reagan Building
Mezzanine Level
Washington, D.C. 20230
Tel: 202-482-3399
             800-USA-TRADE (800-872-8723)
Fax: 202-482-3914
E-mail: MDBO.Banks@mail.doc.gov
Web: www.ita.doc.gov/mdbo

NATIONAL TRADE DATA BANK (NTDB) This data bank from the National Technical Information Service maintains trade and export promotion data collected from over 40 federal agencies, including the CIA, EPA, DOC, Department of State, Ex-Im Bank, OPIC, SBA, and USTR. The NTDB contains over 200,000 trade-related documents and provides information on a number of topics, including export opportunities categorized by industry, country, and product; announcements of foreign companies/ importers looking in search of specific products; how-to-market guides; and country demographic, political, and socioeconomic information.

The NTDB is accessible online via STAT-USA for $50 for three months or $150 for one year. Alternatively, the NTDB may be obtained on two CD-ROM discs for $59 per monthly issue or $575 for a one-year subscription. The NTDB is also available at federal depository libraries throughout the United States.

U.S. Department of Commerce
STAT-USA
HCHB Room H 4885
Washington, DC 20230
Tel: 800-782-8872
             202-482-1986
Fax: 202-482-2164
E-mail: statmail@esa.doc.gov
Web: www.stat-usa.gov

SMALL BUSINESS SUPPORT FACILITY This facility provides tailored business counseling to small U.S. firms looking to expand into Central and Eastern Europe. A significant facility feature is that its services are not limited to the pre-entry stages. It can help small firms until the venture is solidly under way in the given market. Services provided include assisting firms in the development of appropriate export programs, locating sources of financing, and providing a range of post-market entry services.

CEEBIC
Department of Commerce
1401 Constitution Avenue, Room 2325
Washington, DC 20230
Tel: 202-482-2645
Web: www.mac.doc.gov/ceebic/sbsfhome.html

TRADE MISSIONS This service is conducted by the DOC's International Trade Administration to promote the sale of U.S. goods and services throughout the world. Trade Missions are intended to provide participants with a wide range of firsthand country and industry-specific information. During a trade mission, participants are assisted with advanced planning and publicity, logistical support, and prearranged appointments with potential buyers and government officials. The number of business executives participating in the trade mission can range from 5 to 12. Cost depends on location and number of countries visited.

International Trade Administration
Department of Commerce
1401 Constitution Avenue, Room 2810
Washington, DC 20230
Tel: 202-482-6220
Fax: 202-482-2526
Web: www.ita.doc.gov/doctm

WOMEN-IN-TRADE BUSINESS DEVELOPMENT MISSIONS These missions expand the export of U.S. goods and services from small-to medium-sized firms owned or managed by women. Missions are typically comprised of ten to twelve companies representing a mixture of product and service industries. Cost depends on locations and number of countries visited.

Office of Export Promotion Coordination
Department of Commerce
1401 Constitution Avenue, Room 2003
Washington, DC 20230
Tel: 202-482-5479
Fax: 202-482-4452

U.S. Department of Agriculture (USDA)

AGEXPORT ACTION KIT This service provides U.S. exporters with information on potential foreign buyers of food and agricultural products. The kit also contains detailed information on the services provided by the USDA's Export Services Division, including Trade Leads, Foreign Buyer Listings, U.S. Supplier Listings, and Buyer Alerts. This service is available free of charge.

AgExport Connections
USDA-FAS
Room 4939, South Building
Washington, DC 20250
Tel: 202-720-7103
Fax: 202-690-4374
Web: www.fas.usda.gov

AGRICULTURE NETWORK INFORMATION CENTER (AGNIC) AgNIC is an electronic source of agricultural information available over an international network. Agricultural information includes basic, applied, and developmental research; extension; and teaching activities in food, agricultural, renewable natural resources, forestry, and physical and social sciences. AgNIC identifies major collections of agriculture-related information, subject area experts, and other resources in an effort to foster improved communication within this industry.

USDA-FAS
Room 4939, South Building
Washington, DC 20250
Tel: 202-720-7103
Fax: 202-690-4374
Web: www.fas.usda.gov
E-mail: agnic@agnic.org
Web: www.agnic.org

AGRICULTURAL TRADE OFFICES The Foreign Agricultural Service (FAS) maintains overseas Agricultural Trade Offices (ATOs) to help exporters of U.S. farm and forest products in overseas markets. These offices supply U.S. exporters with current market information, potential customers, and promotional opportunities. Each ATO has library facilities, conference rooms, and office space.

Foreign Ag-Affairs Office
U.S. Department of Agriculture
1400 Independence Avenue, SW

Washington, DC 20250
Tel: 202-720-6138
Fax: 202-720-8316
Web: www.fas.usda.gov

MARKET DEVELOPMENT COOPERATORS Market Development Cooperators are agricultural nonprofit associations that work with the FAS to promote and expand international markets for U.S. products. More than 50 foreign agricultural associations, 7,000 processors and handlers, and 1,500 farm cooperatives representing millions of farmers participate in this program. U.S. companies receive assistance in expanding international markets for their food products by contacting the Market Development Cooperator for their respective industry.

Foreign Agricultural Service
USDA
1400 Independence Avenue SW, Room 4932
Washington, DC 20250
Tel: 202-720-4327
Fax: 202-720-9361
Web: www.fas.usda.gov

NATIONAL AGRICULTURAL LIBRARY (NAL) The NAL has resources designed to assist agricultural exporters in locating relevant trade and marketing material. One of the main resources is the AGRICOLA Database, which contains detailed publications and resources that encompass all aspects of agriculture. The NAL is open to the public during regular business hours.

National Agriculture Library
10301 Baltimore Avenue, Room 304
Beltsville, MD 20705
Fax: 301-504-5675
E-mail: lending@nal.usda.gov
Web: www.nal.usda.gov

TRADE LEADS This service enables U.S. business executives to reach out directly to foreign buyers. The USDA maintains over 80 overseas offices that send daily inquiries from foreign buyers interested in purchasing U.S. food products to the USDA's headquarters in Washington, D.C. More than 2,500 trade leads are passed on to interested U.S. suppliers each year. Specifically, trade leads cover grocery, dairy, livestock, poultry, seafood, horticultural, tropical, grain, feed and pulse, cotton, tobacco, seeds, forest, and oilseed products. Each trade lead provides details on how to locate the foreign buyer; specific products in demand; the desired quantity, packaging requirements, timing of deliveries, and type of quotation required; and the foreign buyer's bank reference.

AgExport Connections
Ag Box 1052
USDA-FAS
Washington, DC 20250
Tel: 202-720-7103
Fax: 202-690-4374
Web: www.fas.usda.gov

Small Business Administration (SBA)

AUTOMATED TRADE LOCATOR ASSISTANCE SYSTEM (ATLAS) This service provides product-specific and country-specific reports free of charge. The top 35 import and export markets for a particular good or service are included in the product reports. Country reports specify which products are the most frequently traded in a target market.

Small Business Administration
409 Third Street, SW
Washington, DC 20416
Tel: 800-U-ASK-SBA
Web: www.sba.gov/services

U.S. Agency for International Development (USAID)

CENTER FOR TRADE AND INVESTMENT SERVICES (CTIS) This service serves as a single source of information on USAID programs and procurement opportunities. CTIS facilitates business opportunities for U.S. firms in USAID-supported countries, but it is not a U.S. export promotion office. Rather, it provides counseling (timely and targeted information) and research services by identifying and analyzing critical market intelligence and business opportunities for its clients. Through a nationwide network of federal and private-sector associations, CTIS provides information domestically and throughout the developing world.

Center for Trade and Investment Services
U.S. Agency for International Development
515 22nd Street, NW, Room 100
Washington, DC 20523

Tel: 800-872-4348
            202-663-2660
Fax: 202-663-2670
E-mail: ctis@usaid.gov
Web: www.info.usaid.gov

GLOBAL TRADE & TECHNOLOGY NETWORK (GTN) The GTN facilitates the transfer of U.S. technology to USAID-assisted countries and regions. Through an extensive database, GTN matches developing countries' needs with U.S. companies that have the appropriate technologies, expertise, and products. GTN focuses on identifying international business opportunities in environment, agriculture, health, communication, and information technology fields. Trade leads are transmitted from the field and electronically matched with U.S. firms registered in GTN's sector databases. Information is then faxed or e-mailed to appropriate U.S. companies.

Global Technology Network (GTN)
U.S. Agency for International Development
1300 Pennsylvania Avenue, NW
Washington, DC 20523
Tel: 800-872-4348
            202-712-1624
Fax: 202-216-3526
E-mail: usgtn@usaid.gov
Web: www.usgtn.net

OFFICE OF BUSINESS DEVELOPMENT (OBD) The primary objective of the OBD is to leverage USAID resources by establishing partnerships and networks with the private sector in support of the USAID's global economic development mission. This is accomplished through the integration of the GTN's component services, such as its Business Information Services, and the Domestic Business Outreach Program. OBD tracks those countries and sectors in which USAID is active and specifically targets U.S. small- and medium-sized businesses as the delivery mechanism for the use of private sector solutions to USAID development assistance programming.

Global Technology Network (GTN)
U.S. Agency for International Development
1300 Pennsylvania Avenue, NW
Washington, DC 20523

Tel:	800-872-4348
	202-712-1624
Fax:	202-216-3526
Web:	www.usaid.gov

OFFICE OF SMALL AND DISADVANTAGED BUSINESS UTILIZATION (OSDBU) This office assists U.S. firms interested in contracting with USAID-sponsored projects. OSDBU administers the procurement set-aside programs and keeps businesses informed of procurement opportunities. The office is an initial point of contact at USAID for U.S. businesses, particularly small, and minority-, and women-owned firms. The primary concern of the office is to help firms access the full range of procurement available through USAID, including information and counseling on USAID programs, contracting and subcontracting opportunities, and marketing and operational strategies for conducting business with USAID.

USAID/OSDBU/MRC
Ronald Reagan Building, Room 7.8E
1300 Pennsylvania Avenue, NW
Washington, DC 20523

Tel:	202-712-1500
Fax:	202-216-3056
E-mail:	sdbu@usaid.gov
Web:	www.info.usaid.gov/procurement_bus_opp/ osdbu/index.html

U.S. Trade and Development Agency (USTDA)

REVERSE TRADE MISSION Under the USTDA's Reverse Trade Mission, high-level foreign government officials are brought to the United States with the objective of expanding the number of foreign government procurement opportunities available to U.S. firms. While in the United States, the foreign delegates meet with U.S. industry and government representatives and inform them of specific projects requiring U.S. equipment and services.

U.S. Trade and Development Agency
Information Resource Center
1000 Wilson Boulevard, Suite 1600
Arlington, VA 22209

Tel:	703-875-4357
Fax:	703-875-4009
E-mail:	info@tda.gov

FDI EXCHANGE The FDI Exchange is an e-mail alert service that utilizes the resources of the World Bank's online services including the Investment Promotion Network and PrivatizationLink, as well as information from trusted industry organizations. New direct investment opportunities and business operating conditions are e-mailed as specified by geography, type, sector, and size of investment. Registered members receive these services free of charge.

Multilateral Investment Guarantee Agency
Investment Marketing Services
1818 H Street, NW
Washington, DC 20433
Tel: 202-458-4876
Fax: 202-522-2650
Web: www.fdixchange.com

World Bank

INVESTMENT PROMOTION NETWORK (IPANET) The IPAnet, established by the Multilateral Investment Guarantee Agency (MIGA) of the World Bank Group, allows registered visitors to access and exchange information regarding international investment opportunities and concerns. IPAnet is a vital source of information for companies interested in foreign direct investment. Numerous databases, directories, reference desks, and calendars of events grant visitors access to country- and sector-specific information, legal and regulatory issues, news and events, and specific investment opportunities. An online directory of international opportunities in countries worldwide is also available.

PrivatizationLink is an online information clearinghouse for companies engaged in cross-border investment. It provides information to firms seeking to invest in privatized enterprises in emerging markets. The service currently covers countries in Central and Eastern Europe, Central Asia, and Sub-Saharan Africa and will eventually expand to include other regions. PrivatizationLink provides online access to business profiles of state-owned enterprises and assets currently for sale, as well as details of relevant laws, regulations, and procedures governing these transactions.

Web: www.privatizationlink.com

Although access to IPAnet is free to all registered visitors, members receive additional benefits. These benefits include the ability to use IPAnet's marketing "Billboard" to introduce an organization and its products; market intelligence on the composition of the audience accessing the information and avenues for follow-up; and opportunities for revenue mobilization through sponsorships and advertisements. Membership fees are $2,000 per year and $10,000 for a lifetime membership.

Multilateral Investment Guarantee Agency
1818 H Street, NW
Washington, DC 20433
Tel: 202-458-9292
Web: www.ipanet.net

PRIVATE SECTOR DEVELOPMENT ROADMAP This web site provides scores of information on development opportunities in the developing world, including links to the majority of World Bank resources. Products and services are listed by World Bank divisions such as MIGA and International Finance Corporation (IFC), by activities such as Advisory Services or Financial Instrument, and by subjects such as Grants and Intellectual Property Rights. This service is free and provides open access to the resources of the World Bank's private sector development resources.

The World Bank
1818 H Street, NW
Washington, DC 20433
Tel: 202-473-5067
Fax: 202-522-7479
Web: www.worldbank.org/privatesector/map.htm

PUBLIC INFORMATION CENTER (PIC) The World Bank offers a number of operational documents online that provide early intelligence to companies interested in procurement opportunities in emerging markets. The World Bank and the IFC use the PIC to disseminate information about projects in their respective pipelines. Available information includes economic reports that provide background for the formulation of projects in a country, documentation produced during preparation of a project, and studies on the environmental impact of World Bank projects. Most publications are provided free of charge; however, Staff Appraisal Reports (SARs) and some technical data reports are priced at $15. Documents available through the PIC include the following:

- **Economic and Sector Reports** contain a macroeconomic analysis of a country's economy, analyses of major industry sectors, and other reports on specific issues such as poverty assessment, private sector investment, and public expenditures.

- **Environmental Assessments** are detailed studies required for projects likely to have a significant impact on the environment. Such studies are available prior to the completion of a project viability assessment.

- **Environmental Data Sheets** provide summary information on the expected areas of environmental impact of a proposed project and the status of the studies addressing the issues raised. They are prepared for every project and are updated quarterly.

- **Environmental Impact Assessments** are comprehensive studies required for projects that may have significant environmental impact. These studies are released in-country and in Washington a minimum of 60 days prior to Board consideration of projects.

- **Environmental Review Summaries** present key findings of studies carried out for projects that may have significant environmental impact. These summaries are released a minimum of 30 days in advance of Board consideration.

- **Project Information Documents** give a brief summary of an evolving project and are subject to updating and expanding as the project preparation proceeds.

- **Sector Policy Papers** present reviews of major issues relevant to a specific economic sector and give broad guidelines to the Bank's policy for assistance to that sector.

- **Staff Appraisal Reports** contain a project's description and implementation schedule.

- **Summaries of Project Information** provide basic factual information about a proposed IFC investment and are released a minimum of 30 days prior to consideration of the investment by the Corporation's Board of Directors.

World Bank
Public Information Center
1818 H Street, NW
Washington, DC 20433
Tel: 202-458-5454
Fax: 202-522-1500
E-mail: pic@worldbank.org
Web: www.worldbank.org/infoshop

TRADE SERVICES

(The services listed here are for trade business development opportunities. For more information on trade financing and services, see Chapter 5.)

U.S. Department of Agriculture (USDA)

EXPORT ENHANCEMENT PROGRAM (EEP) The EEP offers assistance designed to challenge unfair trading practices and encourage negotiation on agricultural trade problems. It expands U.S. market opportunities for certain commodities to targeted destinations. It also provides commodities to exporters as bonuses to make U.S. commodities more competitive in global markets by meeting competition from subsidizing countries. Since EEP's establishment in 1985, 112 initiatives have been announced with 75 countries. Sales pertaining to these initiatives have totaled more than USD 11.5 billion.

Eligible exporters must have at least three years' experience in exporting an eligible commodity. Exporters also must have an office and agent in the United States, provide evidence of financial responsibility, and provide various financial securities in connection with participation.

Operations Division, Export Credits
Foreign Agricultural Service, USDA Stop 1035
1400 Independence Avenue, SW
Washington, DC 20250
Tel: 202-720-6211
Fax: 202-720-0938

U.S. Department of Commerce (DOC)

EXPORT FINANCE MATCHMAKER (EFM) The EFM is an Internet-based system that matches exporters in need of trade financing with interested banks. This service is offered by the DOC through the International Trade Association (ITA) to help U.S. exporters and buyers of U.S. goods and services find financial resources. This service is free to U.S. exporters.

Office of Finance
Department of Commerce
1401 Constitution Avenue, NW
Washington, DC 20230
Tel: 202-482-5702
Web: www.ita.doc.gov/efm

NATIONAL EXPORT DIRECTORY (NED) The National Export Directory (NED) was developed by the Trade Information Center to better inform U.S. exporters about trade contacts at the federal, state, and local levels. NED contains contact information for state trade offices, trade finance offices, trade centers, and foreign trade zones. There are also listings of the local or regional offices of the following U.S. government agencies: the U.S. Department of Commerce (including ITA, U.S. Commercial Service, Bureau of Export Administration, and MBDA), EX-IM Bank, SBA, USAID, and the U.S. Department of Agriculture.

Trade Information Center
Department of Commerce
1401 Constitution Avenue, NW
Washington, DC 20230
Tel: 800-USA-TRADE
Fax: 202-482-4473

OFFICE OF EXPORTER SERVICES The Bureau of Export Administration provides export assistance on export licensing requirements through its Office of Exporter Services (OEXS). OEXS interprets the Export Administration Regulations (EAR) and provides assistance such as detailed and up-to-date status information on pending license applications; advice on a broad range of export issues, licensing requirements, required documentation for export transactions, and special policy concerns for specific countries; assistance in selecting the appropriate license; and answers to inquiries regarding the Bureau of Export Administration's policy issues and processing time frames.

OEXS counselors can serve as intermediaries and arrange meetings between the exporters and BXA licensing officials. OEXS also authorizes emergency processing on export license applications. Cases meeting specific criteria are expedited through the licensing system, often being approved within a few days of receipt of the application. OEXS provides counseling and training to help defense-dependent firms located throughout the western United States diversify into new commercial and international markets.

BXA now receives a significant amount of traffic through its online Simplified Network Application Process (SNAP). SNAP provides a secure environment for the electronic submission of license applications, commodity classification requests, and high-performance computer notices. Once BXA has received and processed a request to use SNAP, exporters can access the system for tracking purposes in as little as 24 hours.

Export Counseling Division
Department of Commerce
1401 Constitution Avenue, NW
Washington, DC 20230
Tel: 202-482-4811
Fax: 202-482-3617
Web: www.bxa.doc.gov

Other

ACCESS TO EXPORT CAPITAL PROGRAM (AXCAP) AXCAP is a national database listing of banks and government agencies involved in trade finance and the services they offer operated by the Bankers' Association for Finance and Trade (BAFT). AXCAP matches specific exporter needs with appropriate financial services. For first-time or seasoned exporters looking for new markets, AXCAP helps customize financing options for businesses in global markets. Exporters should contact a trade specialist who will pinpoint specific trade finance problems and provide the exporter with a list of banks and government agencies offering the needed services.

Access to Export Capital Program
Bankers' Association for Finance and Trade
1120 Connecticut Avenue, NW, 5th Floor
Washington, DC 20036
Tel: 202-663-7575
Fax: 202-663-5538
Web: www.baft.org

EXPORT.GOV The U.S. government's web portal, EXPORT.GOV, provides many sources of information on export financing and answers a variety of questions ranging from working capital and insurance to available loans and grants. It provides answers to businesses who are new to the intricacies of export financing.

Web: www.export.gov

PROCUREMENT

Once an agreement is reached between a lender and borrower and the construction or operation of a project begins, it becomes necessary to secure goods and services to facilitate project completion. The process of selecting the vendors and service providers to work on these projects is known as the procurement process. Banks and other lenders are interested in ensuring that contracts are awarded to qualified and cost-efficient companies and individuals to reduce the risks involved in project lending. Lenders typically oversee the bidding process, as they often have greater visibility to a wider range of consultants and companies. Additionally, lenders often provide assurance to bidders that the process will employ equal opportunity practices and adhere to guidelines governing the process.

World Bank

PROCUREMENT POLICY AND COORDINATION UNIT The World Bank lends an annual average of between USD 10 million and USD 15 million to investment projects that purchase goods, equipment, civil works, and consulting services to implement these products. The World Bank often assists the recipients of its financial aid in locating suppliers of these goods and services by overseeing the procurement and bidding processes and making these opportunities as open to the public as possible. The World Bank issues standard bidding documents, supports borrowers in developing a procurement capacity, disseminates information on procurement matters, and maintains liaison with the business community through periodic conferences and monthly business seminars.

The World Bank ensures that its procurement policy adheres to 5 basic guidelines: (1) economy and efficiency must be maintained; (2) loans may be used only for purposes specific to project completion; (3) equal opportunity must be provided to every bidder; (4) the money should open opportunities to local contractors and manufacturers; and (5) transparency must be ensured throughout the procurement process.

Standard bidding documents, instructions for bid applications, and general guidelines for the World Bank can be downloaded from the website listed here.

Procurement Policy and Coordination Unit
The World Bank
1818 H Street, NW
Washington, DC 20433
Tel: 202-473-8874
Fax: 202-522-3317
Web: www.worldbank.org/html/opr/procure/
            contents.html

U.S. Agency for International Development (USAID)

USAID OFFICE OF PROCUREMENT USAID awards approximately
$4 billion dollars every year in federal contracts and grants. Most
USAID contacts are awarded for technical assistance, but also
include the areas of transportation services and construction.
Contracts and grants are often open to the public. USAID ensures
that procurement procedures are conducted in an open manner
and employ equal opportunity practices.
Office of Procurement
U.S. Agency for International Development
Ronald Reagan Building
Washington, DC 20523
Tel: 202-712-5130
Fax: 202-216-3395
E-mail: AandAOmbudsman@usaid.gov
Web: www.usaid.gov/business

3

Regulations and Requirements

Before undertaking any overseas venture, U.S. firms should be aware of foreign country agreements, licenses, host-country regulations regarding certain types of business, tax incentives, requirements, and general regulations affecting trade between the United States and the foreign country. This chapter discusses the following topics:

- **Accounting and Tax Information:** Tax rules governing U.S. individuals and companies abroad, as well as U.S. government incentives for operating abroad
- **Export License Assistance:** Where to obtain information on export licenses and the application process
- **Host Country Incentives:** Investment incentives available in foreign countries for U.S. businesses, including import duty exemptions, tax holidays, and grants
- **International Agreements and Treaties:** How to locate information on investment treaties, trade barriers, and foreign government approvals
- **Rules, Regulations, and Standards:** Where to find information and programs to assist U.S. firms with product standards, customs, export restrictions, and trade disputes

ACCOUNTING AND TAX INFORMATION

GENERAL INFORMATION

This chapter provides the most current and detailed information available. As tax codes, rules and regulations, and treaties are added, changed, or eliminated on a frequent and regular basis, however, be sure to contact an appropriate and authorized agency for the most up-to-date information possible.

TAXATION OF U.S. CITIZENS ABROAD U.S. citizens and resident aliens who work or live abroad or receive certain types of foreign income fall under special categories for tax purposes and are granted special exclusions or deductions under certain circumstances. Individuals are advised to consult a tax attorney or an accountant to determine whether modifications to the rules have been enacted and their effect, if any, on taxes.

OPERATING ABROAD: U.S. INCOME TAX INCENTIVES Major U.S. accounting firms offer comprehensive tax information for U.S. corporations, small businesses, and individuals engaged in international commercial transactions. They provide detailed information on taxation of foreign operations, controlled foreign corporations, sale or liquidation of controlled foreign corporations, foreign tax credits, tax treaties, and special U.S. trade incentives, as well as tax incentives offered by host countries. Because the tax subjects are complex and rules are modified frequently, business executives and individuals are advised to consult a knowledgeable tax adviser.

TAX-FAVORED EXPORT ENTITIES U.S. law allows for the establishment of certain entities that receive special tax benefits from the income earned through the export of qualifying goods and services. These are the Foreign Sales Corporation (FSC) and the Interest-Charge Domestic International Sales Corporation (IC-DISC). These tax subsidies, however, have been ruled illegal by the World Trade Organization and as a result it is possible that they may not exist much longer. The qualification requirements and associated benefits of the export incentives are as follows:

- **FSC** To qualify as an FSC, a corporation must be created or organized under the laws of a qualifying foreign country or a U.S. possession. The corporation must have no more than 25 shareholders, and it must not have preferred stock outstanding at any time during the tax year. The FSC must maintain an office in a qualifying foreign country or a U.S. possession, and it must maintain a set of permanent books of account at that office. Furthermore, at least one of the directors of the corporation must not be a resident of the United States. The FSC must meet the specified foreign management requirements and perform certain economic processes outside the United States. If the corporation meets these and other technical requirements, up to 30 percent of foreign trade may be exempt from U.S. tax, while the remainder will be subject to current taxes. The FSC rules also provide special pricing and income-allocation techniques that help exporters get the maximum tax benefit from the use of this export vehicle.

Certain transfer pricing rules apply when an FSC buys or sells from a related party. The IRS requires that the sale or purchase price be a fair market price or an "arm's-length price." Otherwise, the IRS may reallocate income and expenses between the related parties to reflect such a price. Transfer pricing rules are complex, and companies are encouraged to consult the IRS directly and/or a knowledgeable tax consultant.

Some exporters may elect to treat their FSCs as "small FSCs" if sales are below $5 million. To qualify as a small FSC, a corporation must have elected small FSC status and kept it in effect for the tax year. The corporation cannot be a member of a controlled group that includes an FSC.

- **IC-DISC** Rather than forming an FSC, exporters may establish an IC-DISC. In contrast to the FSC, this is a domestic entity. To qualify, a domestic corporation must derive at least 95 percent of its gross receipts from exporting activities and 95 percent of its assets must be export-related. If the corporation meets these and other requirements, the IC-DISC provisions of the tax code will allow the partial deferral (versus the FSC's exemption) of U.S. income taxes on export profits derived from a maximum of $10 million of gross receipts annually. Unlike the FSC, the "interest-charge" DISC is not subject to U.S. tax. Its shareholders, however, are taxed at current rates. In addition, the shareholders must pay an interest charge on the deferred tax of the IC-DISC. As with the FSC, the IC-DISC rules provide special pricing and income-allocation techniques to maximize available tax benefits.

LICENSING TECHNOLOGY TO A FOREIGN USER If a U.S. business decides not to operate abroad but to make its technology available to a foreign user, royalties or other fees received for the use of the technology may be subject to withholding by the foreign country on the gross amount of the fee. Generally, when such a withholding is made, it is creditable against the U.S. income tax payable upon the fee. An income tax treaty between the United States and the foreign country may reduce or eliminate this withholding.

For some U.S. businesses that have neither the desire nor the capacity to set up operations overseas, licensing technology may provide a useful alternative. However, from a business standpoint, it may be best to establish operations abroad. In that case, significantly different tax considerations come into play. Licensing may not only create competitors, but may also restrict market access.

OPERATING WITHIN A FOREIGN COUNTRY If a U.S. corporation or individual establishes a foreign corporation to carry on activities abroad, its income is generally not subject to U.S. tax until the corporation pays a dividend to the U.S. shareholder. Therefore, U.S. tax on such foreign income may be deferred, even though the foreign corporation is owned entirely by a U.S. corporation or individual.

When a dividend is paid, the U.S. government allows a credit for withholding tax imposed by the foreign country on the dividend. In the case of a U.S. corporate shareholder owning at least 10 percent of the foreign corporation, a credit also is allowed for all or a portion of a foreign corporate income tax imposed on the foreign corporation.

OPERATING ABROAD THROUGH A BRANCH OF A U.S. CORPORATION, PARTNERSHIP, OR JOINT VENTURE A U.S. corporation that has foreign source income through the operation of a branch incurs U.S. corporate taxes on that income as it is earned. If there are foreign losses, those amounts may be used to reduce its U.S. taxable income. If foreign income taxes are paid on the foreign source income, the foreign taxes may be credited against the U.S. taxes (subject to certain limitations if foreign losses have been used to offset U.S. income). U.S. partners or joint ventures must include a share of foreign source income in their U.S. tax returns. U.S. tax is payable on this income, but a credit is allowed for a share of foreign income taxes incurred.

"S CORPORATIONS" Certain provisions of the Internal Revenue Code allow a U.S. corporation that is owned by a small group of U.S. shareholders to elect to pay no U.S. corporate taxes. Instead, each shareholder is taxed on a share of the corporation's income as it is earned and may deduct a share of any losses. Since the corporation is not taxed, the usual double tax burden of operating in the corporate form (i.e., the corporation taxed and the shareholders taxed when dividends are remitted to them) is avoided. Foreign corporate income taxes paid by such a corporation that operates abroad are allowed as credits on the shareholders' U.S. individual tax returns.

POSSESSIONS CORPORATIONS Some U.S. possessions, such as Puerto Rico, provide tax incentives for a U.S. corporation that organizes a business there, including various tax holidays. If a U.S. corporation also elects to be taxed as a possessions corporation and complies with certain other requirements, the corporation will receive a special tax credit against its U.S. corporate income tax. The credit will equal the U.S. income tax that would have been levied on profits earned by that corporation in the possession. Thus, the corporation may pay no U.S. income tax on those profits. A U.S. corporation can elect to be taxed as a possessions corporation if at least 80 percent of its gross income is from sources in a possession and 75 percent of that gross income is from the active conduct of business in the possession.

EXEMPTION FROM GROSS INCOME FOR EMPLOYEES BASED ABROAD Self-employed U.S. individuals or U.S. employees residing in a foreign country can be exempt from U.S. income tax up to $80,000 of foreign-earned income (income from the performance of personal services in the foreign country). To qualify for this exemption, the employee or self-employed individual must be a resident abroad for an entire tax year or be physically present abroad for at least 330 days during a 12-month period. An employee also may be exempt from U.S. income tax on amounts received from his or her employer to cover certain excess housing costs incurred in the foreign country. Many employers take advantage of these exemptions by reducing the compensation of their overseas employees by an amount equal to the U.S. income tax the employees would have paid had they remained in the United States.

FOREIGN TAX CREDIT LIMITATION All U.S. taxpayers are permitted to credit against their U.S. income tax liability foreign income taxes paid or accrued during the taxable year on foreign-source income. In most instances, U.S. corporate taxpayers that receive dividends from a foreign subsidiary in which they own at least 10 percent of the voting stock are allowed to credit the corporate income taxes paid by that subsidiary on the earnings distributed. However, limitations on the credit are designed to ensure that the foreign tax credit claimed will not exceed the U.S. income tax payable by the U.S. taxpayers on the foreign source income. To the extent the limitation prevents a U.S. taxpayer from crediting all of the foreign income tax paid or accrued, double taxation (U.S. plus foreign) or excessive taxation of the same income may result. Due to various factors, including differences in U.S. and foreign concepts of income, it is not unusual for the amount of creditable foreign tax to be limited in a taxable year. A two-year carryback and five-year carryforward period is permitted for those credits so limited, subject to certain requirements.

TRANSFERS OF PROPERTY TO A FOREIGN CORPORATION When a U.S. business organizes a foreign corporation to do business abroad, it often transfers to that foreign corporation tangible property that has appreciated in value (such as equipment or foreign currency) or intangible property that will give rise to future income (such as patents or technical know-how, customer lists, and so forth) necessary for conducting that business. Any such transfer must be reported to the IRS. The gain realized on a transfer to a subsidiary company ordinarily is not taxed by the United States at the time of transfer. However, since the foreign corporation's income may not be currently subject to U.S. income tax, that corporation could subsequently sell or use that property and avoid any U.S. income tax. To prevent such avoidance, when applied to transfers of property to a foreign corporation, the general rule is that the amount of gain or income to be earned is recognized and subject to tax. Certain exceptions to this rule exist, including nonrecognition of gain when tangible assets transferred are used in the active conduct of a trade or business outside the United States.

PASSIVE FOREIGN INVESTMENT COMPANY (PFIC) A PFIC is any foreign corporation in which, for any taxable year, 75 percent or more of the gross income consists of passive income or if at least 50 percent of the average value of the assets produce (or are held to produce) passive income. Ownership percentage by U.S. persons is not a determinant of PFIC status. A PFIC can elect to be treated as a Qualified Electing Fund (QEF) or a Non-Qualified

Electing Fund (Non-QEF). A U.S. shareholder in a PFIC electing QEF status must include in income the pro rata share of the QEF's net capital gain and other earnings and profits (subject to the taxpayer's election to defer payment of tax and incur an interest charge). A U.S. shareholder in a PFIC that does not elect QEF status must pay tax and an interest charge on the deferred portion of any gain on disposition of PFIC stock and on certain distributions from the PFIC.

THE CLOSELY HELD FOREIGN CORPORATION—PASSIVE INCOME As discussed previously, if a U.S. individual organizes a foreign corporation to conduct activities abroad, the income earned by that corporation will normally not be subject to U.S. income tax until the U.S. corporation pays dividends to that individual. However, if more than 50 percent of the corporation's gross income is passive income (e.g., interest, dividends, and so forth) and more than 50 percent in value or voting power of the corporation's stock is owned by five or fewer U.S. citizens or residents, the corporation will be a "Foreign Personal Holding Company." As such, the corporation's net income will be taxed directly to its U.S. shareholders, although not actually distributed to those shareholders as dividends.

CONTROLLED FOREIGN CORPORATIONS (CFCs) Because the income of a foreign corporation is generally not taxed by the United States until distributed as dividends to its U.S. shareholders, some taxpayers seek to shift income currently taxable by the United States to a foreign subsidiary to defer U.S. income tax. The Internal Revenue Code attempts to prevent this by requiring shareholders of so-called CFCs to pay tax on the following types of income earned by the CFC even though such income has not been distributed to the shareholders:

- Passive investment income
- Income from the purchase of goods from or the sale of goods to certain related entities
- Income from the performance of services for or on behalf of certain related entities
- Certain types of shipping and oil-related income
- Insurance income from insuring risk located outside the CFC's country of incorporation
- Income from bad conduct, such as participation in an international boycott and payment of illegal bribes and kickbacks

NON-ARM'S-LENGTH DEALING WITH A FOREIGN CORPORATION If a U.S. corporation deals with its foreign subsidiary in other than an arm's-length fashion, the Internal Revenue Service (IRS) may adjust the U.S. taxpayer's income as if the parties were unrelated. Thus the arm's-length standard requires a related taxpayer to report income and expenses from transactions with the parent as if it were not related to the parent. (Therefore, it is extremely important that the basis for any intercompany pricing be carefully documented.)

GAIN ON DISPOSITION OF FOREIGN SUBSIDIARY BY U.S. PARENT TAXED AS ORDINARY INCOME If a U.S. corporation sells or exchanges (including liquidation) stock of a foreign subsidiary that is CFC, any gain recognized by the U.S. corporation on the stock sale will be taxable as dividend income to the extent the gain does not exceed the foreign corporation's earnings and profits attributable to the stock have not been previously taxed by the United States.

BRIBE- AND BOYCOTT-RELATED INCOME U.S. taxpayers who use foreign corporations to make illegal bribes or other payments to foreign officials or who participate in economic boycotts against Israel (or other designated countries) may be denied credits for foreign income taxes, deferral from U.S. tax on the foreign subsidiary's income, and FSC benefits.

DENIAL OF THE FOREIGN TAX CREDIT WITH RESPECT TO CERTAIN FOREIGN COUNTRIES In general, the foreign tax credit is denied when income is attributable to activities conducted in one of the following:

- In a country that the Secretary of State has designated as one repeatedly supporting terrorism
- In a country where the United States does not have diplomatic relations
- In a country where the government is not recognized by the United States

In addition, U.S. shareholders CFCs will be taxed on the corporation's income attributable to activities conducted in one of the above-described countries. For more information or for questions concerning tax status or regulations, contact the IRS at the following address:

Internal Revenue Service
950 L'Enfant Plaza South, SW
Washington, DC 20024
Tel: 202-622-5000
Fax: 202-622-7854
Web: www.irs.gov

ORGANIZATIONS AND SERVICES

FINANCIAL/GOVERNMENTAL ACCOUNTING STANDARDS BOARD **(FASB/GASB)** These organizations establish and improve standards of financial accounting and reporting for the guidance and education of the public, including issuers, auditors, and users of financial information. FASB serves the investing public through transparent information resulting from high-quality financial reporting standards, developed in an independent, private sector, and open due process. GASB establishes and improves standards of state and local government accounting and financial reporting.

Financial Accounting Standards Board
401 Merritt 7
P.O. Box 5116
Norwalk, CT 06856
Tel: 800-748-0659
            203-847-0700
Fax: 203-849-9714
Web: www.fasb.org
            www.gasb.org

INTERNAL REVENUE SERVICE **(IRS)** This government organization assists international taxpayers through a variety of services, including technical assistance, publications, and other services that can be accessed online. The IRS was recently reorganized into four divisions to better serve its clients: Wage & Investment, Small Business/Self-Employed, Large to Midsize Businesses, and Tax Exempt & Government Entities Division.

Internal Revenue Service
950 L'Enfant Plaza South, SW
Washington, DC 20024
Tel: 800-829-3676
Web: www.irs.gov

INTERNATIONAL TAX COUNSEL This division within the U.S. Department of the Treasury negotiates tax treaties, reviews and works on proposed regulations, and reviews IRS revenue rulings. The International Tax Counsel office also provides up-to-date information on international tax legislation.

International Tax Counsel
U.S. Department of the Treasury
Room 1000
1500 Pennsylvania Avenue, NW
Washington, DC 20220
Tel: 202-622-0180
Fax: 202-622-1956
Web: www.ustreas.gov/offices/tax-policy/
          offices/itc.html

EXPORT LICENSE ASSISTANCE

U.S. Department of Commerce (DOC)

A BASIC GUIDE TO EXPORTING AND U.S. EXPORT ADMINISTRATION REGULATIONS This publication of the International Trade Administration (ITA) is obtainable from the U.S. Government Printing Office to assist businesses in developing export strategies, finding economic market research, shipping overseas, completing export documentation, responding to overseas inquiries, and taking advantage of available government export-assistance programs.

Superintendent of Documents
U.S. Government Printing Office
Tel: 202-512-1800
Fax: 202-512-2250
Web: www.access.gpo.gov

EXPORT LICENSE VOICE INFORMATION SYSTEM (ELVIS) This service of the DOC's Bureau of Export Administration (BXA) is the central resource for information on export licenses and regulations. With a touch-tone telephone ELVIS lets you request information through voice mail and connects you to an export counselor. ELVIS provides information on the variety of licenses available; lets you order applications, regulations, and publications; and allows you to obtain commodity classifications, up-to-date regulations, and helpful export enforcement tips.

Export Counseling Division
Department of Commerce
1400 Pennsylvania Avenue, NW, Room 2705
Washington DC 20230
Tel: 202-482-4811
Fax: 202-482-3617
Web: www.bxa.doc.gov

OFFICE OF EXPORTER SERVICES (OEXS) OEXS interprets the Export Administration Regulations and provides assistance that includes up-to-date status information on pending license applications; advice on a broad range of export issues, licensing requirements, required documentation for export transactions, and special policy concerns for specific countries; assistance in selecting the appropriate license; and answers to inquiries regarding the Bureau of Export Administration's policy issues and processing time frames. OEXS counselors also serve as intermediaries and arrange meetings between exporters and BXA licensing officials.

- **Simplied Network Application Process (SNAP)**—The BXA now receives a significant amount of traffic through this free Internet-based service. SNAP provides a secure environment for the electronic submission of license applications, commodity classification requests, and high-performance computer notices. Once BXA has received and processed a request to use SNAP, exporters can access the system for tracking purposes in as little as 24 hours. Notification of final action is sent electronically.

- **System for Tracking Export License Applications (STELA)**— STELA is an automated voice response system that enables exporters to access the Export Control Automated Support System (ECASS) database by using a touch-tone telephone. STELA provides exporters information on the status of their license applications 24 hours a day, 365 days a year. For those applications approved without conditions, STELA can give exporters authority to ship their goods.

Office of Exporter Services
Department of Commerce
1401 Constitution Avenue, NW
Washington DC 20230
Tel: 202-482-4811

Fax: 202-482-3617
Web: www.bxa.doc.gov

HOST COUNTRY INCENTIVES

The following is a checklist of some of the incentives offered by countries to attract investment. The incentives listed vary by country and depend on how attractive a particular investment is to the country's economy. These investments share some of the following attributes:

- Provide goods as a substitute for imports
- Involve employment of local labor
- Use local raw materials
- Train local managers and technicians
- Develop locally owned suppliers
- Reinvest profits in the local company

TAX AND TARIFF INCENTIVES

Income Tax Incentives

- Corporate income tax holidays (exemptions from income tax) that may be limited or unlimited in time and amount
- Accelerated depreciation
- Investment tax credits
- Increased deduction allowed for business entertainment in connection with export sales
- "Double deduction" of export promotion expenses
- Royalty or fee income of a foreign transferor of technology that may be exempt from withholding of income tax
- Foreign contractor's taxable income that may be determined by a favorable formula
- Reduced personal taxation of foreign managers and technicians
- Reduced withholding of tax on dividends to foreign shareholders from approved investment

Other Tax Incentives

- Exemption from excise taxes on imported machinery and equipment
- Exemption from registration duties, stamp taxes, or capital taxes upon incorporation

- Exemption from property taxes
- Exemption from sales, value added, and excise taxes with respect to export sales
- Tariff incentives
- Waivers on import of machinery, equipment, and raw materials
- Access to regional common markets
- Tariff-free foreign trade zones

NON-TAX INCENTIVES
Financial Assistance

- Grants for purchase of land, buildings, and machinery
- Grants for expenditure of export market development
- Grants to aid research and feasibility studies
- Government land provided for factory sites
- Low-cost rentals in government-owned industrial parks
- Low-cost financing

Other

- Assistance in locating plant sites, employees, suppliers, and markets
- Preference in purchases by government agencies
- Protection of market from competition
- Purchase of government-owned raw materials (e.g., oil and gas) at less than market price
- Guarantee of availability of foreign exchange to purchase equipment and raw materials and to pay interest, fees for technology, and dividends
- Work permits granted to nonresident technicians and managers

This checklist is intended to illustrate the variety of incentives, many of which are negotiable during the preinvestment stage, that are offered by host countries. A prospective investor's market and investment feasibility study should include a thorough investigation of all tax and nontax incentives, as well as obstacles to doing business in a particular country. Further information can be obtained from major accounting firms, foreign ministries, U.S. government agencies, and embassies, as well as financial institutions operating abroad.

U.S. PATENT AND TRADEMARK OFFICE (PTO) This office administers the patent and trademark laws of the United States. After examining patent and trademark applications, PTO grants protection to qualified inventions and federal registration to qualified trademarks. The PTO also provides information concerning international patents and trademarks.

U.S. Patent and Trademark Office
Center for Patent and Trademark Information
2231 Crystal Drive
Arlington, VA 22202
Tel: 703-308-5557
Fax: 703-308-5247
Web: www.uspto.gov

INTERNATIONAL AGREEMENTS AND TREATIES

Department of State

COMMERCIAL AND BUSINESS AFFAIRS (CBA) This office is the point of contact in the U.S. Department of State for U.S. companies requiring assistance with international business. CBA works directly with U.S. business representatives to help them tap into the worldwide resources of the department. CBA creates a dynamic partnership with U.S. businesses by championing U.S. business interests overseas with advocacy, troubleshooting, and market access support; articulating the U.S. business community perspective in foreign policy making and management; engaging business leaders on international issues that affect them; and working with international and U.S. organizations, opinion leaders, and other stakeholders to advance U.S. commercial and business interests in the global marketplace.

Commercial and Business Affairs
2201 C Street, NW, Room 2318
Washington, DC 20520
Tel: 202-647-1625
Fax: 202-647-3953
Web: www.state.gov

INTELLECTUAL PROPERTY & COMPETITION DIVISION This division of the Bureau of Economic and Business Affairs of the U.S. Department of State handles policies relating to the foreign protection of U.S. patents, trademarks, and copyrights. This office works closely with USTR, DOC, and the U.S. Customs Service, among other government agencies, to resolve copyright, patent, and intellectual property rights issues.

The Intellectual Property & Competition Division
U.S. Department of State
2201 C Street, NW
Washington, DC 20520
Tel: 202-647-3895
Fax: 202-647-1537
E-mail: ebtppmtaipc@state.gov
Web: www.state.gov

TREATIES IN FORCE: A LIST OF TREATIES AND OTHER INTERNA-
TIONAL AGREEMENTS OF THE UNITED STATES IN FORCE This annual
publication of the U.S. Department of State includes bilateral and
multilateral agreements in effect as of January 2001 and an
appendix listing documents affecting international copyright regulations of the United States. This list has been archived and is
available for viewing at no cost at the web site below. Check with
the Department of State for updates.

Superintendent of Documents
U.S. Government Printing Office
Washington, DC 20402
Tel: 202-512-1800
Web: www.state.gov/www/global/legal_affairs/
          tifindex.html

National Marine Fisheries Services (NMFS)

TRADE AND COMMERCIAL SERVICES This branch of the NMFS
addresses trade problems affecting U.S. fishery exports. Domestic
and international issues include market access, standards development and application, inspection of U.S. exports, technological trade barriers, traditional industry development, product
utilization, and other issues related to industry competitiveness.
Trade and Commercial Services also prioritizes industry trade
issues to improve access to foreign markets and enhance the competitive position of the U.S. fishing industry. These services also
develop and implement trade strategy, and negotiate positions in
response to industry needs, by representing the Assistant Administrator in trade negotiations with other U.S. government agencies and foreign governments.

Office of Industry and Trade
National Marine Fisheries Services
1315 East-West Highway
Silver Spring, MD 20910
Tel: 301-713-2379
Fax: 301-713-2384
Web: www.nmfs.noaa.gov/trade

United Nations

UNITED NATIONS COMMISSION ON INTERNATIONAL TRADE LAW (UNCITRAL) UNCITRAL is the core legal body within the United Nations system in the field of international trade law. UNCITRAL was tasked by the General Assembly to further the progressive harmonization and unification of the law of international trade. To increase these opportunities worldwide, UNCITRAL formulates modern, fair, and harmonized rules on commercial transactions, including:

- Conventions, model laws, and rules that are acceptable worldwide.
- Legal and legislative guides and recommendations of great practical value.
- Updated information on case law and enactments of uniform commercial law.
- Technical assistance in law reform projects.
- Regional and national seminars on uniform commercial law.
- Information on rules and regulations, case law, models for arbitration and conciliation, research guides, online resources, and more.

Secretariat of the United Nations Commission on International Trade Law (UNCITRAL)
Vienna International Centre
P.O. Box 500
A-1400 Vienna, Austria
Tel: (43-1) 26060-4061
E-mail: uncitral@uncitral.org
Web: www.uncitral.org

U.S. Department of Agriculture (USDA)

FOREIGN AGRICULTURAL SERVICE (FAS) This division of the USDA identifies and works to mitigate foreign trade barriers and practices that impede exports of U.S. farm products. Agricultural representatives play a major role in trying to remove tariff or nontariff barriers affecting market access.

A company that has identified a barrier to exporting its products to a foreign country should contact a Market Development Cooperator group (i.e., trade association). The Cooperator and the USDA will work together to resolve the barrier. A company that believes it has been treated unfairly by a foreign government in a trade issue, such as losing a tender to a higher bidder, should also contact the Cooperator. Exporters without cooperator representation can contact USDA directly.

Foreign Agricultural Service
U.S. Department of Agriculture
1400 Independence Avenue, SW, Room 4939
Washington, DC 20250
Tel: 202-720-0938
Fax: 202-690-0193
E-mail: info@fas.usda.gov
Web: www.fas.usda.gov

U.S. Department of Commerce

SERVICE INDUSTRIES, TOURISM AND FINANCE This division of the DOC provides counseling and advice on U.S. and foreign country laws, regulations, and practices affecting international trade and investment. Staff members offer information and help U.S. firms research laws on taxation; antitrust, patent, and trademark rights; licensing patents; foreign agents, distributors, and joint ventures; product liability; and other issues related to exporting and international investment.

Service Industries, Tourism and Finance Division
Department of Commerce
1401 Constitution Avenue, NW, Room 1128
Washington, DC 20230
Tel: 202-482-5261
Fax: 202-482-4775
Web: www.ita.doc.gov/td/sif/index.htm

U.S. Trade Representative (USTR)

This office negotiates and administers all trade agreements on behalf of the United States. In addition, the USTR serves as the representative for the United States in the major international trade organizations. The USTR has two major responsibilities:

- It acts as the President's chief adviser on international trade policy. Its primary responsibility within the U.S. government is developing international trade policy and coordinating implementation. This includes negotiating with the United Nations, the Organization for Economic Cooperation and Development (OECD), and other multilateral organizations on trade and commodity issues.
- It serves as the country's chief negotiator for international trade agreements. The USTR also is responsible for policy guidance on issues relating to international trade, including 1) expansion of U.S. exports, 2) matters concerning the General Agreement on Tariffs and Trade (GATT), 3) bilateral trade and commodity issues, 4) international trade issues involving energy and the environment, and 5) investment matters related to trade.

U.S. Trade Representative
600 17th Street, NW
Washington, DC 20508
Tel: 888-473-8787
E-mail: contactustr@ustr.gov
Web: www.ustr.gov

BILATERAL INVESTMENT TREATY (BIT) These treaties are reciprocal agreements between the U.S. government and a foreign government that outline the treatment of investors in the two countries. These treaties, ratified by the Senate, create an international obligation for the United States and the foreign treaty partner, thus superseding domestic law. The U.S. government seeks to negotiate BITs that contain the following major elements:

- Most-favored-nation or national treatment (with limited exceptions), whichever is better, for the U.S. investor abroad
- Guarantees of prompt, adequate, and effective compensation for expropriation, as well as the right to transfer such compensation at the prevailing exchange rate on the date of expropriation
- The right of investors to make free transfers of currency in connection with the investment at the prevailing exchange rate

- A legal framework for the settlement of disputes between a firm and the host country, based on prevailing standards of international law, including the possibility of third-party arbitration
- A treaty of at least ten years' duration

The USTR provides copies of BITs that are pending Senate ratification and a list of countries that have entered into BIT negotiations with the United States.

Office of Industry and Services
Office of the U.S. Trade Representative
600 17th Street, NW, Room 422
Washington, DC 20508
Tel: 202-395-7271
Fax: 202-395-3911
Web: www.ustr.gov

Other

TREATIES AND OTHER INTERNATIONAL ACTS SERIES This publication contains the texts of at least 200 treaties entered into by the United States with other nations. It is published and issued in an indeterminate period. A subscription costs $82.

Superintendent of Documents
U.S. Government Printing Office
Washington, DC 20402
Tel: 202-512-1800

WORLD TRADE ORGANIZATION (WTO) This organization was established in 1995 and is responsible for administering agreed-upon rules for trade among its member countries. It requires the notification, publication, and uniform application of trade regulations between member countries and states. For more information on member countries of the WTO and specific trade regulations, contact the WTO directly.

World Trade Organization
Rue de Lausanne 154
CH-1211 Geneva 21
Switzerland
Tel: (41-22) 739 51 11
Fax: (41-22) 731 42 06
E-mail: enquiries@wto.org
Web: www.wto.org

RULES, REGULATIONS, AND STANDARDS

Environmental Protection Agency (EPA)

EDOCKET EPA Docket (EDOCKET) is an online public docket and comment system designed to expand access to documents in the EPA's major dockets. Dockets contain Federal Register notices, support documents, and public comments for regulations the Agency publishes and various nonregulatory activities. This service allows you to search, download, and print documents and submit comments online.

Environmental Protection Agency
EPA Docket Center (EPA/DC)
1200 Pennsylvania Avenue, NW
Washington, DC 20460
Tel: 202-566-1744
Fax: 202-566-2994
Web: www.epa.gov

National Institute of Standards and Technology (NIST)

LAWS AND METRIC GROUP When products are shipped or quotes are provided for foreign customers, products must be denominated in metric standards. The Laws and Metric Group of the Weight and Measures Division provides exporters with guidance and assistance on foreign metric import regulations.

Laws and Metric Group
Weights and Measures Division
National Institute of Standards and Technology
100 Bureau Drive, Stop 2000
Gaithersburg, MD 20899
Tel: 301-975-3690
Fax: 301-948-1416
E-mail: TheSI@nist.gov
Web: www.nist.gov/metric

NATIONAL CENTER FOR STANDARDS AND CERTIFICATION INFORMATION (NCSCI) This organization is the central depository and inquiry point for standards information in the United States. NCSCI responds to over 5,000 individual inquiries annually on identification and source availability of standards. NCSCI also prepares directories for specialized standards information.

NCSCI
Global Standards and Information Group
National Institute of Standards and Technology
100 Bureau Drive, Stop 2150
Gaithersburg, MD 20899
Tel: 301-975-4040
Fax: 301-926-1559
E-mail: ncsci@nist.gov
Web: www.nist.gov

Small Business Association (SBA)

EXPORT LEGAL ASSISTANCE NETWORK (ELAN) This organization provides free initial consultations to small companies on the legal aspects of exporting through an arrangement with the Federal Bar Association (FBA). Qualified attorneys from the International Law Council of the FBA provide advice for companies engaged in the export industry.

Small Business Administration
1110 Vermont Avenue, NW
P.O. Box 34500
Washington, DC 20043
Tel: 202-606-4000
Fax: 202-606-4225
Web: www.fita.org/elan

U.S. Department of Agriculture (USDA)

AGRICULTURAL EXPORT SERVICES DIVISION This division of the USDA provides technical services, information, and research on transportation and packaging problems encountered by exporters and shippers of agricultural products.

Agricultural Export Services Division
Foreign Agricultural Service
Room 4949 South Building, Stop 1052
1400 Independence Avenue, SW
Washington, DC 20250
Tel: 202-720-7420
Fax: 202-690-0193

AGRICULTURAL MARKETING SERVICE (AMS) This service of the USDA provides a voluntary food-quality certification service to help U.S. exporters meet importers' specifications. The service is provided on a user-fee basis. To apply for this service, a copy of the contract specifications must be submitted to the AMS in advance. AMS reviews the contracts and works with the companies to develop written specifications that can be certified.

Agricultural Marketing Service
U.S. Department of Agriculture
P.O. Box 96456
Washington, DC 20090
Tel: 202-720-5115
Fax: 202-720-8477
Web: www.ams.usda.gov

Cotton Program
Tel: 202-720-3139

Dairy Program
Tel: 202-720-4392

Fruit and Vegetable Program
Tel: 202-720-4722

Livestock and Seed Program
Tel: 202-720-5705

Poultry Program
Tel: 202-720-4476

Science and Technology Program
Tel: 202-720-5231

Tobacco Program
Tel: 202-205-0567

Transportation and Marketing Program
Tel: 202-690-1300

ANIMAL AND PLANT HEALTH INSPECTION SERVICE (APHIS) This division provides U.S. agricultural exporters with information concerning foreign import requirements for livestock and fresh vegetables. APHIS also will negotiate with foreign agricultural offices regarding the entry requirements for U.S. agricultural products.

Animal and Plant Health Inspection Service
4700 River Road, Unit 133
Riverdale, MD 20737
Tel: 301-734-8896
Fax: 301-734-4300
E-mail: aphis.web@aphis.usda.gov
Web: www.aphis.usda.gov

FOOD AND AGRICULTURE IMPORT REGULATIONS AND STANDARDS (FAIRS) COUNTRY REPORTS FAIRS Country Reports are prepared by the USDA's Foreign Agricultural Service and provide an overview of a country's generic requirements and standards for consumer-ready food products. Reports contain food laws, labeling requirements, and regulations and standards on food additives and pesticides and may be accessed online.
Office of Agricultural Affairs
USDA/Foreign Agricultural Service
1400 Independence Avenue, SW, Room 4939
Washington, DC 20250
Tel: 202-720-0938
Fax: 202-690-0193
Web: www.fas.usda.gov/itp/ofsts/fairs_by_country.asp

FOOD SAFETY AND INSPECTION SERVICE (FSIS) This service supplies information regarding foreign import regulations for meat and poultry. FSIS also inspects meat and poultry products to ensure that they meet both U.S. and foreign standards.
Food Safety and Inspection Service
U.S. Department of Agriculture
Room 331-E, Jamie Whitten Building
1400 Jefferson Drive, SW
Washington, DC 20250
Tel: 202-720-7900
Fax: 202-720-9600
Web: www.fsis.usda.gov

Meat and Poultry Inspections
Tel: 402-221-7400
Fax: 402-221-7438

GRAIN INSPECTION, PACKERS AND STOCKYARDS ADMINISTRATION (GIPSA) GIPSA facilitates the marketing of livestock, poultry, meat, cereals, oilseeds, and related agricultural products and promotes fair and competitive trading practices for the overall benefit of consumers and American agriculture. GIPSA is part of USDA's Marketing and Regulatory Programs, and it works to ensure a productive and competitive global marketplace for U.S. agricultural products. GIPSA also helps ensure a fair and competitive marketing system for all involved in the merchandising of grain and related products, livestock, meat, and poultry.

- **Federal Grain Inspection Service (FGIS)** established the Official Standards for Grain, which are used daily by sellers and buyers to determine the type and quality of grain bought and sold. FGIS also establishes standard testing methodologies to accurately and consistently measure grain quality. Finally, the program provides for the impartial application of these grades and standards through a network of federal, state, and private inspection agencies.
- **Packers and Stockyards Programs (P&S)** ensure open and competitive markets for livestock, meat, and poultry. P&S is a regulatory program whose roots are in providing financial protection and ensuring fair and competitive markets.

Grain Inspection, Packers and Stockyards Administration
Stop 3601, Room 1094-S
1400 Independence Avenue, SW
Washington, DC 20250
Tel: 202-720-0219
Fax: 202-205-9237
Web: www.usda.gov/gipsa/index.htm

OFFICE OF FOOD SAFETY AND TECHNICAL SERVICES (FSTS) This office responds to issues related to food safety regulations and barriers that affect the international trade of U.S. agricultural products. Issues include commodity complaints, foreign product labeling and food standards, sanitary regulations, pesticide residues, and other technical requirements for exporting U.S. products to foreign markets.

Food Safety and Technical Services
FAS/USDA
Room 5545-S
1400 Independence Avenue, SW

Washington, DC 20250
Tel: 202-720-1301
Fax: 202-690-0677
Web: www.fas.usda.gov

Other

AMERICAN NATIONAL STANDARDS INSTITUTE (ANSI) This organization represents the interests of over 1,000 companies, organizations, government agencies, and international members. ANSI facilitates development by ensuring consensus, due process, and openness among its qualified groups. ANSI also promotes the use of U.S. standards internationally and encourages the adoption of international standards as national standards when these meet the needs of the user community.

American National Standards Institute
1819 L Street NW, 6th Floor
Washington, DC 20036
Tel: 202-293-8020
Fax: 202-293-9287
Web: www.ansi.org

EUROPEAN MARKETING RESEARCH CENTER This organization is located in Rotterdam, The Netherlands, and provides technical assistance to U.S. exporters, including help with lost and damaged exports shipped to the European market. The center also provides information on foreign requirements for packaging, labeling, and spoilage tolerances.

European Marketing Research Center
Avenue Louise 283 (b.22)
1050 Brussels Belgium
Tel: 32 (0) 2 626-15-15
Fax: 32 (0) 2 626-15-16
E-mail: info@emrc.be
Web: www.emrc.be

INTERNATIONAL MAIL MANUAL This manual is provided by the United States Postal Service and provides information on correct international postal rates, prohibitions, restrictions, availability of insurance and other special services, as well as information on mailing to individual countries. Subscription service consists of three complete cumulative manuals per year. For an annual subscription, the cost is $24/U.S. or $30/foreign.

Superintendent of Documents
U.S. Government Printing Office
Washington, DC 20402
Tel: 202-512-1800

INTERNATIONAL ORGANIZATION FOR STANDARDIZATION (ISO)
This worldwide federation of national standards bodies from some 130 countries is a nongovernmental organization established in 1947. The mission of ISO is to promote the development of standardization and related activities in the world to facilitate the international exchange of goods and services and to develop cooperation in the spheres of intellectual, scientific, technological, and economic activity. ISO's work results in international agreements that are published as international standards.

ISO Central Secretariat
International Organization for Standardization
1, rue de Varembé
Case postale 56
CH-1211 Genève 20
Switzerland
Tel: (41-22) 749 01 11
Fax: (41-22) 733 34 30
E-mail: central@iso.ch
Web: www.iso.ch

THOMAS The THOMAS World Wide Web system provides free access to legislative information. The first database made available was Bill Text, followed shortly by Congressional Record Text, Bill Summary & Status, the Congressional Record Index, and the Constitution (now found, along with other historical Congressional documents, under "Historical Documents" on the THOMAS home page). Enhancements in the types of legislative data available, as well as in search and display capabilities, are continually updated.

Web: thomas.loc.gov

TRADE REMEDY ASSISTANCE OFFICE This office was established as a separate division of the U.S. International Trade Commission (ITC) to assist eligible small businesses in preparing petitions to the ITC to halt unfair trade practices such as the dumping of foreign goods at below-market prices, as well as foreign import restrictions and export subsidies. This office works closely with the U.S. Department of Commerce, the U.S. Customs Service, the U.S. Trade Representative, and the U.S. Department of Labor to provide technical assistance to firms seeking relief under U.S. trade laws. Legal services assist small companies with filing petitions.

Trade Remedy Assistance Office
500 E Street, SW, Room 601
Washington, DC 20436
Tel: 800-343-9822
           202-205-2200
Fax: 202-205-2139
Web: www.usitc.gov/trao.htm

U.S. Customs Service

This department of the U.S. government is responsible for administering the import laws of the U.S. Virgin Islands and Puerto Rico and for clearing all goods imported into the United States. The Customs Service has seven geographical regions that are further divided into districts with ports of entry.

In addition to providing publications (see U.S. Customs Publications in the publications section of this chapter), the U.S. Customs Service also provides U.S. companies with decisions on the classifications and rates of duty for specific merchandise prior to shipment to the United States. To obtain a decision, the following information must be provided:

- Complete description of the goods, including samples, sketches, diagrams, and other illustrative material if the goods cannot be described adequately in writing
- Method of manufacture or fabrication
- Specifications and analyses
- Quantities and costs of the component materials
- Commercial designation and chief use in the United States

U.S. Customs Service
1300 Pennsylvania Avenue, NW
Washington, DC 20229
Tel: 202-927-1000
Web: www.customs.ustreas.gov

The U.S. Customs Office offers the following free publications that provide information on U.S. customs requirements for imports:

- **U.S. Import Requirements:** General information on U.S. Customs requirements for imported merchandise
- **Tariff Classifications on U.S. Imports:** How to obtain a binding U.S. Customs duty ruling on items before they are imported
- **Import Quota:** Summary of import quotas administered by the Customs Service
- **Notice to Masters of Vessels:** Precautions that masters or owners of vessels should take to avoid penalties and forfeitures
- **Notice to Carriers of Bonded Merchandise:** Precautions that carriers and customhouse brokers should take to safeguard merchandise moving in-bond and the penalties incurred for violations
- **Drawback:** How to obtain a duty refund on certain exports
- **Foreign Trade Zones:** Advantages, use, and customs requirements of foreign trade zones
- **Foreign Assembly of U.S. Components:** A detailed explanation of use of Item 807.00 in the U.S. Tariff Schedule, which permits a reduction in duty to reflect the value of components manufactured in the United States and assembled abroad

The following publications are available for a fee from the U.S. Customs Service:

- **Harmonized Tariff Schedules of the United States Annotated:** For use in classification of imported merchandise, for rates of duty and for statistical purposes; cost is $60/U.S., $75/foreign
- **Customs Regulations of the U.S.:** Loose-leaf volume of regulations interpreting many of the customs, navigation, and other laws administered by the U.S. Customs Service; cost is $98/U.S., $122.50/foreign
- **Customs Bulletin and Decisions:** Weekly pamphlet containing proposed and final amendments to customs regulations, notices and administrative decisions of interest to the international trading community, and pertinent decisions of the U.S. Court of International Trade and the U.S. Court of Appeals for the Federal Circuit; cost is $122.50/U.S., $170/foreign

Superintendent of Documents
U.S. Government Printing Office
Washington, DC 20402
Tel: 202-512-1800

4

Technical Assistance

Due to the complex nature of conducting business in emerging markets, companies often need guidance that extends beyond securing financial support. This guidance, in its numerous forms, tends to fall into the broad category of technical assistance. In this context, technical assistance refers to services that assist officials or executives in operating successfully by improving practices, policies, systems or institutions. On its most basic level, technical assistance involves the transfer of knowledge from qualified and experienced organizations or consultants to countries, companies, or individuals that stand to benefit from such knowledge. Assistance is often offered in the form of market research studies, financial analysis, technological assistance, training programs or workshops, seminars, conferences, publications or newsletters, business plan development, client identification, and more.

Technical assistance is usually funded with grants and is often offered in conjunction with capital investment activities. Many of the organizations and services detailed in this chapter are an excellent starting point when looking for financial assistance, although most of them offer technical assistance services separately from capital investment or other financial activities. The first section of this chapter deals with the funding sources available to the institutions or governments providing technical assistance services or to ventures that make the transfer of knowledge possible. The Technical Assistance Services section outlines services available primarily to the private sector. Many of these sources offer enhanced services within a particular industry in order to improve those emerging markets. The Business Development Services section outlines programs and services that help locate and secure new business opportunities, as opposed to improving existing business operations. The last section outlines training services. Typically, training services advise professionals in order to improve financial, technological, or managerial aspects of business operations. The primary focus for these programs is to ensure the transfer of knowledge directly to business professionals.

Once a potential export, investment opportunity, or economically viable industry within a foreign market has been identified, business executives need to evaluate a project's commercial feasibility. The costs associated with comprehensive feasibility studies, which include overseas travel, consultant fees, and business plan formulation, often preclude not only their undertaking, but also the underlying projects. U.S. government agencies and multilateral organizations administer a variety of programs aimed at sharing the cost of developing overseas projects as well as improving international business expertise. Resources may include travel reimbursement, the hiring of consultants, and/or sharing in the execution of feasibility studies.

Chapter Four is organized under the following main headings:

- Funding Sources
- Technical Assistance Services
- Business Development Services
- Training Services

FUNDING SOURCES

Export-Import Bank of the United States (Ex-Im Bank)

ENGINEERING MULTIPLIER PROGRAM The Ex-Im Bank established this program to stimulate exports of U.S. architectural, industrial design, and engineering services to increase the potential for future U.S. exports. Under this program, Ex-Im Bank aims to expand sales of project-related feasibility studies and preconstruction design and engineering services by offering fixed-rate loans and guarantees to foreign buyers of these services. In the long term, the program is designed to generate additional overseas sales of U.S. goods and services (the multiplier effect) since the foreign buyer is more likely to order U.S. equipment and services for a construction project on which U.S. engineers, designers, and architects did the feasibility and design work.

Export-Import Bank of the United States
Engineering Department
811 Vermont Avenue, NW
Washington, DC 20571
Tel: 202-565-3946
Fax: 202-565-3380
Web: www.exim.gov

Inter-American Development Bank (IDB)

MULTILATERAL INVESTMENT FUND (MIF) MIF is an autonomous fund administered by the IDB. It was established in 1993 to promote private sector investment in the market economies of Latin America and the Caribbean and is the major source of technical assistance grants for micro and small business development in the region, investing primarily with equity and quasi-equity in intermediary institutions that support small enterprises. As of the close of 2002, MIF was engaged in more than 520 projects totaling a commitment of over $830 million. Together with its partners, MIF has directed over $1.6 billion in technical assistance and investment projects. The MIF approves transactions worth about USD 70 million per year, from grants to equity participation, in amounts ranging from below USD 1 million up to a limit of USD 5 million. Grants fund small, targeted projects that encourage innovation or spur new developments and technologies.

MIF operates a Small Enterprise Investment Facility to meet the specialized needs of small businesses. Investment tools including loans and equity and quasi-equity investments are offered to projects that are financially sound. However, MIF also is willing to accept some of the higher risks associated with lending to small and early-stage investments and makes possible projects that might otherwise have a difficult time finding financing. To this end, MIF also extends access to microfinance institutions and services that are willing to aid these enterprises.

The Multilateral Investment Fund announced the approval today of a $5 million grant to promote business alliances and partnerships that will enhance private sector competitiveness in seven countries of Central America and the Caribbean. The resources will help fund 32 pilot projects, chosen on a competitive basis, that will promote competitiveness of around 800 small- and medium-sized businesses in Costa Rica, Dominican Republic, El Salvador, Guatemala, Honduras, Nicaragua and Panama. The program will be carried out by the Instituto Centroamericano de Administración de Empresas (INCAE), which will also contribute $5 million. Other donors will contribute $3.4 million. The business alliance projects will encourage partnerships involving the private sector, nongovernmental organizations and government.

Source: Multilateral Investment Fund Press Release, 5/7/03

Multilateral Investment Fund
1300 New York Avenue, NW
Stop B-600
Washington, DC 20577
Tel: (202) 942-8211
Fax: (202) 942-8100
E-mail: mifcontact@iadb.org
Web: www.iadb.org/mif

National Institute of Standards and Technology (NIST)

NIST GRANTS The NIST provides grants that aid in getting technology products as quickly as possible from the research and development stage to the marketplace. These grants remove barriers and obstacles in commercializing new technologies and are available to industry and academic and other institutions on a competitive basis.

To improve risk and failure management and structural efficiency, a joint venture led by Caterpillar initiated a three-year project on November 2002. The goal is to develop and demonstrate prototype sensor and analysis technologies for determining in real time the condition and remaining functional life of large pieces of equipment. The estimated cost of the project is almost USD 9 million. NIST grants will cover 49% of the estimated total cost. The Structural Health Integrated Electronic Life Determination (SHIELD) system will consist of wireless sensors that could be attached to different parts of a structure to collect data continuously on actual use, fatigue damage and cracks, and hardware and software to analyze the data. Other project participants are Motorola, Inc. (Schaumberg, IL) and Native American Technologies (Golden, CO). The University of Illinois at Urbana-Champaign (Urbana, IL) and Drexel University (Philadelphia, PA) will serve as consultants.

Source: Project Briefs, Advanced Technology Program, NIST

National Institute of Standards and Technology
Department of Commerce
1400 Constitution Avenue, NW, Room 1107
Washington, DC 20230
Tel: 301-975-6329
Web: www.nist.gov

U.S. Agency for International Development (USAID)

THE EURASIA FOUNDATION The Eurasia Foundation is a privately managed grant-making organization established with financing from USAID. The principal aim of the Foundation is to provide flexible grant assistance to the organizations within the Newly Independent States (NIS) of the former Soviet Union. The Foundation supports technical assistance, training, educational, and policy programs in the NIS, covering a wide range of activities in economic and democratic reform. Grants are made available to U.S. organizations with partners in the NIS and directly to NIS organizations.

The Eurasia Foundation's programmatic focus includes eight areas:

- **Business Development:** Topics include training and counseling for entrepreneurs, information dissemination, trade and export promotion, and legal and policy reforms
- **Business Education and Management Training:** Topics include development of curricula and training materials and specific training for managers in specific industries
- **Economics Education and Research:** Topics include faculty training, development of curricula, and policy-related economic research education
- **Electronic Communications:** Topics include access to the Internet for nonprofit organizations, online resources in NIS languages, and training for Internet usage
- **Media:** Topics include the financial and editorial independence of media organizations, training of journalists and editors of the independent media, exploration of press laws, and examination of policy issues relevant to media freedom
- **NGO Development:** Topics include improving management of nongovernmental organizations (NGOs), developing local philanthropy, and improving public awareness of the NGO sector
- **Public Administration and Local Government Reform:** Topics include improvement of management capacity at the national, regional, and local levels; exploration of innovative directions in the delivery of public services; and promotion of regional economic development
- **Rule of Law:** Topics include developing progressive legislation, promoting basic civil rights, improving access to information on laws, and supporting alternative means of dispute resolution

The Eurasia Foundation
1350 Connecticut Avenue, Suite 1000
Washington, DC 20036
Tel: 202-234-7370
Fax: 202-234-7377
Web: www.eurasia.org

In 2001, USAID and the Eurasia Foundation provided support to the Azerbaijani Association of Certified Accountants (ACA) who then introduced the first accounting certification system in the country designed in accordance with international standards. The association also provides International Accounting Standards (IAS) training to local accountants. The association has formed partnerships with the Ministry of Finance to educate government counterparts about the benefits of IAS. In civil society development, successful projects include work with the NGO "Society and Law," which is creating a mechanism for Azerbaijani citizens to gain access to the European Court of Human Rights. The law firm "Mahir" is introducing an alternative dispute resolution, and will select and train independent mediators.

Source: Country Studies, Azerbaijan in 2001, USAID web site

U.S. Department of Commerce (DOC)

MARKET DEVELOPMENT COOPERATOR PROGRAM This competitive matching grants program builds public/private partnerships by providing federal assistance to nonprofit export multipliers such as states, trade associations, chambers of commerce, world trade centers, and other nonprofit industry groups that are particularly effective in reaching small- and medium-sized enterprises. This program helps to underwrite start-up costs for new export ventures that are often difficult for groups to undertake without government assistance.

International Trade Administration
Department of Commerce
1401 Constitution Avenue, NW
Washington, DC 20230
Tel: 800-872-8723
Web: www.ita.doc.gov

NATIONAL OCEANIC AND ATMOSPHERIC ADMINISTRATION (NOAA) GRANTS The NOAA is in charge of conducting studies and ensuring the protection of ocean, marine, and other environmental resources. To this end, the institution provides grants to industry, academic, and government environmental research and projects.

National Oceanic and Atmospheric Administration
8455 Colesville Road, Suite 1500
Silver Spring, MD 20910
Tel: 301-763-6400
Web: www.rdc.noaa.gov

U.S. Trade and Development Agency (USTDA)

This agency funds various types of technical assistance, feasibility studies, training, orientation visits, and business workshops that support development of modern infrastructure and fair and open trading environments. All USTDA activities are carried out by U.S. firms. The following is a brief summary of the activities that USTDA funds:

- **Definitional missions and desk studies** undertake quick analysis of project proposals to affirm eligibility and are conducted in the United States by third-party contracting firms. By contrast, definitional missions provide a more detailed evaluation of a project proposal and involve traveling to the host country in question.
- **Technical assistance** provides fund services for the evaluation or implementation of projects. In some instances, USTDA also offers funding to foreign governments for technical assistance that supports activities that may lead to increased U.S. exports.
- **Feasibility studies** support exporter or investor feasibility studies through cost-sharing grants as long as certain eligibility criteria are met, including the potential for significant U.S. exports upon project implementation.
- **Orientation visits** offer U.S. suppliers an opportunity to showcase their products to foreign procurement officials. USTDA sponsors visits to the United States for foreign officials interested in purchasing American goods and services for specific projects.

- **Conferences** allow USTDA to provide U.S. firms with face-to-face contact with key procurement officials and decision makers. These results-driven events build business relationships by familiarizing project sponsors with U.S. goods and services and informing U.S. companies about specific upcoming export opportunities.

In January 2003, U.S. Trade and Development Agency (USTDA) signed a $287,480 grant agreement with the Karachi Port Trust (KPT) of Pakistan to partially fund a feasibility study for a proposed 25 million gallons per day (MGD) desalination plant in Karachi. Most of Pakistan's urban water supply and sewage works were installed or last upgraded more than 25 years ago, and are operating above design capacity or have reached the end of the serviceable system life. This situation has left the country facing a critical shortage of potable water supply. Karachi, a port city with a population of about 12 million, and growing at 5 percent per year, faces severe water shortages with no confirmed or identified new sources of water to meet the present deficit of over 150 MGD.

Source: USTDA Press Releases, January 23, 2003

U.S. Trade and Development Agency
1000 Wilson Boulevard, Suite 1600
Arlington, VA 22209
Tel: 703-875-4357
Fax: 703-875-4009
E-mail: info@tda.gov
Web: www.tda.gov

World Bank

CONSULTANT TRUST FUND PROGRAM (CTFP) The Consultant Trust Fund Program (CTFP) of the World Bank encourages participating donor countries to make available grant funds, usually tied to services sourced from these countries, to complement the World Bank Group's own resources for technical assistance activities, preinvestment studies, and project preparation assistance. Since its inception in 1985, the CTFP has grown to include 52 separate trust funds supported by 26 donors. The CTFP finances the costs of services of consultants engaged by the Bank for assignments. Under the program, Bank staff hires the services of consultants from the participating donor countries and often employs local consultants from borrowing countries. One of the primary motivations of this program is the donors' desire to share more actively their technical expertise with developing countries for mutual benefit and to introduce new consulting talent to enrich the World Bank's own manpower resources.

Trust Funds and Co-Financing Department
The World Bank
1818 H Street, NW
Washington, DC 20433
Tel: 202-473-1211
Fax: 202-477-6391
Web: www.worldbank.org

JAPAN POLICY AND HUMAN RESOURCE DEVELOPMENT (PHRD) FUND The PHRD is the largest single source of untied grants available to meet the technical assistance needs of developing countries. The fund provides grants to World Bank client countries to help in the preparation and implementation of investment projects financed by the World Bank. With complete financial backing from the government of Japan, the PHRD supports the preparation of World Bank-financed operations in all sectors and regions. In addition to its project preparation activities, the PHRD Fund also finances the training activities offered by the Economic Development Institute along with the services provided by experts through the Japan Consultant Trust Fund.

Trust Funds and Co-Financing Department
The World Bank
1818 H Street, NW
Washington, DC 20433
Tel: 202-473-1211
Fax: 202-477-7019
Web: www.worldbank.org/rmc/phrd/phrd.htm

TECHNICAL ASSISTANCE TRUST FUND PROGRAM (TATF) The TATF is one of the primary ways the International Finance Corporation (IFC) finances technical assistance efforts. Trust funds have been established by industrialized countries to underwrite the costs of conducting preparatory and business development work in emerging markets. Normally each trust fund supports the hiring of consultants from the donor country who then carry out work as part of an IFC project team. TATF helps IFC expand the range of its technical assistance efforts and gives donor country consultants the opportunity to work side by side with IFC.

International Finance Corporation
Capital Markets Department
2121 Pennsylvania Avenue, NW
Washington, DC 20433
Tel: 202-473-8790
Fax: 202-974-4374
Web: www.ifc.org

TECHNICAL ASSISTANCE SERVICES

Department of Energy (DOE)

WORK FOR OTHERS (WFO) The DOE sponsors a research and technical assistance program, called the WFO program, for commercial U.S. companies. The DOE is authorized and encouraged to provide technical assistance and to make arrangements (including contracts, agreements, and loans) for conducting research and development activities with private or public institutions within the U.S. commercial sector. This work activity includes participating in joint or cooperative research, developmental, or experimental projects.

Work for Others Coordinator
Department of Energy
Oak Ridge Operations Office, MS M-6.1
Post Office Box 2001
Oak Ridge, TN 37831
Tel: 865-576-0646
Fax: 865-576-2554
E-mail: cooperda@oro.doe.gov
Web: www.oro.doe.gov

Small Business Administration (SBA)

EXPORTEXPRESS PROGRAM The SBA ExportExpress Program includes technical assistance in the form of marketing, management, and planning assistance specifically targeted to meet the needs of small businesses. Technical assistance is provided by SBA's U.S. Export Assistance Centers, in cooperation with SBA's network of resource partners. Assistance may include training offered through the SBA's Export Trade Assistance Partnership, SBDC

International Trade Center, SCORE, District Export Council, or Export Legal Assistance Network and is often provided in conjunction with financial support from the ExportExpress Program.

Small Business Administration
409 Third Street, SW
Washington, DC 20416
Tel: 800-U-ASK-SBA
Web: www.sba.gov

MANAGEMENT AND TECHNICAL ASSISTANCE PROGRAM SBA offers management and technical assistance services through grants and cooperative agreements to qualified service providers. Assistance includes specialized training, professional consulting, and executive development. Qualified service providers deliver training and technical assistance to eligible firms and individuals participating in SBA's Business Development Program, to other small disadvantaged businesses, to low-income individuals, and to firms in labor surplus areas or in areas with a high proportion of low-income individuals.

Small Business Administration
409 Third Street, SW
Washington, DC 20416
Tel: 800-U-ASK-SBA
Web: www.sba.gov

U.S. Department of Agriculture (USDA)

EMERGING MARKETS PROGRAM The Emerging Markets Program is funded by the Commodity Credit Corporation as part of the Foreign Agricultural Service (FAS). This program is dedicated to promoting U.S. agricultural exports in emerging markets through the use of various forms of technical assistance to promote market development, improve market access, and assist in the development of emerging market-based economies. All projects funded by the program must include cost sharing between the program and the private agribusiness partner. Funds cannot be used for any promotion or advertising targeted at end-user consumers, and performance reports are required for all activities supported with program funds.

Emerging Markets Office
U.S. Department of Agriculture
Room 6506, South Building

1400 Independence Avenue
Washington, DC 20250
Tel: 202-720-0368
Fax: 202-690-4369
Web: www.fas.usda.gov/excredits/em-markets/
            em-markets.html

EXPORT INCENTIVE PROGRAM (EIP) The EIP, as part of the Market Access Program (MAP), a division of the Foreign Agricultural Service, helps U.S. commercial entities conduct brand promotion activities by providing matching funds for use in trade shows, in-store demonstrations, and trade seminars. Other activities financed by MAP vary from commodity to commodity and include market research, consumer promotions technical assistance, and trade servicing.

USDA, Market Operations Staff
1400 Independence Avenue, SW
AG Box 1042
Washington, DC 20250
Tel: 202-720-5521
Fax: 202-720-8461
E-mail: info@fas.usda.gov
Web: www.fas.usda.gov

FOREIGN MARKET DEVELOPMENT COOPERATOR PROGRAM The Foreign Market Development Cooperator Program, also known as the Cooperator Program, aims to develop, maintain, and expand long-term export markets for U.S. agricultural products by building partnerships between the USDA and U.S. agricultural producers and processors, who are represented by nonprofit commodity or trade associations. Under this partnership, the USDA and the cooperators pool their technical and financial resources and provide partial reimbursement to companies conducting market development activities outside the United States. Projects are classified under three main categories: market research, trade-servicing, and technical assistance.

USDA
FAS/CMP/MOS, Room 4932
1400 Independence Avenue, SW
Washington, DC 20250
Tel: 202-720-4327
Web: www.fas.usda.gov/mos/programs/fmd.html

U.S. Department of Commerce (DOC)

MULTILATERAL DEVELOPMENT BANK OPERATIONS (MDBO)

MDBO facilitates access to representatives from multilateral banks and offers information and assistance to U.S. companies interested in supplying goods and services to overseas construction, engineering, manufacturing, and investment projects. MDBO counsels U.S. companies on the project procurement process and maintains a library of information on current and planned multilateral development bank (MDB) projects. MDB representatives also assist U.S. exporters with business leads and provide counseling on MDB projects. The DOC has assigned members of the U.S. & Foreign Commercial Service to each of the major MDBs. The major MDBs (African Development Bank, Asian Development Bank, the European Bank for Reconstruction and Development, and the Inter-American Development Bank) maintain in-country representative offices. These services can supplement published MDB project information and may be able to identify trade opportunities stemming from potential projects.

Office of Multilateral Development Bank Operations
Department of Commerce
1400 Constitution Avenue, NW, Room 1107
Washington, DC 20230
Tel: 202-273-0927
Fax: 202-482-3471
Web: www.commerce.gov

RESEARCH AND NATIONAL TECHNICAL ASSISTANCE PROGRAM

The Economic Development Agency (EDA) established this program to develop a comprehensive base of information about economic development issues; to disseminate information to local, state, and national economic development practitioners; and to measure the performance of economic development programs.

- **Information dissemination grants** make critical information about economic development programs, projects, and emerging issues available to practitioners through the use of newsletters, web sites, and conferences.
- **Research grants** examine important existing and emerging issues in economic development and document the results for practitioners and policy makers.
- **Evaluation grants** systematically assess the economic impact of funding under EDA's programs to measure effectiveness and make recommendations for improving the program.

Economic Development Agency
Department of Commerce
1401 Constitution Avenue, NW
Washington, DC 20230
Web: www.doc.gov/eda

Atlanta Region
Tel: 404-730-3002

Austin Region
Tel: 512-381-8144

Chicago Region
Tel: 312-353-7706

Denver Region
Tel: 303-844-4715

Philadelphia Region
Tel: 215-597-4603

Seattle Region
Tel: 206-220-7660

TRADE ADJUSTMENT ASSISTANCE PROGRAM The EDA uses a national network of 12 Trade Adjustment Assistance Centers to help U.S. manufacturers and producers injured by increased imports prepare and implement recovery strategies. These centers offer assistance in completing and submitting petitions to EDA for certification of eligibility and to apply for EDA assistance. Technical assistance provided under this program includes market research; development of new marketing materials to include e-commerce; identification of technology, computer systems, and software to meet specific needs; and completion of quality assurance programs such as ISO-9000.
Economic Development Administration
Department of Commerce
1400 Constitution Avenue, NW
Washington, DC 20230
Web: www.doc.gov/eda

World Bank

CAPITAL MARKETS DEPARTMENT IFC's Capital Markets Department prepares surveys on venture capital activities in over 20 countries and studies fiscal incentive programs for increasing equity investment. Advisory services are available for physical and financial restructuring, business plan development, market development and identification, product development, technologies, and potential partners. Studies are prepared for finance ministries, central banks, other government agencies, and professional and academic institutions. Many of these studies are also available to the public.

International Finance Corporation
Capital Markets Department
2121 Pennsylvania Avenue, NW
Washington, DC 20433
Tel: 202-473-8790
Fax: 202-974-4374
Web: www.ifc.org

ENERGY SECTOR MANAGEMENT ASSISTANCE PROJECT (ESMAP)

ESMAP is sponsored by the United Nations Development Program (UNDP) and the World Bank to help developing countries manage their energy sectors in order to promote energy-efficient and environmentally sound development. ESMAP provides managerial assistance and advice in energy sector planning, institutional and policy development, and technical assistance to projects and enterprises providing solutions for sustainable and deliverable energy to the poor. Assistance is offered in the form of technical studies, expert advice, best practice advice, workshops, publications, and preinvestment advice.

Energy Sector Management Assistance Project
The World Bank
1818 H Street, NW
Washington, DC 20433
Tel: 202-473-3672
Fax: 202-522-0395
E-mail: ifiles3@worldbank.org

IFC ADVISORY SERVICES IFC offers advisory services to small and medium enterprises (SMEs) that are independent of project finance support. Advice is provided for project development, business advisory services, restructuring, and technical assistance to companies involved in business ventures or business development. Project Development Facilities have been created to assist with financial plans, market research, feasibility studies, project life cycle management, partnership development, locating funds, and operational support. Advisory services also include assistance with environmental impact management, corporate governance, and privatization. Services are fee-based at a subsidized rate.

Technical Assistance & Trust Funds Department
International Finance Corporation
2121 Pennsylvania Avenue, NW
Washington, DC 20433
Tel: 202-473-0535
Fax: 202-974-4344
Web: www.ifc.org

INTERNATIONAL CENTER FOR SETTLEMENT OF INVESTMENT DISPUTES (ICSID) ICSID is a division of the World Bank that facilitates the conciliation and arbitration of disputes between member countries and investors who qualify as nationals of other countries. In addition to resolving disputes, the center also conducts research and advisory services relevant to World Bank and ICSID objectives.

ICSID
1818 H Street, NW
Washington, DC 20433
Tel: 202-458-1534
Fax: 202-522-2615
Web: www.worldbank.org/icsid

INVESTMENT MARKETING SERVICES (IMS) IMS is the Multilateral Investment Guarantee Agency's (MIGA) principal instrument for providing technical assistance in investment promotion to member countries. The IMS's objective is to promote foreign direct investment and to distribute information about investment opportunities in developing and transitional economies. IMS clients include investment promotion agencies, business chambers and associations, promotion departments in sectoral ministries, and other government and private sector organizations that are involved in promoting or facilitating foreign direct investment. IMS services fall into three categories:

- **Capacity-building activities** reflect an integrated approach to investment promotion. Starting with institutional assessments that examine the strengths and weaknesses of client investment intermediaries, they cover all aspects of the investment promotion process. IMS offers a range of services, including investment promotion skills training, executive development workshops, investment promotion workshops, sector strategy workshops, and the AfriIPA Support program.

- **Information dissemination** relies on the World Bank's IPAnet and PrivatizationLink to distribute information regarding investment conditions and opportunities. PrivatizationLink focuses on investment opportunities stemming from divestiture of state-owned companies in developing countries. It features company profiles of enterprises slated for sale, including data on specific activities of the enterprise, ownership structure, work force, fixed assets, and so forth.

- **Investment facilitation** includes the organization of promotional conference and associated executive training programs, promotion strategy, and investor services workshops. IMS pursues a multicountry, single-sector focus when possible to generate the critical mass of investment opportunities needed to guarantee investor response, ensure cost-effectiveness, and achieve the widest possible collaboration by all interested parties.

Investment Marketing Services
Multilateral Investment Guarantee Agency
1800 G Street, 12th Floor
Washington, DC 20433
Tel: 202-473-0394
Fax: 202-522-2650
E-mail: kmillett@worldbank.org
Web: www.miga.org/screens/services/ims/ims.htm

RELATIONS, ADVISORY, TECHNICAL ASSISTANCE AND SPECIALISTS UNIT (RATAS) IFC has accumulated a significant amount of in-house capital market technical expertise in areas such as venture capital, commercial banking, insurance, and securities market development through the work of this unit. RATAS coordinates financial sector technical assistance to IFC member governments and private entities and links IFC with other organizations involved in capital market development work. RATAS's technical assistance and advisory activities promote the development of efficient private sector capital markets and institutions with programs that cover a wide range of activities, including:

- Assisting with the drafting of securities laws and regulations.
- Advising on regulations for new types of financial institutions and refinement of existing regulations for new forms of market activity.

- Establishing supervisory and enforcement entities and mechanisms.
- Creating and developing stock exchanges, including the computerization of existing stock exchanges.
- Advising on collective investment vehicles and entry and exit requirements for international portfolio investment and securities issues.
- Preparing financial sector reviews and assisting government authorities in designing sector development strategies.

International Finance Corporation
Capital Markets Department
2121 Pennsylvania Avenue, NW
Washington, DC 20433
Tel: 202-473-8790
Fax: 202-974-4374
Web: www.ifc.org

BUSINESS DEVELOPMENT SERVICES

U.S. Agency for International Development (USAID)

GLOBAL DEVELOPMENT ALLIANCE (GDA) GDA is USAID's response to the new reality of development assistance that recognizes that flows between the developed world and the developing world have changed. These changes reflect the emergence of the private for-profit sector and the nongovernmental (or so-called "third sector") as significant participants in the development process. GDA serves as a catalyst to mobilize ideas, efforts, and resources of the public sector, the private sector, and nongovernmental organizations in support of shared objectives.

U.S. Agency for International Development
    Information Center
Ronald Reagan Building
1300 Pennsylvania Avenue, NW
Washington, DC 20523
Tel: 202-712-4810
Fax: 202-216-3524
Web: www.usaid.gov/gda

MULTIPLE BUSINESS SERVICES PROGRAM Through its Multiple Business Services program, The National Association of State

Development Agencies (NASDA) and USAID Private Sector Project cooperate with the International Executive Service Corps (IESC) to locate international business opportunities in developing countries that benefit U.S. companies. NASDA's network of state-level economic development departments disseminates IESC business opportunities to small- and medium-sized businesses throughout the United States. NASDA also assists with state-level conferences for business audiences that inform volunteer executives about the opportunities identified in developing markets. Through specially funded business development services, IESC provides firms with long-term industry-specific assistance, including strategic planning, trade facilitation, trade show representation, sourcing of U.S. equipment and technology, and assessment of financing options.

International Executive Service Corps
901 15th Street, NW
Washington, DC 20005
Tel: 202-326-0280
Fax: 202-326-0289
E-mail: iesc@iesc.org
Web: www.iesc.org

U.S. Department of Commerce (DOC)

UNITED STATES FOREIGN COMMERCIAL SERVICE Across the globe, more than 1,700 men and women of the Commercial Service promote and protect U.S. business interests around the world. The Commercial Service is committed to increasing the number of U.S. firms, especially small- to medium-sized firms that benefit from international trade. The Commercial Service's worldwide network includes offices in more than 100 U.S. cities and in more than 80 overseas posts. This presence brings professional trade assistance to U.S. firms domestically and in more than 95 percent of the world market.

Department of State
7070 Ashgabat Place
Washington, DC 20521
Tel: 800-USA-TRADE
Web: www.export.gov/commercialservice

Small Business Administration (SBA)

SMALL BUSINESS DEVELOPMENT CENTERS (SBDC) These centers target small business owners who are new to exporting and offer counseling, training, and managerial and trade finance assistance. While counseling services are provided at no cost to the small business exporter, nominal fees are generally charged for export training seminars and other SBDC-sponsored export events.

Office of Small Business Development
U.S. Small Business Administration
409 Third Street, SW, 4th Floor
Washington, DC 20416
Tel: 202-205-6766
Fax: 202-205-7727
Web: www.sba.gov

U.S. Agency for International Development (USAID)

MICRO AND SMALL ENTERPRISE DEVELOPMENT (MSED) TRAINING PROGRAM The MSED Training Program offers training and assistance to the lenders providing loans to businesses and to the borrowers who utilize loans or guarantees. Training programs are flexible and cater to the specific needs of clients. Training for business entrepreneurs who are borrowing from lenders is provided with financial management tools that may be utilized for running their business or with information on how to obtain and repay loans.

Office of Development Credit
1300 Pennsylvania Avenue, Room 210
Washington, DC 20523
Tel: 202-712-4265
Fax: 202-216-3593
E-mail: odc@usaid.gov

TRAINING SERVICES

U.S. Department of Commerce (DOC)

SPECIAL AMERICAN BUSINESS INTERNSHIP TRAINING (SABIT) SABIT is managed by the International Trade Administration (ITA) of the DOC and assists economic restructuring in the New Independent States (NIS) of the former Soviet Union by exposing top-level business executives, scientists, and engineers to American methods of innovation and management. SABIT places executives and scientists from the NIS in internships with small, medium, and large businesses and organizations throughout the United States SABIT offers two types of training programs: the SABIT Grant Program and the Specialized Training Programs.

- **The Grant Program** provides training to individual English-speaking managers and scientists from the NIS at a single U.S. company or institution for a period of 3–6 months. This program focuses on management training and commercial application of research and development and reimburses U.S. hosts for a portion of the training costs.
- **Specialized Training Programs** bring groups of 15–25 specialists from the NIS together for six weeks of industry-specific training at a variety of companies and sites across the country. Through this format, interns become familiar with a U.S. industry sector and all regulations involved. SABIT pays for the majority of the costs associated with this program.

Special American Business Internship Training Program
Department of Commerce
1400 Constitution Avenue, NW, Room 3319
Washington, DC 20230
Tel: 202-482-0073
Fax: 202-482-2443
E-mail: sabitapply@usita.gov
Web: www.ita.doc.gov/media/Publications/
            brochures/sabit01_2003.pdf

Other

UNITED STATES TELECOMMUNICATIONS TRAINING INSTITUTE (USTTI) USTTI is a partnership between the telecommunications industry and the federal government. The goal of this collaborative effort is to share U.S. communications and technological advances on a global basis by providing free telecommunications and broadcast training courses to qualified individuals who manage communication infrastructures in the developing countries of the world.

United States Telecommunications Training Institute
1150 Connecticut Avenue, NW, Suite 702

Washington, DC 20036
Tel: 202-785-7373
Fax: 202-785-1930
E-mail: train@ustti.org
Web: www.ustti.org

5

Trade Assistance

Export credit agencies (ECAs) and the other organizations described in this chapter provide support to trading businesses at every level of the project cycle, including early stages of the negotiating process. The numerous government sources of support available for financing, insuring, and providing technical assistance for the export of goods and services are described. Specifically, ECAs, the most important government source of trade finance, provide three basic functions: first, they help exporters neutralize officially supported foreign credit competition; second, they assume risks beyond those that can be assumed by private lenders (for example, discounting foreign receivables); and third, they provide financing to foreign buyers when private lenders cannot or will not finance those export sales.

Government-backed trade financing ranges from pre-export working capital needed to fill purchase orders and export-related capital equipment expenditures to short-term (less than 180 days) export receivable financing to customer financing with terms of ten years or more. The ability to secure financing can be an important marketing tool in winning international bids and contracts. Insurance products are available to protect investments for borrowers and lenders. A variety of technical assistance services direct businesses searching for and securing foreign customers, contracts, and financing.

The Export-Import Bank of the United States (Ex-Im Bank) is one of the primary Washington-based sources for information and services within this industry. As such, it is described in detail in the first portion of each section of this chapter, followed by an alphabetical listing of other useful products by organization.

Chapter Five is organized under the following main headings:

- Trade Finance
- Trade Insurance

TRADE FINANCE

Export-Import Bank of the United States (EX-IM Bank)

Ex-Im Bank is an independent government agency chartered by Congress to facilitate the export financing of U.S. goods and services. By neutralizing the effects of export credit subsidies from other governments and absorbing credit risks the private sector will not accept, Ex-Im Bank enables U.S. firms to compete in overseas markets on the basis of price, performance, delivery, and service. Ex-Im Bank has been particularly instrumental in developing U.S. small business exports, and it offers a number of programs and services specifically designed to meet the needs of small and medium enterprises (SMEs) that require unique lending instruments. Following are some of the most important products offered by Ex-Im Bank:

DIRECT LOAN PROGRAM Ex-Im Bank offers fixed-rate loans directly to foreign buyers of U.S. capital equipment and services and to exporters involved with large-scale projects. It does so to help U.S. exporters compete against foreign suppliers offering officially supported export credits and to fill in gaps in the availability of private export financing.

Ex-Im Bank authorized a $178 million long-term direct loan to support the $136.5 million export by Bechtel International Inc., in Gaithersburg, MD, of gas turbines and other equipment to build a 469-megawatt combined cycle power plant in Araucaria, Parana, Brazil. It was Ex-Im Bank's first power project in Brazil to use limited recourse project financing, in which repayment came from project revenues. "We are delighted to break new ground by supporting one of the first private thermal power projects in Brazil to be structured as a limited recourse project financing," said Ex-Im Bank Chairman John E. Robson. "This transaction will support numerous U.S. jobs and help Brazil diversify its energy sources." The Ex-Im Bank loan will cover both the construction and operating phases of the project. The sole source of repayment is the tariff revenue from the 20-year power purchase agreement with COPEL. The U.S. Overseas Private Investment Corporation (OPIC) also is participating in the financing of the $360 million project.

Source: Ex-Im Bank Press Release, October 2001

Ex-Im Bank extends fixed-rate loans to a company's foreign customer that cover up to 85 percent of the value of all eligible goods and services in the U.S. supply contract or 100 percent of the U.S. content in all eligible goods and services in the U.S. contract, whichever is less. While there is no minimum or maximum limit to the size of the export sale that may be financed by the loan, Ex-Im Bank Direct Loans typically involve loan amounts over USD 10 million with repayment terms of five or more years.

Capital equipment, large-scale projects, and related services are eligible for direct loan financing. The borrower must be a creditworthy entity in a country eligible for Ex-Im Bank assistance.

GUARANTEES Ex-Im Bank guarantees provide repayment protection for private sector loans to creditworthy buyers of U.S. exports. Ex-Im Bank also guarantees lease financing. Guarantees cover repayment risks on the foreign buyer's debt obligations. Ex-Im Bank guarantees that, in the event of default, it will repay the principal and interest on the loan. The foreign buyer is required to make at least a 15 percent cash payment.

- **Comprehensive Guarantees** cover all risks of nonpayment of principal and ordinary interest.
- **Political Risk-Only Guarantees** cover only political risks of nonpayment of principal and interest and are available for transactions with private or nonsovereign public buyers. It is the only type of guarantee available for transactions in which common ownership between the supplier (or exporter) and the foreign buyer (or guarantor) may exist (to the extent such ownership constitutes effective control). Political risks include transfer risk, expropriation, and political violence.
- **Foreign Currency Guarantees** cover risks related to currency fluctuation and related payment default. Export credits extended by commercial banks to buyers of U.S. goods are guaranteed by Ex-Im for up to 100 percent of the principal and interest.

SHORT-TERM WORKING CAPITAL GUARANTEES These guarantees give U.S. exporters access to working capital loans from commercial financial institutions. By providing 90 percent repayment guarantees to lenders on secured short-term loans against inventory and foreign receivables, exporters obtain the necessary working capital to purchase inventory, build products, and extend short-term credit to overseas buyers. Typically, advance rates of 90 percent against eligible receivables and 60 to 80 percent against inventory are allowed. On a case-by-case basis, Ex-Im Bank allows advances against inventory not supported by purchase orders in order to give extra flexibility to the exporter. This program provides the means for small- and medium-sized companies to pursue exports more aggressively.

Exporters have basic ways of obtaining a working capital guarantee: exporters can either approach Ex-Im Bank directly and obtain a preliminary commitment, which can then be converted into a loan by finding a willing lender, or they can apply through their bank. The process is accelerated when the bank is a Delegated Authority Lender (see the following).

Ex-Im Bank made a working capital guarantee in the amount of $900,000 to Crown Parts and Machine Inc., a small business in Billings, Montana. Ex-Im Bank's working capital guarantee covers a loan from Rocky Mountain Bank, also of Billings, which otherwise does not finance exports. The 12-month loan will provide Crown Parts with the cash flow needed to increase production at its Billings factory, and to expand shipments to Chile. The loan is also expected to allow the company to hire approximately 10 additional workers.

With two-thirds of its sales already derived from exports, the company will be able to further expand its overseas sales. "We were very happy with how smoothly everything went with this transaction with Ex-Im Bank," said John Coombs, Crown Parts Controller. Crown Parts manufactures and remanufactures parts and replacement parts for highway haul trucks and electric shovels used for open-pit coal, gold, and copper mining. In addition to Chile, its key export markets are China and Canada.

Source: Ex-Im Bank News, April 2003 Vol.3, Issue 4

- **Delegated Authority Programs** accelerate the process of obtaining a Working Capital Guarantee by allowing an applicant to apply directly with commercial lenders who extend Ex-Im lending privileges, without having to approach Ex-Im directly. There are four levels of delegated authority lenders, each with specific loan limits ranging from USD 2–10 million per exporter and an aggregate of USD 150 million for loans under this program. This program permits the lenders to commit Ex-Im Bank to a loan with minimal documentation and provides for a reduction in guarantee fees.
- **Priority Lender Programs** assure faster turnaround for loans of up to USD 5 million to qualified banks. Qualification for this status includes attendance at Ex-Im Bank seminars,

completion of at least two working capital loans, and submission of annual reports.

- **Alternate Funding Sources** offer three programs, one for the lender and two for the exporter. The lender program is designed to support a lender with an overline/liquidity facility that enables the lender to leverage limited capital resources. Exporter programs concentrate on finding commercial support either by assisting exporters who have a preliminary commitment but cannot find a lender or by providing guarantees to underserved markets, such as businesses owned by minorities or women, businesses located in economically depressed or rural areas, and businesses targeting environmental improvement.

- **City/State Partners Program** enables exporters or lenders to go to state and municipal institutions whose staff has been trained in Ex-Im Bank programs. These local government agents will guide exporters or lenders through the Ex-Im Bank application process. To locate these government agents, contact Ex-Im directly.

Ex-Im Bank issues guarantees to creditworthy exporters. Lenders must be able to demonstrate an ability to service loans to exporters and must certify that the loan would not otherwise be made without the guarantee. Exporters must be based in the United States, and start-up and developmental stage entities are ineligible. The terms of a loan are typically up to 12 months, but may be longer. For multiple export transactions ("Revolving Loans"), terms can be extended up to 36 months.

Ex-Im Bank charges either a nonrefundable processing fee of USD 500 for each application for a preliminary commitment or a processing fee of USD 100 for a final commitment application. In addition to the initial charge is an up-front facility fee of 1.5 percent of the total loan amount, based on a one-year loan.

CREDIT GUARANTEE FACILITY This program offers a line of credit between U.S. and foreign banks. Foreign buyers can go to a local bank to get approved and to make purchase payments. A U.S. bank will receive the payments from the foreign bank and disburse the payment to the supplier. Ex-Im Bank guarantees the U.S. bank against the risk of payment default from the foreign bank. Repayment terms range from two to five years. Coverage is 100 percent of principal and interest for up to 85 percent of the U.S. export value.

SPECIAL PROGRAMS

- **Aircraft Finance** offers financial support to exporters of new and used U.S.-manufactured commercial and general aviation aircraft (including helicopters) under its direct loans, guarantees, and insurance programs. The terms and conditions of Ex-Im Bank's aircraft programs are governed by the OECD Sector Understanding on Export Credits for Civil Aircraft. Ex-Im Bank typically provides guaranteed loans that have been extended by a financial institution to the borrower directly or that have been extended to facilitate a finance lease.

- **Operations and Maintenance Contracts** involve sending qualified U.S. personnel to conduct the day-to-day activities of an operating facility. Maintenance activities typically include start-up and shutdown of production machinery; receiving, storing, and maintaining the flow of raw materials; product quality testing and control; and controlling costs, conducting equipment repair, and overseeing preventive maintenance. Beyond these activities, Ex-Im Bank's program also covers the U.S. costs of executing the contract, including salaries for U.S. citizens working at the site, home office costs associated with the work, travel expenses, the cost of spare parts, and the upgrade of old equipment and other rehabilitation work of a capital nature.

- **Engineering Multiplier Programs** stimulate exports of U.S. architectural, industrial design, and engineering services, increasing the potential for future U.S. exports. Under this program, Ex-Im Bank aims to expand sales of project-related feasibility studies and preconstruction design and engineering services by offering fixed-rate loans and guarantees to foreign buyers of these services. In the long term, programs generate additional overseas sales of U.S. goods and services since foreign buyers may be more likely to order U.S. equipment and services for a construction project on which U.S. engineers, designers, and architects did the feasibility and design work.

TIED AID CAPITAL PROJECTS FUND This fund counters a foreign-aid donor's use of trade-distorting tied aid or concessionary credits ("soft loans"). This fund, or "war chest," may be utilized on a case-by-case basis and is applied only when U.S. exports are directly threatened by foreign tied aid. Ex-Im Bank will support sales that combine substantial follow-on market penetration with strong international competitive advantages for the U.S. firms. To qualify, applicants should have a planned horizon extended beyond the current sale; expect substantial follow-up on market penetration, financed in the future on commercial terms; and be willing to engage energetically in price competition against foreign exporters.

Ex-Im Bank is committed to upholding OECD rules on trade-related aid and supporting the reduction of trade-distorting tied aid. Ex-Im Bank's tied-aid credit is structured as low-rate interest loans for 100 percent of the export value, with a term of up to 25 years. The exact interest rate depends on the concessionality (as defined by the OECD) of the foreign tied-aid credit encountered. The fees are strictly risk-based and are structured to reflect pertinent sovereign risks, the financing of 100 percent of export value and term exposure to risk.

EX-IM ELIGIBILITY AND APPLICATION The Fund is to be used for matching or countering foreign tied-aid credit offers, but not for initiating tied-aid credits into export competitions. Ex-Im Bank reviews requests for financing based on the financial and technical aspects of a transaction, as well as the degree of foreign government-subsidized export credit the U.S. exporter faces from competitors. Because of its mandate to create economic benefits in the United States, Ex-Im Bank does not support transactions whose contract value is less than 50 percent of U.S. origination. Ex-Im Bank is also prohibited from financing military sales.

PEFCO The Private Export Funding Corporation (PEFCO) is a consortium of private lenders that act as a supplemental lender to official export financing sources. PEFCO makes loans to public and private borrowers located outside of the United States who require medium- and/or long-term financing on purchases of U.S. goods and services. PEFCO also provides funding to exporters who have obtained a preliminary commitment for an Ex-Im Bank Working Capital Guarantee that other financial institutions are unwilling to fund. In all cases, the loans made by PEFCO must be covered by the comprehensive guarantee of repayment of principal and interest by Ex-Im Bank. PEFCO loans range from USD 1 million to USD 225 million (with 5- to 22-year terms).

To apply for financing, PEFCO is usually approached indirectly through a commercial bank. When contacted, PEFCO will provide a fixed-rate quote (valid for 45 days) or will offer to establish a quote at a future time as selected by the borrower. If the offer is accepted, a Credit Agreement will be negotiated with the borrower, PEFCO, Ex-Im Bank, and any other lender or guarantor.

- **Long-Term Note Purchase Facility** offers assured liquidity for banks by purchasing foreign importer notes bearing either fixed or floating interest rates that are guaranteed under Ex-Im Bank's long-term guarantee program. This facility is available if the note's original value was USD 10 million or more and the original term was five to seven years or more.
- **The Discount Facility** is used when a transaction requires that the note have a fixed interest rate that can be set prior to the shipment date of the items and/or can be held even when the note has multiple disbursements. PEFCO charges a fee of USD 500 or USD 250, whichever is higher, plus 0.10 percent on the amount of the PEFCO-committed facility plus 0.25 percent per annum on the undisbursed amount of the facility.
- **The Medium-Term Note Purchase Facility** is available when the note has a floating interest rate or when the transaction requires a fixed interest rate that can be set at the time the items are shipped. A "switch option" conforming to the fixed interest rate switch option of the Ex-Im Bank guarantee gives the borrower the choice of changing from a floating to a fixed interest rate at the borrower's option. The PEFCO interest rate under this facility is typically a LIBOR-based floating rate plus a per annum spread.
- **Working Capital Facility** is offered in two formats: the Liquidity/Overline Format and the Lender-of-Last-Resort Format. Both provide an assured source of liquidity for lenders making export-related working capital loans guaranteed against nonpayment with an Ex-Im Bank Working Capital Guarantee. Loan amounts range from USD 100,000 to USD 10 million.
  - *The Liquidity/Overline Format* is used when banks and other lenders want to reduce the size of their loan portfolios or need another lender to participate in a line of credit to a client. PEFCO purchases the 90 percent of loan principal guaranteed by Ex-Im Bank under the Working Capital Guarantee.

○ *The Lender-of-Last-Resort Format* provides financing for exporters that Ex-Im Bank has determined cannot obtain financing from other sources, even with a Working Capital Guarantee. Ex-Im Bank guarantees for loans under the Lender-of-Last-Resort Format cover 100 percent of the loan principal.

Ex-Im Bank authorized $103 million in financing for two transactions supporting the export of U.S. wireless telecommunications equipment, and television broadcast rights and capital goods and services to Mexico. "These transactions support both U.S. jobs and Mexican economic development, and further the Partnership for Prosperity between Mexico and the United States launched by Presidents Fox and Bush," said Ex-Im Bank Vice Chairman Eduardo Aguirre, Jr. "We hope through this partnership to expand our extensive trade ties and narrow the economic gaps between and within our societies."

Through PEFCO, Ex-Im Bank has provided the following funding:

- A $20 million medium-term credit guarantee facility to support the $23 million purchase of television programming rights and capital goods and services from various U.S. exporters by Nuvision, S.A. de C.V., a Mexico City producer, marketer and distributor of films. The primary source of repayment is Corporacion Interamericana de Entretenimiento, S.A. de C.V., one of the founders of a joint venture film production and distribution company of which Nuvision is a subsidiary. The guaranteed lender is Toronto-Dominion Bank, Houston, TX.

- An $80.6 million long-term guarantee supporting the $100 million export by Motorola, Inc., Arlington Heights, IL, and other U.S. suppliers of cellular telecommunications equipment and related services. Exports are being bought by four Mexican cellular phone-operating companies that together form Telefonica Moviles Mexico (TMM). U.S. suppliers include: Gabriel Electronics Inc., Scarborough, ME; Andrew Corp., Orland Park, IL; Microflect Co. Inc., Salem, OR; and Marconi Communications Inc., Warrendale, PA. The primary source of repayment is TMM.

The financial applicant and arranger is PNC Bank, Pittsburgh, PA. The guaranteed lender is the Private Export Funding Corp. (PEFCO), New York, NY.

Source: Ex-Im Bank Press Release, August 6, 2002

Private Export Funding Corporation
280 Park Avenue
New York, NY 10017
Tel: 212-916-0300
Fax: 212-286-0304
Web: www.pefco.com

Export Import Bank
811 Vermont Avenue, NW
Washington, DC 20571
Tel: 800-565-3946
            202-565-3946
Fax: 202-565-3380
Web: www.exim.gov

Business Development Group
811 Vermont Avenue, NW
Washington, DC 20571
Tel: 202-565-3900
Fax: 202-565-3931

Small Business Administration (SBA)

EXPORT WORKING CAPITAL PROGRAM The Export Working Capital Program (EWCP) helps small businesses export their products and services through credit lines to expand their business exports. Proceeds are used to finance labor and materials needed for manufacturing, to purchase goods or services, or to finance foreign accounts receivable. The unique advantages of the EWCP program include simplified procedures (shorter application and fewer required documents) and quick turnaround times (generally ten days or less).

Applicants must qualify under SBA's size standards and meet other eligibility criteria applicable to all SBA loans. In addition, applicants must have been in business for at least 12 months prior to filing an application. Business must be current on all payroll taxes and have a depository plan for the payment of future withholding taxes.

SBA can guarantee up to 90 percent of the principal and interest of a loan or USD 750,000, whichever is less. Borrowers also may have other current SBA guarantees, as long as the SBA's total exposure does not exceed USD 750,000. If the borrower also has secured an international trade loan, the combined limit on

SBA's exposure may not exceed $1.25 million. For loans that exceed this amount, the exporter must solicit funding assistance from another source, such as the Ex-Im Bank.

The maturity of an EWCP loan is based on an applicant's business cycle, but cannot exceed 36 months, including all extensions. Borrowers can reapply for a new credit line when their existing line of credit expires. However, a new credit line may not be used to pay off an existing line of credit. Interest rates are set through negotiations between the applicant and the participating lender. For maturities of 12 months or less, SBA charges a nominal fee of 0.25 percent on the guaranteed portion of the loan. In addition, the normal fees permitted on all SBA loans also may be assessed on EWCP loans.

Collateral may include accounts receivable, inventories, assignments of contract proceeds, bank letters of credit, or appropriate personal guarantees. Only collateral that is located in the United States and its territories and possessions—or other assets under the jurisdiction of U.S. courts—is acceptable.

Ronald Contrado and two other founders started Homisco, Inc. in 1981 with a plan for filling the void after federal deregulation of the long-distance telecommunications industry. In 1997, Homisco took this division international with prepaid wireless services. Homisco provides the software and hardware to wireless telecommunications carriers serving the emerging international markets in Africa, Asia, South America, the Caribbean and the Middle East. These developing countries lack the infrastructure for landlines, so wireless phone service has filled the need. Sixty-five percent of the company's revenues, which grew to $9 million in 2001, are now derived from export sales. SBA backed a $1.1 million Export Working Capital Loan in participation with Salem Five Cents Savings Bank in 2001 to support the rapid growth of the business.

Source: SBA web site, July 26, 2002, www.sba.gov/ma/ss2002_5.html

---

EXPORT EXPRESS SBA developed this program to make obtaining working capital easier for small businesses. Under the Export Express program, SBA eliminated much of the paperwork typically associated with other working capital applications. SBA will guarantee up to $250,000 on Export Express loans. This program focuses on single transactions requiring financing of six months or less.

Complications from the September 11th attacks against the World Trade Center and the Pentagon did not stop 4D Solutions, Inc. of Boyertown, Pennsylvania from completing a government contract overseas. The SBA approved a $148,000 Economic Injury Disaster Loan (EIDL) to provide the firm with working capital to pay necessary operating expenses and obligations until operations returned to normal. The Export Legal Assistance Network (ELAN) also assisted the company with obtaining that special license.

Source: SBA web site, March 5, 2002, www.sba.gov/pa/phil/phlsc4d.txt

INTERNATIONAL TRADE LOAN PROGRAM The International Trade Loan Program provides long-term, primarily fixed asset financing to help small businesses establish or expand international operations. Loans are made through lending institutions under SBA's Guaranteed Loan Program. Proceeds from the loan may be used for working capital or for facilities and equipment, which include purchase of land or buildings. Similar to other SBA programs, loan proceeds may not be used to pay off other debts. Lenders must take a first lien position (or first mortgage) on the items financed. Furthermore, SBA may require additional credit assurances, such as personal guarantees and subordinations.

Applicants for this loan must establish that the loan proceeds will significantly expand their existing export markets or develop new ones or that the applicant's sales and profitability are adversely affected by increased competition from foreign firms. In either case, the applicant may be asked to provide detailed narratives as well as financial statements.

Under this program, SBA can guarantee up to USD 1.25 million, less the amount of SBA's guaranteed portion of other loans outstanding under SBA's regular lending program. SBA's maximum share for facilities and equipment is USD 1 million. The maximum share for working capital is USD 750,000. Maturities of loans may extend to the 25-year maximum period applicable to most SBA loan programs. Interest rates range from 2.25 to 2.75 percentage points above the prime rate, depending on the maturity of the loan.

U.S. Small Business Administration
Office of International Trade
409 Third Street, SW, 8th Floor
Washington, DC 20416

Tel: 202-205-6720
Fax: 202-205-7272
Web: www.sba.gov

Small Business Answer Desk
Tel: 800-8-ASK-SBA

COMMUNITY ADJUSTMENT AND INVESTMENT PROGRAM (CAIP)

This program helps communities suffering job loss due to liberalized trade with Mexico and Canada following the North American Free Trade Agreement (NAFTA). CAIP promotes economic implementation of the adjustment by increasing the availability and flow of credit and encourages business development and expansion in impacted areas. Through the CAIP, credit is available to businesses in eligible communities to create new, sustainable jobs or to preserve existing ones.

- **SBA 504 Program** assists businesses in the acquisition of long-term fixed assets. A typical transaction involves a commercial lender providing 50 percent of the cost or purchase price of real estate or equipment, the borrower providing at least 10 percent of the amount, and the SBA providing the balance through the involvement and assistance of a Certified Development Corporation (CDC). The up-front costs for this portion of a typical transaction are borne by the borrower and can amount to several thousand dollars, depending on the size of the transaction. As with the Loan Guarantee Program, the CAIP may cover much of the cost for the borrower on eligible projects.

Designer Glass, a division of G.M.D. Industries, was founded in 1982 in College Point, Queens. This company was faced with the challenge of finding an affordable new space. As per the 504 program structure, a private sector lender (Citibank) provided a loan for 50% of the project cost, a Certified Development Company (Empire State Development Corporation) provided a loan for 40% of the project cost (backed by a 100% SBA-guaranteed debenture) and the Designer Glass contributed 10% equity. The business has doubled both the number of its employees and its sales in the two years since they purchased their College Point location.

Source: SBA web site, February 7, 2003, www.sba.gov/ny/ny/SuccessDesignerGlass.html

---

U.S. Department of Agriculture (USDA)

AGRICULTURAL EXPORT CREDIT GUARANTEE The Commercial Export Credit Guarantee Programs (GSM-102 and GSM-103) of the Commodity Credit Corporation (CCC) are designed to expand U.S. agricultural exports by stimulating U.S. bank financing to foreign purchasers. Financing through these programs is available in cases where credit is necessary to increase or maintain U.S. exports to a foreign market and where private financial institutions would be unwilling to provide financing without CCC guarantees.

Under a letter of credit, CCC covers the risk of a foreign bank's failure to pay for any reason. CCC requires that the foreign buyer's bank issue an irrevocable letter of credit, in U.S. dollars, in favor of the exporter covering payment for the commodities. Payment of interest to the U.S. bank that finances the transaction can be covered by the letter of credit or by a separate loan agreement between the U.S. bank and the foreign buyer's bank. These guarantees cover 98 percent of the principal and a portion of the interest on loans extended by guaranteed U.S. banks. No coverage is available for ocean freight under the guarantee.

- **Export Credit Guarantee Program (GSM-102)** provides the exporter or the exporter's assignee with the guaranteed repayment of six-month to three-year loans made to banks in eligible countries where U.S. farm products are purchased. Most major agricultural commodities are covered.
- **Intermediate Credit Guarantee Program (GSM-103)** is similar to the GSM-102 program, but it provides guarantees for three- to ten-year loans.

The U.S. Department of Agriculture authorized $10 million in credit guarantees for sales of U.S. agricultural commodities to Tunisia under the Commodity Credit Corporation's Intermediate Export Credit Guarantee Program (GSM-103) for fiscal year 2003. Commodities receiving coverage include feed grains, wheat, wheat flour, and semolina. Coverage of up to 98 percent of the principal is offered on credit terms in excess of three years but not more than seven years.

Source: USDA Press Release, February 12, 2003

These products are offered in countries where these guarantees are required to secure financing and where there is enough foreign exchange to make the scheduled payments. Commodities are reviewed on a case-by-case basis to determine eligibility. The rate of interest is generally slightly above the prime lending rate or the LIBOR.

Export Credits
Web: www.fas.usda.gov/excredits/exp-cred-guar.html

FACILITY GUARANTEE PROGRAM (FGP) The Facility Guarantee Program (FGP), run by the CCC, provides payment guarantees to facilitate the financing of U.S. manufactured goods and services exported to improve or establish agriculture-related facilities in emerging markets. By supporting such facilities, the FGP is designed to enhance sales of U.S. agricultural commodities and products to emerging markets where the demand for such commodities and products may be constricted due to inadequate storage, processing, or handling capabilities for the products.

The U.S. Department of Agriculture today announced the availability of $10 million in credit guarantees for export sales of U.S. manufactured goods and services to improve existing agriculture-related facilities in Turkey under the Commodity Credit Corporation's Facility Guarantee Program (FGP) for fiscal year 2004. CCC guarantees will not exceed $5 million per project. CCC will provide coverage up to 95 percent of principal (facility base value) as determined in accordance with 7 CFR 1493.260(b)(2) on credit terms up to eight years.

Source: USDA Press Release, December 8, 2003

Export Credits
Web: www.fas.usda.gov/excredits/facility.html

SUPPLIER CREDIT GUARANTEE PROGRAM (SCGP) The SCGP administers export credit guarantee programs for commercial financing of U.S. agricultural exports. Compared to the GSM-102 coverage, SCGP guarantees a substantially smaller amount of the value of exports (currently 50 percent) and does not cover interest. Exporters who have previously qualified for GSM-102 or GSM-103 guarantees are automatically eligible for SCGP coverage. Other exporters must receive qualification from CCC prior to accepting guarantee applications.

Export Credits
Web: www.fas.usda.gov/excredits/scgp.html

USDA
Stop 1031
1400 Independence Avenue, SW
Washington, DC 20250
Tel: 202-720-6301
Fax: 202-690-0727
E-mail: askec@fas.usda.gov
Web: www.usda.gov

Other

STATE DEVELOPMENT FUNDING PROGRAMS U.S. firms can often access state programs to fill financing gaps not covered by federal and private entities or to complement federal funding options. Some state programs provide assistance through export counseling or technical assistance, while others offer financial support for international activities. Many state trade programs work with Ex-Im Bank to help exporters arrange financing. To learn more about state programs, contact a local International Trade Office (listed in Appendix C) or the National Association of State Development Agencies (NASDA) for information regarding available state resources.

National Association of State Development Agencies
    (NASDA)
12884 Harbor Drive
Woodbridge, VA 22192
Tel: 703-490-6777
Fax: 703-492-4404
E-mail: spope@nasda.com
Web: www.nasda.com

TRADE INSURANCE

Export Import Bank of the United States (Ex-Im Bank)

Ex-Im Bank provides export credit insurance to protect U.S. exporters against the risk of foreign buyer payment default. Ex-Im Bank insures a wide variety of U.S. exports to global markets, with special emphasis on stimulating small business transactions and expanding U.S. exports. Ex-Im Bank's Credit Insurance policies protect against the political and commercial risks of a foreign buyer defaulting on a credit obligation.

Besides protecting the exporter against nonpayment, Ex-Im Bank insurance also allows exporters to use international receivables to obtain financing. Because these receivables are insured, they can often be included in the borrowing base with a bank to obtain more attractive financing. In some cases, the insured receivables can be assigned to a bank or other financial institution, making them functionally equivalent to an Ex-Im Bank Loan Guarantee. This is a particularly attractive option since export receivables can be very difficult to finance. In addition, export credit insurance also allows exporters to offer more attractive credit terms to overseas buyers. By not needing cash in advance or letters of credit for international transactions, exporters can offer better financing packages, which, ultimately, win more business.

Credit insurance is also available through insurance brokers and Ex-Im Bank's five regional offices in Chicago, New York, Miami, Houston, and Long Beach. (See Appendix I for a complete listing of U.S. Export Assistance Centers).

SHORT-TERM CREDIT INSURANCE Ex-Im Bank's Credit Insurance policy provides protection against the political and commercial risks of a foreign buyer's defaulting on a credit obligation. Policies are available for single or repetitive export sales to individual or multiple buyers. They generally cover 90 to 100 percent of the principal for specified political and commercial risks, as well as a specified amount of interest.

- **Short-Term Single-Buyer Credit** provides foreign credit risk protection for exporters against default of payment due to commercial and political hazards such as political violence, government intervention, and transfer and inconvertibility problems. However, it does not cover product disputes or cancellation of contract. It gives exporters the opportunity to expand overseas sales by providing comprehensive credit risk protection on the short-term sale of goods to a single buyer.

  To be eligible for this insurance program, exporters must show at least one year of successful operations, a positive net worth, and at least one principal engaged full-time in the company. Repayment terms are up to 180 days and may be extended to 360 days for agricultural commodities, fertilizer, and consumer durables.

- **Short-Term Multi-Buyer Export Credit** provides comprehensive commercial and political risk insurance on the sale of goods and services from one exporter to a number of buyers. Premium rates are calculated per USD 100 of the gross invoice on the sale value. The exporter must pay a refundable minimum advance premium of USD 500. All exporters are charged a First-Dollar Deductible for losses on all eligible transactions shipped within 12 months. The minimum First-Dollar Loss Deductible is USD 5,000, and the actual amount is based on total annual export credit sales. Deductibles must be held for the insured's own account.

- **Small Business Export Credit Insurance** enables small businesses to participate in exporting by insuring their export credits up to 180 days. The Small Business Policy covers the repayment risks on short-term export sales by U.S. companies that have had average annual exports of less than $5 million for the previous two years. This program has the same structure as the regular insurance policies, with only a few adjustments. This policy provides 100 percent coverage of political risk and 95 percent commercial risk coverage. Exporters must meet Small Business Policy Standards, have had USD 5 million or less total export credit sales volume over the past two years (excluding cash or irrevocable letter of credit sales), meet the SBA's small business guidelines, have at least one principal working full-time, have a positive net worth, and have at least one year of successful operating history.

Hoffman International Inc., a small business distributor of wholesale heavy equipment in Piscataway, N.J., has completed a $650,000 sale of used Mack trucks, flatbed trailers, and new Terex cranes to a private sector buyer in Gabon by using export credit insurance from Ex-Im Bank. The buyer, SEMTS, is a contractor in Gabon involved in maritime, petrochemical and road construction projects. A $150,000 Small Business Policy from Ex-Im Bank enabled Hoffman International Inc. to offer longer terms of repayment to cover the last portion of its contract. The broker on this transaction is SBEA Services Inc. of McLean, Va.

Source: Ex-Im Bank Press Release, May 2, 2000

- **Other Short-Term Insurance Programs**
  - *Umbrella Policy*—This policy is for exporters with little export experience and extends many of the administrative duties and the minimum annual premium to an administrator. It is renewable annually.
  - *Financial Institution Buyer Credit*—This policy supports financial institutions that encourage exports by extending a direct buyer credit loan or reimbursement loan to a foreign buyer.
  - *Bank Letter of Credit Policy*—This policy protects banks against loss on irrevocable letters of credit issued by foreign banks for the purchase of U.S. exports.
  - *Small Business Environmental Policy*—This policy insures the sale of environmentally beneficial goods without the restriction of the volume of the shipment as a qualifying factor.
  - *Leasing Policy*—This policy is for entities that provide leases for U.S.-manufactured goods. It insures against governmental repossession and against a default on the stream of lease payments.

MEDIUM-TERM INSURANCE Ex-Im Bank offers guarantees that cover political and commercial risk. The foreign buyer must make cash payment for 15 percent of the contract value to the supplier, which they can finance through a different source. Guarantees have full support from the U.S. government, and notes guaranteed by Ex-Im are transferable.

Any financing institution, U.S. bank, foreign bank, exporter's financial supporter, or capable party can act as the lender. Buyers must be creditworthy and located in a country eligible for Ex-Im Bank assistance. This guarantee is available to private or nonsovereign public buyers.

Repayment terms range from one to ten years and are dependent upon the value of the export contract, the item exported, the recipient country, and the market terms. Lenders can choose a market rate of interest and a 360- or 365-day year for interest calculations. The guarantee is available for fixed or floating rate loans and will cover 100 percent of the interest.

The commitment fee is 1/8 of 1 percent per annum on the undisbursed balance of a guaranteed loan. Commitment fees are based on a 360-day cycle and begin accruing 60 days after Ex-Im's

Final Commitment. Exposure fees may be financed by Ex-Im, and they are risk-based, calculated, and payable as the guaranteed loan is disbursed or in an up-front, lump sum payment. The party responsible for the exposure fee must be determined, and Ex-Im must be notified at the time of the Final Commitment application.

WORKING WITH EX-IM BANK

1. Applicant (exporter, bank, broker, buyer) is assigned an Ex-Im Bank Relationship Manager upon the acceptance of an application package that has been deemed complete by Applications and Processing Division.
2. The Relationship Manager helps the client structure the transaction and acts as an interface and "gatekeeper."
3. The Relationship Manager then passes the package to the credit underwriting group, which analyzes the ability of the buyer (or guarantor) to repay the obligation with a reasonable degree of certainty. For most insurance transactions, Ex-Im Bank has established certain guidelines, including some of the following:
   a. There has been positive operating profit and net income in each of last two fiscal years.
   b. There has been positive cash from operations in last fiscal year.
   c. EBITDA/debt service (including Ex-Im Bank debt if more than 25 percent of total debt) is at least 1.5 for last fiscal year.
   d. Total liabilities (excluding Ex-Im Bank debt) do not exceed 1.75 times tangible net worth at end of last fiscal year.
   e. Ex-Im Bank exposure does not exceed 40 percent of tangible net worth at end of last fiscal year.
   f. Interim statements disclose no material adverse change in financial condition.
4. Once credit analysis is completed successfully, the transaction is presented to a credit committee and then approved by the Bank's Board of Directors.
   Business Development Group
   U.S. Export-Import Bank
   811 Vermont Avenue, NW
   Washington, DC 20571
   Tel: 202-565-3900

Fax: 202-565-3931
Web: www.exim.gov

The Export-Import Bank of the United States (Ex-Im Bank) granted a five-year, $1.8 million dollar medium-term export credit insurance policy to the Orgil International Greenhouses Corporation of San Diego, CA to build and ship four advanced greenhouse-growing systems to Cuauhtemoc, Mexico. The greenhouses will be used to grow high quality tomatoes, peppers and cucumbers. "This is great news for our local San Diego economy and for our suppliers around the country. We expect to hire more employees as a result of this approval. It will also assist Mexican farmers increase their growing productivity and food safety in an environmentally responsible way," said Joe Gelman, president of Orgil International Greenhouses.

Ex-Im Bank's export credit insurance covers the risk of nonpayment for U.S. companies selling products to Mexico or worldwide. The insurance policy can also be converted into cash immediately once goods are shipped. This guarantees that U.S. businesses are paid and allows them to offer competitive financing terms to their foreign customers. "With Ex-Im Bank's export credit insurance U.S. businesses can finance accounts receivables and offer foreign buyers terms that are usually much lower than the cost of financing available in their country and that helps make sales happen," Ex-Im Bank Board Member Dan Renberg said. Fast turn-around is another advantage to Ex-Im Bank's export credit insurance. Orgil's export credit insurance financing request was approved within seven days after receiving the company's completed application.

Source: Ex-Im Bank Press Release, July 19, 2002

Overseas Private Investment Corporation (OPIC)

CONTRACTORS AND EXPORTERS PROGRAM The Overseas Private Investment Corporation (OPIC) offers a program for U.S. contractors and exporters that insures against:

- Wrongful calling of bid, performance, or advance payment guarantees, as well as custom bonds and other guarantees.
- Loss of physical assets and bank accounts due to confiscation or political violence and inconvertibility of proceeds from the sale of equipment used at the site.
- Losses due to unresolved contractual disputes with the foreign buyer.

This insurance protects U.S. companies acting as contractors in international construction, sales, or service contracts. It also protects U.S. exporters of heavy machinery, turbines, computers, medical equipment, and other goods. Typically, coverage is issued when the U.S. company has a contract with a foreign government buyer.

Overseas Private Investment Corporation
Finance Department
1100 New York Avenue, NW
Washington, DC 20527
Tel: 202-336-8750
Fax: 202-408-9866
Web: www.opic.gov

6

Project Finance

Financing for projects in industrialized countries is often available from many sources (e.g., commercial banks, capital markets, private equity, and so forth). In emerging markets, however, project financing can be more difficult to obtain because of the higher political and commercial risks. To spur development and exports, the U.S. government, various multilateral organizations, and foreign governments can help by providing loans, loan guarantees, equity, and grants to viable greenfield or expansion projects. These products not only round up the financing plan, but also attract private financial institutions to participate in the transaction.

Project finance allows companies to secure financing based on the anticipated cash flows of a project rather than the balance sheet of the sponsoring company. Sponsor companies find this type of lending beneficial because it is often structured to reduce or eliminate recourse through the creation of a special purpose vehicle (SPV) that allows for the financing of a project without affecting the sponsor's credit rating or balance sheet. For this reason, project finance is an important and legitimate form of "off-balance sheet" financing for companies. Due to the structure of project finance transactions, lender risk is mitigated as the sponsor and other parties bear the risk throughout the construction and start-up periods. Lenders are willing to offer this financing only after establishing a project's long-term economic and technical viability and after determining that the sponsor company has sufficient technical and financial resources available to mitigate certain risks.

Although project financing can be a mutually beneficial arrangement for both the project sponsor and the lender, it is not without risk. The unique structure of project finance allocates risk among project participants and lends itself best to projects such as large-scale power plants, toll roads, oil and gas, development projects, and so forth. The cost and logistical effort required for the completion of these financings is significant. However, development lenders often look for ways to make project financing available for smaller project and small business sponsors by streamlining documentation, offering project/corporate hybrid instruments, and dedicating staff to help small sponsors structure deals.

To complement private and public sources of debt capital, special government-supported private equity investment funds have been established. In most cases, these funds have specific development goals that permit them to assume a higher level of risk. Typically, these funds should be seen as investors, although a recent crop of funds has sought to take a controlling minority stake in projects. In between senior debt and equity, several agencies and agency-supported investment vehicles also provide subordinated and quasi-equity financing for projects.

This chapter details critical U.S. government, World Bank, and national and regional development finance institution resources that can be used to finance projects in developing markets worldwide. A detailed listing of international development finance institutions can be found in Appendix J. Additionally, Appendix K contains a listing of international government-backed equity funds.

Unlike the other chapters that provide an alphabetical product listing, the large number of programs described in this chapter are arranged by the organizations providing the financing. Types of financing discussed in this chapter include the following:

- Project and corporate finance
- Guarantees
- Grants
- Private equity

Export Import Bank of the United States (Ex-Im Bank)

Ex-Im Bank is an independent U.S. government agency chartered by Congress to facilitate the financing of exports of U.S. goods and services. By neutralizing the effects of export credit subsidies from other governments and by absorbing credit risks the private sector typically does not accept, Ex-Im Bank enables U.S. firms to compete fairly in overseas markets on the basis of price, performance, delivery, and service. Ex-Im Bank's products and services that support conventional (sovereign, corporate, or local bank guarantees) trade transactions are discussed in Chapter 5 on export financing.

PROJECT AND STRUCTURED FINANCE AT EX-IM BANK Limited recourse (project) and structured financing are two options that offer maximum flexibility for project sponsors and help U.S. exporters compete globally in natural resource and infrastructure sectors. Ex-Im Bank has two primary goals: maximize U.S. company participation in the transaction and lend responsibly to creditworthy projects.

* **Limited Recourse (Project) Finance**—If a project will result in significant U.S. exports, Ex-Im Bank will lend to newly created companies, including greenfield projects and significant facility or production expansion activities. Repayment of financing is expected from future project cash flows, rather than a reliance on foreign governments, financial institutions, or established corporations directly for repayment of the debt. This financing arrangement is especially appropriate when hard currency revenues can be captured offshore or long-term off-take contracts insure project cash flows. Ex-Im Bank is always looking at other innovative structures, such as risk sharing with suppliers and reinsurance, in order to facilitate transactions in important industry sectors that may not meet these criteria.

  Ex-Im Bank makes every effort to offer the maximum support allowed under arrangements outlined by the Organization for Economic Co-Operation and Development (OECD). One of the most attractive features of project finance lending is its flexible lending conditions, including the financing of interest accrued during project-related construction, allowing up to 15 percent eligible foreign content in the U.S. components, and financing host country local costs up to 15 percent. In addition to flexible lending conditions, repayment terms are highly negotiable and are often tailored to the specific project, including the provision of more flexible grace periods and repayment terms. Rules allow for full flexibility in setting a project's grace period, repayment profile, and maximum repayment term, subject to a maximum average life of 5.25 years, or extending a project's average life up to 7.25 years, subject to constraints for setting a maximum grace period of 2 years and a maximum repayment term of 14 years.

Ex-Im Bank approved a $35 million long-term loan guarantee to support the $32.6 million export by Siemens Power Transmission & Distribution, Inc., EMIS-Division, (SPTD EMIS), Minneapolis, MN, of software and services to upgrade Israel's electric power distribution system. The Ex-Im Bank guarantee also covers $2.4 million in financing fees and project-related hardware costs in the buyer's country.

The buyer, the government-owned Israel Electric Corp. Ltd (IEC), awarded Siemens a $46 million contract for the project, including the $32.6 million in U.S. exports covered by the Ex-Im Bank guarantee. The guaranteed lender on the transaction is BNP-Paribas, New York, NY. IEC is the primary source of repayment.

Source: Ex-Im Bank Press Release, January 10, 2003

- **Structured Trade Finance** allows Ex-Im Bank to offer financing to overseas buyers of U.S. products based on their creditworthiness as reflected on their balance sheet as well as from other sources of collateral or security. Ex-Im Bank has been doing "structured" deals for many years in the areas of multiple-country fiber-optic cable, oil and gas projects, air traffic control, telecommunications, and manufacturing.

Some of the benefits of the project and structured finance programs include an expedited response time with Letters of Interest (LI) being received within 7 days or less and a preliminary project letter (PPL) being received within 45 days of submitting a formal application for financing. Additionally, Ex-Im Bank has no country or project limits and continually offers coverage to a great variety of projects.

To apply for financing, interested parties should set up an initial meeting with a Project Finance Business Development Officer to discuss Ex-Im Bank's policies and procedures and to receive a complete explanation of the application process. LI applications should be completed and submitted to Ex-Im Bank for review. There is a nonrefundable processing fee of USD 100 associated with the LI. In some cases, Ex-Im may be willing to perform a more extensive analysis and will issue a Competitive Letter of Interest (CLI). The cost for CLI analysis is USD 1,000. Once a project has been approved to advance to a Phase I evaluation, Ex-Im Bank will retain an outside adviser for the project. An evaluation fee and a contract will be required before a review begins. Upon completion of the Phase I evaluation process, a PPL will be issued within 45 days of the date of evaluation by the financial adviser. The PPL identifies the issues that need to be resolved to Ex-Im Bank's satisfaction before the project is submitted to the Bank's board for approval.

Project and Structured Finance Division
Export-Import Bank of the United States
811 Vermont Avenue, NW
Washington, DC 20571

Tel:	800-565-EXIM
	202-565-3690
E-mail:	structuredfinance@exim.gov
Web:	www.exim.gov/products/guarantee/
	proj_finance.html

Inter-American Development Bank (IDB)

The IDB is an international financial institution composed of 46 member countries, of which 26 are borrowing countries in Latin America and the Caribbean. The IDB, headquartered in Washington, D.C., is currently the dominant source of public finance for development projects in the region, contributing between USD 6–7 billion annually. While most of the Bank's past activities have been concentrated in the public sector, the IDB has been more active in the private sector in recent years. To this end, the IDB has created the Inter-American Investment Corporation (IIC) and the Multilateral Investment Fund (MIF), while increasing the role of its own Private Sector Department (PRI). Public and private entities in Latin American member countries, including national and regional authorities, are eligible to borrow from the IDB.

PRIVATE SECTOR DEPARTMENT (PRI) The PRI is a specialized operational department established by the IDB in 1994 to meet the growing need for long-term financing and guarantees for private sector operations, particularly for infrastructure projects. Usually, the PRI handles large loans and guarantees that exceed USD 10 million, while smaller loans and equity investments are underwritten by the IIC. PRI can lend directly to private sector entities without government guarantees for infrastructure projects as a method of attracting other investors to participate. Projects are focused on the industries of energy, transportation, water supply, waste management, and telecommunications. Unlike projects in the public sector, investors do not need to be from member countries of the IDB and there is no requirement of majority ownership by local investors.

STRUCTURED AND CORPORATE FINANCE The PRI finances infrastructure and capital market-related projects on a corporate finance or project finance basis. Corporate finance loans are normally used for expansions and modernizations of existing productive capacities and are typically utilized for privatized public utility companies. Project finance loans are typically useful for new or greenfield operations that use a special-purpose company as the borrower of the loan; these loans are also useful for the construction, ownership, and operation of the project.

The loans provided by PRI are usually structured in an A/B loan structure. IDB provides the A loan from its own resources and acts as the lead lender, lender of record, and administrative agent for the entire loan facility. IDB then attracts other banks and institutional investors to participate on a cofinancing basis through the B loan. The one or two financial institutions acting as the B loan arrangers are involved in analyzing, structuring, negotiating, and syndicating the B loan. The financial institutions involved in an A/B loan arrangement are given immunity from withholding taxation (due to the IDB's relationship with borrowing countries), and the arrangement reduces or eliminates country risk reserve requirements for some banks.

Terms may vary depending on the specifications of each project, but IDB limits its participation in loans to 25 percent of the project costs, with a USD 75 million limit. In some smaller countries with limited market access, this participation can be increased to 40 percent, but the USD 75 million limit still applies. Usually, the tenor ranges from 8 to 15 years, but in some cases may be extended to up to 20 years. Interest rates can be fixed or floating and are set based on many considerations, including loan term, sponsor, project financial strength, financial market conditions, and specifications of the project. Applicable fees are project dependent, but usually include a project evaluation fee, a commitment fee, a one-time front-end fee, a structuring fee, and annual administration fees.

CAPITAL MARKETS INITIATIVES IDB supports capital market initiatives that develop long-term financing and increase the liquidity of capital markets in IDB borrowing countries. To help develop the region's capital markets, IDB provides the following types of financing:
- Debt financing and/or guarantees to regional or national investment funds to mobilize venture capital resources

and/or debt capital that are not commonly available to private sector projects or other long-term capital investments
- Debt financing and/or guarantees for funds, leasing companies, or other financial intermediaries
- Start-up debt financing and/or guarantees for local financial institutions and companies that guarantee locally issued private sector debt
- Guarantees for local financial institutions to help them secure assets and develop a medium-term corporate debenture market to enable and encourage long-term, local financing
- Colending arrangements with local financial institutions and institutional investors that have a developmental impact on the domestic capital market's long-term financing capabilities

IDB can cover 25 to 40 percent of the proposed project costs for loans and up to 50 percent of project costs for transactions supported by a guarantee, not exceeding USD 150 million per project. IDB does not participate in the equity of investment funds or individual companies.

The Inter-American Development Bank announced the approval of its first private sector bond guarantee program in Peru—an up to $10 million guarantee of a $50 million bond issue by Graña & Montero S.A.A., the leading engineering services and contracting company in the country. The operation is the first private sector bond guarantee project by any multilateral financial institution in Peru.

The Netherlands Development Finance Company (FMO) will co-guarantee up to another $10 million of the bond issue. The two guarantees for a total of $20 million of the bond, together with a proposed securitization mechanism, will enable Graña & Montero to issue an AA structured bond, an upgrade from its BBB investment rating at the local level. That in turn will attract quality investors to one of Peru's most important firms for infrastructure development and will set a precedent for raising private resources on the local capital market for corporate investment and expansion needs.

Source: Inter-American Development Bank Press Release, May 14, 2003

Inter-American Development Bank
1300 New York Avenue, NW
Washington, DC 20577
Tel: 202-623-1000
Fax: 202-623-3096
Web: www.iadb.org

Inter-American Investment Corporation (IIC)

The IIC, an affiliate of the IDB, provides financing for the establishment, expansion, and modernization of small- and medium-sized private sector enterprises in Latin America and the Caribbean. It is primarily concerned with meeting the needs of small- to medium-sized enterprises whose expanded or established business will benefit the economic development of the member country. IIC typically provides financing for companies with sales ranging from USD 5–35 million and is flexible in constructing terms to fit the specific needs of each company. Projects financed by IIC must be commercially viable and preferably majority-owned by nationals of Latin America or the Caribbean. Although all economic sectors are eligible, only small- and medium-sized companies can qualify for IIC financing.

LOANS The IIC provides loans ranging from USD 2–10 million per project, either directly to project companies or indirectly through financial intermediaries. IIC is willing to finance up to 33 percent of total costs for new projects and up to 50 percent of the cost of expansion projects, provided that its participation does not exceed 33 percent of the total value of project assets. Most IIC loans are priced to float at six-month LIBOR plus a spread of 3 to 6 percent. Loans at fixed rates are also occasionally made, or project sponsors can arrange their own swaps with third parties. The maximum loan term is 12 years, with a grace period not to exceed 5 years. Financing may be used for both local and foreign currency costs, including fixed assets, working capital, and preoperating expenses.

IIC extended a USD 4 million long-term loan to Refineria Oro Negro, S.A., an oil refinery in Bolivia, in order to finance a portion of a USD 11.9 million project. The project will increase the refinery's processing capacity and extend the product line to include gasoline and premium gasoline. A new crude processing unit and a catalytic reforming unit will be installed. The expansion will increase total processing capacity from 2,000 to 3,000 BPD.

Source: IDB web site, www.iic.int/projects/2003_bo1067a_invest.asp

---

EQUITY INVESTMENTS The IIC also provides direct equity to international projects. These investments can represent up to 33 percent of the company's capital. Typically, once a project has matured, IIC attempts to exit the company by selling its shareholdings to a local stock market, interested third parties, or the other shareholders. IIC is flexible in the various types of institutions and funding it cooperates with in fulfilling its mission.

COFINANCING Part of IIC's mission is to mobilize funds for companies and ventures that have no other financing options. One of the ways IIC accomplishes this mission is by cofinancing projects with other financial institutions. This lending option allows IIC to make more funds available to a project by combining its direct lending resources with an alternate commercial lending institution. Having IIC, a multilateral status organization, take part in the funding of a project makes financial institutions more likely to take a risk on the project. It also lowers the risk and loan amount for an outside financial institution. When IIC cofinances a project, it acts as the administrator of the loan. IIC loans cannot be subordinated to the participating lender's portion. On the other hand, IIC often arranges longer maturities than commercial lending institutions, thereby mitigating the financial burden to the borrower.

Inter-American Investment Corporation
1350 New York Avenue, NW
Washington, DC 20577
Tel: 202-623-3900
Fax: 202-623-2360
E-mail: iicmail@iadb.org
Web: www.iic.int

Multilateral Investment Fund (MIF)

MIF was established in 1993 by the IDB to advance innovative development solutions that reached beyond most standard lending instruments. It has funded over USD 830 million for more than 520 projects. While the most MIF support falls under the category of technical assistance and is covered in Chapter 4, MIF also has the ability to extend a variety of investment and debt instruments that improve business and market environments and promote small and microenterprise development to nonprofit private sector institutions in Latin American and Caribbean countries.

MIF grants fund small projects that are innovative or that spur additional investments or ideas, where its investment program facilitates calculated market risks and innovative products that promote investment from other financing sources.

SMALL ENTERPRISE INVESTMENT FUND This fund is comprised of 35 different funds that are each independently managed by a company in the private sector that invests in small businesses in a broad range of industries. Small businesses must have fewer than 100 employees and less than USD 5 million in annual sales. MIF has contributed USD 173 million, which has helped in leveraging over USD 294 million.

Multilateral Investment Fund
Inter-American Development Bank
1300 New York Avenue, NW, Stop B-600
Washington, DC 20577
Tel: 202-942-8211
Fax: 202-942-8100
E-mail: mifcontact@iadb.org
Web: www.iadb.org/mif

Millennium Challenge Corporation (MCC)

Recently passed legislation approved USD 800 million in fiscal year 2004 for the creation and administration of the Millennium Challenge Corporation to govern the Millennium Challenge Account (MCA). The MCA was previously under the supervision of USAID. This initiative aims to reduce poverty by significantly increasing economic growth in recipient countries through a variety of targeted investments. The United States channels these funds only to developing countries that demonstrate a strong commitment to upholding the rule of law, rooting out corruption, protecting human rights and political freedoms, investing in their people, and encouraging economic freedom. As this government entity remains in its infancy, its impact on the private sector remains unclear, although, at the very least, new procurement opportunities will probably be available to companies interested in participating in projects that promote the ideals and missions of the MCC.

Millennium Challenge Account
Tel: 202-712-5000
Web: www.mca.gov

Overseas Private Investment Corporation (OPIC)

OPIC was established in 1971 by the U.S. government to provide services to American businesses looking to expand into foreign countries and emerging markets. OPIC contributes substantially to both the national and foreign policy interests of the United States. It also helps less developed nations expand their economies and become valuable markets for U.S. goods and services, thereby increasing U.S. exports and creating U.S. jobs. Since its inception, OPIC has supported investments worth nearly USD 145 billion, generating USD 65 billion in U.S. exports and creating over 254,000 American jobs.

OPIC provides financing to U.S. investors through direct loans and loan guarantees and by supporting private investment funds that, in turn, provide equity to coinvest with U.S. companies investing abroad. The amount of OPIC's commitment varies, taking into consideration the contribution of the project to the host country's development, the financial requirements, and the extent to which the financial risks and benefits are spread among the investors and the lenders. OPIC's participation is limited to USD 250 million, which can be in the form of a corporate loan or project (limited recourse) financing. Loans can be made only in denominations of U.S. dollars with a typical spread of 2 to 6 percent above current Treasury rates. At least 25 percent of the project company must to be owned by U.S. investors.

OPIC will assist in designing the financial plan and coordinating it with other lenders and investors and will participate in up to 50 percent of the total costs of a new venture. Up to 75 percent of total project costs may be considered in the case of the expansion of a successful existing business. Project sponsors are encouraged to arrange for additional participation from other local and international sources, which tend to be highly valuable components in these types of projects. Following are some of the financing products available:

PROJECT FINANCE OPIC is willing to provide project finance to the private sector after carefully analyzing the economic, technical, marketing, and financial soundness of a project to determine its creditworthiness. Sufficient cash flow must be available to pay all operational costs and to service all debt. Also, collateral must be provided to secure the loan, either in the host country or in the United States. The project sponsors are expected to support the overseas operation until certain specific tests for physical completion, operational implementation, and financial soundness are met. To the extent that project financing is appropriate, sponsors may not need to pledge their own general credit beyond required completion undertakings.

OPIC signed an agreement with OAO Lukoil, Russia's leading oil producer, committing OPIC to $130 million in financing to increase its oil export capacity. OPIC will provide a loan guaranty to HBK Fund LP, a Delaware limited partnership based in Dallas, Texas, for a loan the fund will make to an indirect subsidiary of OAO Lukoil, Russia's leading oil producer. The project will consist of the construction and operation of a crude oil and petroleum product export terminal on the western coast of Vysotsky Island on the Gulf of Finland, north of St. Petersburg.

OAO Lukoil has one of the largest petroleum reserve bases among private oil companies worldwide—nearly 17 billion barrels of oil equivalent as of early 2002—and is one of the largest crude oil producers in Russia.

Source: OPIC Press Release, September 22, 2003

CORPORATE FINANCE Under this program, OPIC makes loans to U.S. sponsors of overseas projects, primarily small businesses. OPIC looks to the ability of the U.S. company to repay the loan and to offer collateral, rather than to rely on the overseas project company. When the borrower is in the United States, OPIC can structure a corporate finance transaction more easily, faster, and generally cheaper than when the borrower is in a foreign country. The purpose of the financing still would be to support a project in a foreign country; however, the primary source of repayment would be from the U.S. company.

HYBRID LOANS Hybrid structures combine elements of corporate finance and project finance. The cash flow and collateral from a combination of the domestic parent company and the project company are used to craft an acceptable loan structure. Hybrid finance structures can be more costly than corporate finance structures. However, in many cases, the domestic sponsor may already have pledged its assets to an existing bank. OPIC may be able to see value in the cash flow and collateral that a local U.S. bank does not.

FRANCHISE LOANS These loans are available to franchises that are at least 25% owned by a U.S. small business or where there is significant involvement of the small business franchiser in the project. Projects must be financially sound, foster private initiative and competition, and promise significant benefits to the social and economic development of the host country. Loans do not generally exceed USD 4 million, and loans over USD 1.5 million should result in operations with at least five units.

SMALL BUSINESS CENTER (SBC) FINANCE PROGRAM OPIC, together with the U.S. Small Business Administration (SBA), recently launched this initiative to help America's small businesses compete in the global marketplace. This program seeks to improve the climate for U.S. businesses by combining the resources of these two institutions to increase opportunities for U.S. small businesses expanding into dynamic emerging markets. OPIC recognizes that small businesses looking to participate in the global marketplace face unique challenges, including lack of resources to pursue international opportunities, political risk concerns, and lack of private sector support. One value-added function of this product is that applications will be processed within a 60-day period. Any small business with an annual revenue less than USD 35 million is eligible. Loan amounts for overseas investments range from USD 100,000 to USD 10 million, with terms of 3 to 15 years.

Financing from OPIC will enable a U.S. small business to more than double its water purification facilities in an area of Mexico that was ravaged by a powerful earthquake in January 2003.

OPIC will provide a USD 1.5 million loan to Faro de Agua, a small business run by Brad Schwarz of Mercedes, Texas and the Leaño family of Guadalajara in Jalisco, Mexico, to expand the company's curbside water purification and distribution sites—called faros—from 28 to 59 in Colima state and the city of Matomoros. Colima was the epicenter of a January earthquake that registered 7.8 on the Richter scale and killed more than two dozen people. This project meets a basic need of the populations of both Colima and Matomoros at a time when that need is greatest by using environmentally friendly technology in a retail application at affordable prices.

Source: OPIC Press Release, April 2, 2003

ELIGIBILITY AND APPLICATION OPIC finances investment projects with substantial U.S. participation that are commercially and financially sound, promise significant benefits to the social and economic development of the host country, and foster private initiative and competition. OPIC will not support projects that may result in the loss of U.S. jobs, adversely affect the U.S. economy or the host country's development or environment, or contribute to violations of internationally recognized worker rights. Additionally, most OPIC commitments for direct loans or loan guarantees must be approved by the government of the host country. Special emphasis is placed on projects in developing countries and on projects involving smaller U.S. firms or cooperatives as sponsors.

Potential project sponsors interested in obtaining financing should provide OPIC with a copy of the business plan for the proposed project and complete an application for OPIC financing (available through its home page). The business plan should establish general eligibility and give OPIC the basis on which to respond to the amount and terms of the requested financing, including:

- A general description of the project.
- Identity, background, and the audited financial statements of the project's proposed principal owners and management.
- Planned sources of supply, anticipated output and markets, distribution channels, competition, and the basis for projected market share.
- Summary of project costs and sources of procurement of capital goods and services.
- Proposed financing plan, including the amount of the proposed OPIC participation.
- Pro forma financial statements for the proposed project.
- A brief statement regarding the contribution the project is expected to make to local economic and social development.

The sponsors may be asked to provide additional economic, financial, and technical information subsequent to the filing of these materials. The time required to review an application and to commit and close a loan varies. Investors are encouraged to consult with OPIC early in the investment process so as to understand OPIC's requirements for a particular project.

Overseas Private Investment Corporation
1100 New York Avenue, NW
Washington, DC 20527
Tel: 202-336-8799
Fax: 202-408-9859
E-mail: info@opic.gov
Web: www.opic.gov

U.S. Agency for International Development (USAID)

USAID is the government agency responsible for managing U.S. foreign economic and development assistance. USAID's economic assistance programs come in the form of project-specific loans or grants enabling the procurement of U.S. goods and services for project implementation. USAID works closely with private voluntary organizations, indigenous organizations, universities, American businesses, international agencies, other governments, and other U.S. government agencies. USAID has working relationships with more than 3,500 American companies and over 300 U.S.-based private voluntary organizations.

MICRO AND SMALL ENTERPRISE DEVELOPMENT PROGRAM (MSED)

The MSED extends financial resources to micro and small enterprises (MSEs) that often lack the acceptable collateral, business experience, or plans to obtain financing through normal financial institutions. This program offers financial institutions risk-sharing mechanisms such as direct loans, loan guarantees, and bond guarantees to encourage lending to MSEs in developing countries.

- **Loan Portfolio Guarantee (LPG) Program,** MSED's primary tool for providing loan guarantees, covers up to 50 percent of the principal loss on a portfolio of small business loans. Guarantees cover small business loans financing any productive or commercial activity, subject to limited restrictions, as well as selected private banks and financial institutions that are engaged in or want to expand their small business lending in USAID-assisted countries. Guarantees may be issued in the form of loans, lines of credit, finance leases, overdrafts, commercial letters of credit, and other instruments.
- **Bond Guarantees** are provided when market conditions prevent credit flow to MSEs. These guarantees support the issuance of bonds by financial institutions in order to help raise local funds to expand lending activities to MSEs.
- **Direct Loans** are used in transactions where the offer of a loan guarantee is not enough to foster lending from financial institutions to MSEs. Direct loans are typically approved only for projects with a regional or international scope. Cross-border risk is a primary consideration in determining project viability. Once a loan is issued, repayment is required in U.S. dollars.
- **Wholesale Guarantees** are offered to financial institutions that, in turn, offer retail loans to micro finance institutions (MFIs) for on-lending to micro enterprises involved in projects with a broad scope. The goal of this facility is to increase the availability of microenterprise credit through financial institutions in markets where these formal finance institutions generally do not serve the sector directly.

- **Portable Guarantees** are reserved for MFIs that require commercial sources of funding in order to on-lend to microenterprises. These guarantees also provide credit enhancements, making it more likely for MFIs to secure funding at more competitive terms.

MSED loans and guarantees range in size from USD 500,000 to a maximum of USD 6 million, with repayment terms of up to ten years. A one-time up-front Facility Fee of 0.5 percent of the guarantee limit and a semiannual utilization fee ranging from 1 to 2 percent of the outstanding utilization of guarantee will be charged.

Center for Economic Growth
Tel: 202-712-0374

GRANTS Grants, in whole or in part, are allocated for the program of a nongovernmental organization (NGO), a university, or an institution with a stated purpose of enhancing the public good. The beneficiaries acknowledge the responsibility for achieving program objectives.

The U.S. Agency for International Development (USAID) awarded five grants, totaling USD 22.2 million, as part of a regional conflict prevention strategy in Central Asia. These grants are part of USAID's Community Action Investment Program (CAIP), a program designed to build social stability and alleviate sources of potential conflict in the five Central Asia republics of Kazakhstan, Kyrgyzstan, Tajikistan, Turkmenistan, and Uzbekistan.

USAID will implement CAIP through several international nongovernment organizations (NGOs), which will work with local NGOs to launch innovative conflict mitigation activities. NGOs working under CAIP will provide communities and groups with the skills necessary to improve their public dialogue and effective communication. CAIP fosters new community-government partnerships by providing training and technical assistance to help local governments increase their ability to respond more effectively to community needs, and by involving citizens in the rehabilitation and development projects. This gives citizens a sense of ownership and personal stake in their society, and increases the likelihood that the communities' newly constructed or repaired infrastructures will be maintained by the local governments.

Source: USAID Press Release, July 11, 2002

CAPITAL INVESTMENT FUND (CIF) USAID has established the CIF in the amount of USD 95 million in fiscal year 2003. These funds provide USAID with greater flexibility to manage investments in technology systems and facility construction not allowed by the annual appropriation for operating expenses.

COOPERATIVE AGREEMENTS A Cooperative Agreement in many aspects is identical to the provision of a grant with the exception that it often requires greater involvement by USAID. Essential prerequisites include approval of annual work plans, designation of key positions and approval of key personnel, or USAID approval of monitoring and evaluation plans. While for-profit firms are eligible for grants and cooperative agreements, USAID's policy is not to pay a fee or profit under such assistance instruments.

U.S. Agency for International Development
Information Center
Ronald Reagan Building
1300 Pennsylvania Avenue
Washington, DC 20523
Tel: 202-712-4810
Fax: 202-216-3524
Web: www.usaid.gov

USAID Office of Procurement
Tel: 202-712-5130
Fax: 202-216-3395
E-mail: AandAOmbudsman@usaid.gov

USAID Office of the Inspector General
Tel: 800-230-6539
          202-712-1023
E-mail: ig.hotline@usaid.gov

World Bank

The World Bank Group is one of the world's largest sources of development assistance. In fiscal year 2002, the institution provided more than USD 19.5 billion in loans to its client countries. It works in more than 100 developing economies focusing primarily on helping the poorest people and countries. For each of its clients, the Bank works with government agencies, non-governmental organizations, and the private sector to formulate assistance strategies. Its country offices worldwide deliver the

Bank's program, liaise with the government and civil society, and work to increase an understanding of development issues.

In addition to these products, the World Bank offers many other project finance instruments to the private sector through two of the five organizations that comprise the World Bank: the International Bank for Reconstruction and Development (IBRD) and the International Finance Corporation (IFC). Both of these organizations are discussed next.

INTERNATIONAL BANK FOR RECONSTRUCTION AND DEVELOPMENT (IBRD) IBRD, the original institution of the World Bank Group, opened its doors for business in 1946. Today it is the largest source of market-based loans to developing countries and is a major catalyst of similar financing from other sources. IBRD lends, guarantees, or provides developmental assistance to public and private entities in middle-income and creditworthy low-income countries. It is funded mainly through member contributions and borrowings on international capital markets. IBRD has 183 member countries.

IBRD has two basic loan programs, investment loans and adjustment loans, and three guarantee programs. Investment loans are designed for long-term (five to ten years) projects to finance goods, works, and services, while adjustment loans are designed for short-term (one to three years) projects needing quick disbursement to support policy or reform initiatives. Loans may be used in combination with other products for a customized finance package or by themselves to match a particular need.

GRANTS The World Bank provides numerous grants to various projects at the request of its borrowing countries. The following is a list of the types of grants provided by the World Bank. This list is merely an overview. Check with the nearest World Bank office for a complete listing and description of the various programs available within each category.

- Capacity Building
- Education
- Environment
- Health, Nutrition, and Population
- Information Technology
- Infrastructure
- Microfinance
- Social Development

The following are examples of the programs available through World Bank grant-making activities:

- **Development Marketplace** promotes innovative development ideas through early-stage seed funding. It links social entrepreneurs with poverty-fighting ideas to partners with resources to help implement their vision. Since 1998, the Development Marketplace has awarded more than USD 14 million to over 200 groundbreaking projects through Global Competitions and Country Innovation Days.
  Web: www.developmentmarketplace.org

- **Development Grant Facility (DGF)** was established to integrate the overall strategy, allocations, and management of World Bank grant-making activities. Its primary goals are to encourage innovation, catalyze partnerships, and broaden the scope of World Bank services. The budget for 2003 covered 48 different grant programs. Projects requesting grants must further the World Bank's development objectives, but they cannot compete with regular lending instruments. The World Bank also must have a distinct comparative advantage for being associated with the program—projects must have multicountry benefits—and the World Bank's involvement must provide significant leverage. In addition, grants are usually given to organizations with a record of achievement and financial stability, management of recipient institutions must be independent of the World Bank, programs must have an explicit disengagement strategy, and programs and activities must promote and reinforce partnerships with other organizations in the development region.
  Web: www.worldbank.org/dgf

INVESTMENT LENDING This product is structured to suit a wide range of enterprises that build infrastructure and sustain development. IBRD currently believes that assisting private sector institution building, social development, and public policy infrastructure will provide the most long-lasting and successful resolutions for alleviating poverty. Developing the private sector boosts economic independence and social development. Investment loans have accounted for 75 to 80 percent of IBRD lending for the past 20 years. The following are a number of investment loans offered by IBRD:

- **Specific Investment Loans** support the creation, rehabilitation, and maintenance of infrastructure. The loan also may be used to finance consultant services, management, and training so that policies affecting the productivity of the investment can be reformed.
- **Adaptable Program Loans (APLs)** are designed for long-term projects with more than one phase. APLs adapt and evolve according to lessons learned so that the World Bank can continue its support of a long-term project. Between each phase, the project and financing terms are reviewed. These loans can be used in the health, power, water, education, and natural resource management sectors, where time is required for consensus and reformation.
- **Learning and Innovation Loans (LILs)** support small pilot-type investment and capacity building projects. If one is successful, the LIL could lead to increasing the scale of the project. These projects should not exceed USD 5 million or have an implementation time exceeding two or three years. They are used to test new approaches or new borrowers, build trust, or act as pilot projects in preparation for larger projects. They support locally based development initiatives.
- **Technical Assistance Loans (TALs)** finance outside and/or local consultants to strengthen organizations in preparation for public sector reform. These loans help consultants build institutional capacity before implementing public sector reform and often complement an investment or adjustment operation.
- **Financial Intermediary Loans (FILs)** develop financial sector policies and institutions. Specifically, IBRD aims to improve the efficiency of institutions, promote sound business practices, encourage private investment, and improve credit terms for either households or enterprises. Financing goes to financial intermediaries, but will be routed to fill the needs of real sector investment needs. The financial institution does, however, assume a credit risk with each subproject.
- **Emergency Recovery Loans (ERLs)** are designed for assets and production levels immediately after a civil disturbance, war, or natural disaster. Loans can be used for investment and productive activities, making recurring emergencies such as floods or expected crisis such as droughts most appropriate for ERLs.

Project loan terms are available up to 25 years to borrowers who are not in arrears with the World Bank and who are eligible IBRD and International Development Association (IDA) borrowers. Loans are awarded and dispersed for specific foreign or local functions that are funding investment projects. Projects include preidentified equipment, materials, civil works, technical and consulting services, studies, and incremental recurrent costs. Loan agreements will most likely include conditions of disbursement to stipulate allocation of funds to specific project components.

IBRD charges a front-end fee of 1 percent of the loan amount, payable upon loan effectiveness. Lending rates depend on the product being financed and vary with the currency in FSLs and Variable-Spread Single Currency Loans (VSCLs). The commitment fee on the undisbursed balance varies with the type of loan: for FSLs, 0.85 percent in the first four years and 0.75 percent thereafter. All other loans have a commitment fee of 0.75 percent, but for all loans, a partial waiver may apply. For borrowers paying on a timely basis, a partial waiver may apply to disbursed and outstanding loan balances.

The World Bank
1818 H Street, NW
Washington, DC 20433
Tel: 202-473-1000
Fax: 202-477-6391
Web: www.worldbank.org

Europe
Vice President for Europe
66 avenue d'Iéna
75116 Paris
Tel: 331 (1) 4069-3010
Fax: 331 (1) 4069-3064

United Kingdom, New Zealand
New Zealand House, 15th Floor
Haymarket
London SW1 Y4TE
Tel: 44 (207) 930-8511
Fax: 44 (207) 930-8515

Belgium
Special Representative to the EU Institutions
10, rue Montoyer
B-1000 Brussels

Tel: 32 (2) 552-0052
Fax: 32 (2) 552-0025

Germany
Representative of the World Bank Group
Bockenheimer Landstr 109
D-60325 Frankfurt am Main
Tel: 49 (69) 7434-8230
Fax: 49 (69) 7434-8239

Switzerland
Special Representative and the Head of Office
3, chemin Louis Dunant
C.P. 66
CH-1211 Geneva 10
Tel: 41 (22) 748-1000
Fax: 41 (22) 748-1030

Tokyo
Director
Fukoku Seimei Building, 10th Floor
2-2-2 Uchisawai-cho
Chiyoda-Ku, Tokyo 100
Tel: 81 (3) 3597-6650
Fax: 81 (3) 3597-6695

East Timor, Papua New Guinea, and Pacific Island Operations
East Asia and Pacific Region
Country Director
Level 18, CML Building
14 Martin Place
Sydney
NSW 2000
Australia
Tel: 61 (02) 9223-7773
Fax: 61 (02) 9223-2533

INTERNATIONAL FINANCE CORPORATION (IFC) The IFC uses its own funds to provide its clients with a variety of financial products. In contrast to the World Bank, IFC does not require sovereign guarantees. IFC aims to stimulate private investment and therefore limits its investment to 25 percent of the total project cost. In recent years, for example, every dollar of project financing approved by IFC for its own account led to USD 5.42

financing by other private investors. IFC-supported projects range from approximately USD 100,000 to USD 100 million and cover a wide range of industries, including agribusiness, cement, chemicals, fertilizers, financial institutions, tourism, manufacturing, mining, oil and gas exploration, power generation and transmission, pulp and paper, telecommunications, textiles, and transport and storage.

In addition to its traditional debt or equity investments, IFC is prepared to consider other financing approaches on the basis of market need and can provide standby loans to signal its readiness to close any financial gap that the market might otherwise be unwilling to cover immediately. IFC also can issue guarantees to support third-party loans to private companies in developing countries or securities issued by such companies.

A LOANS IFC offers fixed and variable-rate loans from its own account to private sector projects in developing countries. These A loans are used to finance both greenfield companies and expansion projects. IFC also makes loans to intermediary banks, leasing companies, and other financial institutions through credit lines for further lending. Credit lines are often targeted at small- and medium-sized enterprises or at specific sectors. Most A loans are issued in leading (hard) currencies, but local currency loans also may be provided. A loans are usually limited to 25 percent of the total estimated project costs for greenfield projects and generally range from USD 1–100 million. Loans typically have maturities of 7 to 12 years at origination. Grace periods and repayment schedules are determined on a case-by-case basis in accordance with the borrower's cash flow needs.

SYNDICATED LOANS (B LOANS) In a B loan, participating banks provide their own funds and assume their own commercial risk, while IFC remains the lender of record. Mobilizing funds for private sector projects in developing countries from other investors and lenders is one of IFC's most essential functions. IFC actively seeks partners for joint ventures and raises additional finance by encouraging other institutions to make investments in IFC projects. The cornerstone of IFC's finance mobilization efforts is the loan participation program. The program arranges syndicated loans from commercial banks, providing additional financing to IFC-financed projects in developing countries.

Escorts Telecommunications Limited (ETL) is a 100% owned greenfield cellular subsidiary of the Escorts Group of India. It is one of India's major industrial houses with interests in agri-machinery, telecommunications, and healthcare. In March 2001, the government of India auctioned off 24 new cellular licenses. ETL was the highest bidder in four regions and was awarded a 20-year license to build and operate cellular networks in these regions. The World Bank Country Assistance Strategy notes that deficiencies in India's infrastructure are a key hindrance to economic growth, and that the government of India does not have the resources to finance infrastructure expansion.

The total project cost is estimated at USD 205 million equivalent. The proposed IFC investment is up to USD 80 million equivalent, consisting of: (i) up to USD 30 million equivalent in a US dollar and/or a local currency denominated IFC A loan (for the account of IFC); (ii) up to USD 30 million equivalent in an IFC B loan (for the account of participants); and (iii) up to USD 20 million equivalent in equity.

Source: Summary of Project Information (SPI), IFC, June 28, 2002

EQUITY AND QUASI-EQUITY (C LOANS) IFC takes equity stakes in private sector companies and other entities such as financial institutions and in portfolio and investment funds in developing countries. IFC is a long-term investor and usually maintains equity investments for a period of 8 to 15 years. IFC also offers a full range of quasi-equity products with both debt and equity characteristics to private sector projects in developing countries. IFC provides a full range of quasi-equity finance, including convertible debentures, subordinated loans, loans with warrants, and other instruments. These products are provided to ensure that a project is soundly funded. IFC generally provides from 5 to 15 percent of a project's equity and does not take an active role in company management. IFC risks its own capital and does not accept government guarantees. However, to meet national ownership requirements, IFC shareholdings can be treated as domestic capital or local shares.

GUARANTEES IFC offers credit enhancement structures for debt instruments (bonds or loans) in the form of partial credit guarantees. These structures allow IFC to use its triple-A credit rating to help clients diversify their funding sources, extend maturities, and obtain financing in local currency. A partial credit guarantee covers creditors regardless of the cause of default. However, the amount that IFC pays out under the guarantee is capped at an agreed-upon amount; for example 40 percent of the initial principal or one year of debt service. The guaranteed amount may vary over the life of the transaction based on the borrower's expected cash flows and creditor's concerns and may be used to cover any debt-servicing shortfalls. Client companies may issue bonds with the partial guarantee to attract local currency in their domestic capital market or foreign currency in the international capital market. Alternatively, they may use the partial guarantee for loans to attract financing from local or international financial institutions.

FINANCIAL INTERMEDIARY INVESTMENTS A large chunk of IFC financing is channeled to private sector projects in developing countries through intermediaries. IFC uses its full range of financial products to provide capital to a wide variety of financial intermediaries. Working through intermediaries allows IFC to extend its long-term finance to more companies, in particular to SMEs and microfinance entrepreneurs. IFC operates on a commercial basis and invests exclusively in for-profit projects and charges market rates for its products and services. Examples include credit and equity lines to banks, private equity and investment funds, venture capital funds, and leasing companies.

CREDIT LINES IFC provides credit lines to local financial institutions and private equity funds to make long-term financing available to SMEs as they seek to enhance their competitiveness in more open economies around the world. Credit lines to developing country banks help redress the limited availability of term funding and lessen constraints on the ability of these banks to provide working capital and investment financing to local enterprises.

ELIGIBILITY AND APPLICATION IFC invests only in private companies or those under private management where the bulk of the capital, entrepreneurship, and the initiative comes from private sources. Fundamentally, an IFC-supported project, be it a new enterprise or the expansion of an existing one, must be in the private sector, be technically sound, and have good prospects of being profitable while benefiting the local economy. Another important criterion for all IFC investments is that the project must conform to host country and World Bank environmental and worker rights guidelines along with IFC's own Environmental Procedures. Additionally, IFC will invest only in a venture when appropriate arrangements exist for the repatriation of its investment capital and related earnings.

Before approving an investment, IFC conducts a thorough appraisal to establish the proposed project's financial, economic, technical, and environmental feasibility. As a rule, projects in which IFC invests must be internationally competitive in order to attract other funding and contribute to the balanced economic development of the host country.

There is no standard application form for IFC financing. A company or a single entrepreneur, either foreign or domestic, seeking to establish a new venture or expand an existing enterprise can approach IFC directly. This can be done by requesting a meeting or by submitting a preliminary project summary. After these initial contacts and a preliminary review, IFC will request a detailed feasibility study or business plan to determine whether to appraise the project for financing.

International Finance Corporation
2121 Pennsylvania Avenue, NW
Washington, DC 20433
Tel: 202-477-1234
Fax: 202-944-4327
E-mail: info@ifc.org
Web: www.ifc.org

Latin America & the Caribbean Department
Bernard Pasquier, Director
Tel: 202-473-0736

Sub-Saharan Africa Department
Haydee Celaya, Director
Tel: 202-473-0319

Middle East & North Africa Department
Sami Haddad, Director
Tel: 202-473-6864

Southern Europe & Central Asia Department
Khosrow Zamani, Director
Tel: 202-473-5650

Asia & the Pacific Department
Javed Hamid, Director
Tel: 202-473-0400

Agribusiness Department
Jean-Paul Pinard, Director
Tel: 202-473-0517

Health & Education Department
Guy Ellena, Director
Tel: 202-458-8139

Global Financial Markets Group
Karl Voltaire
Tel: 202-473-9301

Global Information & Communication Technologies Group
Mohsen Khalil, Director
Tel: 202-473-6786

Infrastructure Department
Declan Duff, Director
Tel: 202-473-9779

Oil, Gas & Mining Chemicals Department
Rashad Kaldany, Director
Tel: 202-473-6787

Power Department
Francisco Tourreilles, Director
Tel: 202-473-0814

Private Equity & Investment Funds Department
Teresa Barger, Director
Tel: 202-473-8801

Small & Medium Enterprises Department
Harold Rosen, Director
Tel: 202-473-8841

EQUITY

While raising senior debt is of primary interest in most project finance transactions, project sponsors sometimes need third-party equity and quasi-equity instruments to make deals happen. In some instances, sponsors need additional equity because of internal capital shortages or a desire to off-load some of the risk. In other situations, sponsors need to quickly round off the financing plan in case of unanticipated cost increases or fund-raising problems. Raising equity or subordinated debt typically takes less time than obtaining senior debt, although the timing advantage is off-set by the forfeited tax shield and high yield expectations of equity investors.

In other situations, senior lenders such as IFC ask for equity-linked instruments in order to participate in the upside of a project and better align their interests with those of equity holders. The ability of IFC and other multilaterals to invest equity or quasi-equity instruments in project finance transactions was highlighted earlier in this chapter. This section provides sample case studies of entities whose principal interest is to provide equity and subordinated finance to project deals. Many of these entities are privately sponsored and managed venture and private equity funds that benefit from government-guaranteed debt, equity investment, political risk insurance, or some other form of support. Still others, albeit a minority, specialize in providing subordinated or mezzanine debt to emerging market projects. For a comprehensive listing of selected government-backed equity funds, see Appendix K.

While terms and conditions vary depending on the unique circumstances and risk profile of each transaction, there are some commonalities in the approach taken by private equity investors. Typically, government-backed equity funds prefer to take a meaningful minority stake (25 to 49 percent) that gives them board representation and some blocking power over important decisions, such as sale of project, closure, IPO, major capital investments, and so forth. Otherwise, fund investors do not participate in the day-to-day management of projects. Return expectations are generally in the high teens and often into the twenties. Government-backed funds typically focus on specific geographic regions and/or industry sectors; e.g., the OPIC-backed Agribusiness Fund for the New Independent States managed by America First or Darby Overseas Investments supported by IDB, who look to make subordinated loans for projects in Latin America. Following are some representative case studies of transactions that a few of the government-backed funds have supported.

Agribusiness Partners

Agribusiness Partners, an America First company, is a USD 100 million fund that invests in agribusiness and food processing companies in the former Soviet Union. The fund has a guarantee from OPIC, which allows it to provide needed financing to this region.

Agribusiness Partners (API) made a USD 22.5 million direct equity investment in Golden Rooster—an integrated poultry processing and broiler operation in Lipetsk, Russia that processes 350,000 birds per week. Phase I of the Project began in 1996, when API made an initial investment of $12.5 million. Under Phase I, the Company consolidated 11 existing broiler farms, a feed mill and a processing plant into one large operation with total output capacity of 350,000 broilers per week. In less than two years, Golden Rooster gained recognition as Russia's market leader for broiler production. Its production capacity is twice the size of its nearest competitor, and its leadership is defined by brand-name recognition and product quality.

Darby Overseas Investments

Darby Overseas Investments is a private investment firm head-quartered in Washington, D.C., that invests capital in emerging markets through a variety of investment products. The objective of this group is to invest in early and mid-stage technology companies, primarily in the Latin American region, to assist international and local technology companies in experiencing growth.

Darby Overseas Investments, Ltd. announced that its Darby Latin American Mezzanine Fund (DLAMF), together with Citigroup Venture Capital Latin America, a unit of Citigroup, Inc., is making a mezzanine investment in Promotora Ambiental S.A. de C.V. (PASA), the leading private waste management company in Mexico. Darby invested USD 16 million of the USD 40 million being raised. PASA is the largest private provider of non-hazardous solid waste services in Mexico. It serves municipal (residential), commercial, and industrial customers in 36 Mexican cities, has over 18,500 corporate clients and has over 2,900 employees.

PASA operates four lines of business, including commercial and industrial waste collection, municipal waste collection, landfill operations, and oil drill-cutting treatment. The new financing in which Darby is participating is being used in part to undertake corporate refinancing in the light of Waste Management's withdrawal and in part to provide new funds for PASA's expansion.

Source: News Release, Darby Overseas Investments, September 10, 2002

Emerging Markets Partnership

Emerging Markets Partnership is an international private equity firm headquartered in Washington, D.C. It provides equity to companies in amounts ranging from USD 10–150 million.

The IDB Infrastructure Fund, headquartered in the Kingdom of Bahrain, has agreed to acquire an approximately 32 percent ownership interest in AES Oasis Limited for approximately USD 150 million. AES Oasis is a newly created company, majority owned by The AES Corporation, USA. AES Oasis, headquartered in the United Arab Emirates, will own AES's existing two electric generation and desalination plants in Oman and Qatar, together with the oil-fired generating facilities of AES LalPir and AES PakGen in Pakistan, and will develop other power projects in the wider Middle East region.

The Fund expects the acquisition to be completed in the second or third quarter of 2003 after certain conditions, including obtaining government and lender approvals, have been met. The Fund, with commitments of USD 980 million, is one of the largest investment funds available for direct investment in the region. Headquartered in the Kingdom of Bahrain with its Asia regional office in the Sultanate of Brunei Darussalam, it focuses on private sector projects in power, petrochemicals, transportation, telecoms and other infrastructure-related sectors.

The Fund's General Partner is Emerging Markets Partnership (Bahrain) E.C. and the Islamic Development Bank (IDB) is the Principal Sponsor of the Fund.

Source: AME Info, March 31, 2003

7

Insurance

International business, including exports and direct investments, involves a substantial amount of commercial and political risk. The focus of this chapter is on insurance products in support of foreign direct investments. Trade-related insurance was covered in Chapter 5. To mitigate risks and to facilitate third-party equity and debt for investments, Washington-based agencies offer a variety of risk mitigation products. Insurance products cover equity and debt investments on a conditional basis against various types of risks, up to 100 percent in some cases, but they typically involve a deductible. The exact conditions under which an insurance claim may be paid are clearly defined and very specific to each contractual agreement.

The uncertainty of the political climate in emerging market countries often poses a considerable risk to companies or investors looking to operate or expand in these markets. To encourage foreign direct investment, organizations such as the Multilateral Investment Guarantee Agency (MIGA), the Overseas Private Investment Corporation (OPIC), and other development finance institutions (see Appendix J) offer political risk insurance (PRI) to cover such noncommercial risks.

PRI covers the actions of foreign governments that may adversely affect an investment. Actions typically covered include expropriation, breach of contract, currency transfer restrictions, inconvertibility, war, and political violence. A PRI policy sometimes allows projects to secure a better rating, which often results in savings, and the additional security makes it much easier to attract incremental equity and debt. PRI ensures that many of these fears are alleviated, thereby making foreign investments, which are often critical to these economies, possible.

Following is a list of topics covered in this chapter:

- Political risk coverage
- Commercial risk coverage
- Foreign exchange risk

- Interest rate risk
- Leasing insurance

Inter-American Development Bank (IDB)

GUARANTEES IDB offers political risk and credit guarantees to cover private sector lenders who make loans to projects in Latin America and the Caribbean. Coverage may be provided up 100 percent for specific political risks, such as sovereign contractual obligations or transferability. IDB issues long-term credit guarantees (which extend the effective life of financing), liquidity guarantees in the form of put options or take-out financing, and rolling guarantees that cover a fixed number of scheduled payments. IDB credit guarantees do not require government counterguarantees.

- **Political Risk Guarantees** provide IDB coverage for breach of contract, currency inconvertibility, and other political risks such as expropriation or related arbitrary governmental actions. Coverage needs are specifically tailored to each project and can be extended to up to 50 percent of project costs or USD 150 million, whichever is less. Annual fees, commitment fees on the undisbursed balance, and certain other up-front fees are charged on a case-by-case basis.
- **Credit Guarantee Coverage** is available in several forms and typically provides comprehensive coverage for selected terms of a loan made by commercial lenders. These guarantees are specifically tailored to each project to provide the most effective enhancement to the guaranteed amount of the loan. IDB can support up to 25 percent of the project costs with a USD 75 million limit. In some instances, participation can be increased to 40 percent, but the USD 75 million limit still applies. Annual fees for credit guarantees are charged similar to the approximate spreads charged for long-term loans. Other fees may be applied on a case-by-case basis.

Inter-American Development Bank
1300 New York Avenue, NW
Washington, DC 20577
Tel: 202-623-1000
Fax: 202-623-3096
Web: www.iadb.org

Multilateral Investment Guarantee Agency (MIGA)

The guarantee program of MIGA, an arm of the World Bank Group, is designed to encourage the flow of foreign private investment to emerging markets by mitigating political risks associated with a project. MIGA offers long-term political risk insurance to project sponsors (i.e., equity coverage) for new investments in developing member countries. Beyond insurance protection, MIGA's participation in a project enhances confidence that the investor's rights will be respected, an advantage inherent in MIGA's status of a voluntary association of developing and developed countries.

LONG-TERM RISK INSURANCE This insurance may be purchased separately or in combination with other products. However, an investor must select the desired coverage before MIGA will issue a guarantee. The maximum amount of coverage that MIGA can retain for a single project is currently USD 50 million, although the amount of coverage mobilized can be expanded considerably through MIGA's collaboration with other insurers. The following types of coverage are offered by MIGA:

- **Transfer Restrictions** protect against loss arising from an investor's inability to convert local currency into foreign exchange for transfer outside the host country. Currency devaluations, however, are not covered.
- **Expropriation** protects against loss of the insured investment as a result of acts by the host government that may reduce or eliminate ownership of, control over, or rights to the insured investment.
- **War and Civil Disturbance** protects against loss from, damage to, or the destruction or disappearance of tangible assets caused by politically motivated acts of war or civil disturbance in the host country, including revolution, insurrection, coups d'état, sabotage, and terrorism.
- **Breach of Contract** protects equity losses arising from the host government's breach or repudiation of a contract with the investor.

MIGA can insure straight equity, shareholder loans, or third-party (bank) loans. Usually, MIGA requires bank loan coverage to be purchased as a package with equity insurance. MIGA also insures new investments originating in any member country and

The Multilateral Investment Guarantee Agency (MIGA) is supporting the financing and development of a new airport outside Quito, Ecuador. The new airport will replace the Mariscal Sucre airport, currently located in the city center, which no longer meets travel requirements and has constrained the region's economic development.

MIGA is offering $66.5 million in guarantee coverage to Aecon Group Inc. of Canada, Airport Development Corporation Management Limited of the British Virgin Islands, and Houston Airport System Development Corp. of the United States, for their equity investment and shareholder loans to Corporación Quiport S.A. of Ecuador. The coverage is for a period of up to 15 years, against the risks of transfer restriction, war and civil disturbance, and breach of contract.

Source: MIGA Press Release, June 18, 2003

---

destined for any developing member country other than the country of origin. New investment contributions associated with the expansion, modernization, or financial restructuring of existing projects are eligible, as are acquisitions that involve the privatization of state enterprises.

MIGA's standard term of coverage is 15 years. Coverage may, in extraordinary circumstances, be extended to 20 years if MIGA finds that the coverage is justified by the nature of the project. MIGA may insure equity investments for up to 90 percent of the investment contribution, plus an additional 450 percent of the investment contribution to cover earnings attributable to the investment. In the case of loans and loan guarantees, MIGA may insure up to 90 percent of the principal, plus an additional 135 percent of the principal to cover interest that will accrue over the term of the loan. For technical-assistance contracts and similar agreements, MIGA insures up to 90 percent of the total value of payments due under the insured agreement.

MIGA has established a fee structure for determining the premium rates that apply to a specific investment. MIGA's risk assessment focuses primarily on the risks associated with the individual project and coverage, taking into account general economic and political conditions in the host country. Accordingly, the base rates may be raised or lowered for a particular project depending on the project's risk profile.

MIGA charges two types of premiums: current and stand-by. Stand-by premiums are typically 50 percent of the current rates and are similar to commitment fees in that they are applied to cover what is approved but not currently active. Stand-by coverage is very useful for loans that take many years to amortize. An investor seeking coverage from MIGA must submit a preliminary application before an investment will be made or irrevocably committed. Once investment and financing plans are established, an investor should promptly complete and return the Definitive Application for Guarantee to MIGA along with any relevant project documentation, such as a joint venture contract, a feasibility study, or an environmental assessment. The Definitive Application provides the detailed information needed for review and preparation of a Contract of Guarantee. This information includes the eligibility of the investor, the amount and type of investment, types of coverage desired, the developmental effects of the project, and substantiation of the project's financial and economic viability.

There is no charge for filing a preliminary application. However, MIGA charges an application fee of either USD 5,000 or USD 10,000 to process Definitive Applications, as outlined in the schedule below:

- Guarantees up to USD 25 million: USD 5,000
- Guarantees more than USD 25 million: USD 10,000
- Natural Resources, Oil, and Gas, and Infrastructure: USD 10,000

MIGA also charges a processing fee for exceptional underwriting costs incurred in evaluating projects that are environmentally sensitive (e.g., oil and gas, mining, and infrastructure) or whose complex financial structures require retention of outside advisers. The initial processing fee is USD 25,000. If the exceptional costs incurred are less, the unused balance will be refunded to the applicant. If the exceptional costs incurred are greater, the applicant will be billed for the additional amount.

COOPERATIVE UNDERWRITING PROGRAM (CUP) The Cooperative Underwriting Program provides the stability needed to encourage private sector insurers to participate in transactions they would normally not undertake. This program allows MIGA to extend its reach by acting as the insurer-of-record for the entire loan amount, while retaining only a portion of the risk. In 2001, the CUP was able to provide USD 153 million in investment coverage.

TREATY REINSURANCE AGREEMENT MIGA has a quota share treaty reinsurance agreement with A.C.E. Insurance Company, Ltd.

(ACE), a wholly-owned subsidiary of ACE Limited. This agreement is an innovative means to supplement MIGA's own guarantee capacity in order to continue its support of investments into developing countries.

The agreement between MIGA and ACE significantly increases available insurance capacity for investors seeking to expand their businesses in developing countries. Under the agreement, ACE assumes exposure of up to USD 25 million per project and up to USD 100 million per country for new contracts of guarantee. In effect, this means MIGA can offer increased coverage of up to USD 75 million per project (increased from USD 50 million) and up to USD 325 million per country (increased from USD 225 million). This is particularly important for countries in which MIGA has already utilized most of its current capacity (e.g., Brazil, Peru, and Russia).

Investors are not subject to any new procedures or duplication of information. The main parameters of MIGA's current program, such as sector and country eligibility and terms and conditions of the guarantee contracts, remain unchanged.

Multilateral Investment Guarantee Agency
1800 G Street, NW
Washington, DC 20433
Tel: 202-473-6168
Fax: 202-522-2630
Web: www.miga.org

Overseas Private Investment Corporation (OPIC)

OPIC provides political risk insurance to U.S. investors, contractors, exporters, and financial institutions involved in international business transactions in developing countries. OPIC insurance is available for investments in new ventures or expansions of existing enterprises and can cover equity investments, parent company and third-party loans and loan guarantees, technical assistance agreements, cross-border leases, assigned inventory or equipment, as well as other forms of investment.

CURRENCY INCONVERTIBILITY COVERAGE This coverage assures that earnings, returns on capital, principal and interest payments, and other remittances, including payments under technical service agreements, can continue to be converted into U.S. dollars. The insured will be compensated by OPIC for host country currency restrictions, whether active (host country authorities deny access to foreign exchange through regulations) or passive (host country monetary authorities fail to act on an application for hard currency). In either case, OPIC makes payments in the U.S. dollar equivalent of the local currency amount at an exchange rate in effect before OPIC received the application for compensation. Inconvertibility coverage does not protect against currency devaluation.

EXPROPRIATION COVERAGE This coverage protects against the nationalization, confiscation, or expropriation of an enterprise, including "creeping" expropriation (i.e., host government actions that deprive the investor of fundamental rights in a project for at least six months). Expropriation coverage does not protect against losses due to lawful regulatory or revenue actions by host governments or actions provoked or instigated by the investor or foreign enterprise.

OPIC contributed $1.5 million in political risk insurance to a company providing life and health insurance to previously uninsured local companies and individuals in Venezuela, continuing a trend of foreign investment that has turned around the insurance industry in that country. BMI Venezuela, a wholly-owned subsidiary of BMI Financial Group, Inc. of Coral Gables, Florida, will use the expropriation insurance to cover BMI Financial Group's investment in the Venezuelan enterprise, as well as services provided by another subsidiary, BMI Services, Inc., which will provide training to BMI Venezuela employees in cost management techniques, systems expertise, and health coverage enhancement programs.

Source: OPIC News, December 2001

POLITICAL VIOLENCE COVERAGE This insurance protects investors from property and income losses resulting from violence undertaken for political purposes. Actions of political violence covered by OPIC include declared or undeclared war, hostile actions by national or international forces, civil war, revolution, insurrection, and civil strife, including politically motivated terrorism and sabotage. OPIC compensates for two types of losses: business income losses (losses of income resulting from damage to insured property) and damage to tangible property.

SPECIAL INSURANCE PROGRAMS Several insurance programs are tailored to meet the special needs of certain types of investments.

Investors are urged to contact OPIC to receive additional information on special insurance programs.

- **Financial Institutions** allow U.S. banks and other institutional investors to better manage their cross-border exposures by insuring a wide range of banking activities, including project loans made or arranged by banks, gold loans, commercial paper transactions or floating-rate notes purchased by eligible institutions, cross-border leases, debt-for-equity investments, and commodity price swaps.

OPIC approved a $35 million guaranty to enable a leading American bank to expand its lending to middle-market businesses worldwide. The OPIC guaranty, for National City Bank of Cleveland, OH will allow National City to expand its medium and long-term lending to middle-market businesses—those with annual revenues between $35 million and $350 million—in OPIC-eligible countries globally. OPIC will review each National City transaction for U.S. effects, environmental, human and workers' rights, and establish concentration limits to ensure that the facility's transaction portfolio is diversified. National City is one of only three U.S. banks to undertake this type of lending facility with OPIC in 2002.

Source: OPIC Press Release, September 17, 2002

- **Oil and Gas**—To encourage petroleum exploration, development, and production in developing countries, OPIC provides enhanced political insurance coverage that better meets the needs of the oil and gas sector. OPIC's enhanced expropriation coverage compensates the investor for losses caused by material changes unilaterally imposed by a host government on project agreements, including abrogation, impairment, and repudiation or breach of concession agreements, production sharing agreements, service contracts, as well as other agreements between the U.S. company and the foreign government.
- **Natural Resources (Except Oil and Gas)**—For exploration-phase natural resource projects, OPIC insurance not only insures against confiscation and political violence losses to tangible assets, but also insures against the unlawful withdrawal or breach of mineral exploration, development, and other vital rights by the host government. Coverage under this program extends to equity, parent company or institutional

loans, owners' guarantees of loans (including completion guaranties), leases of equipment to project companies, and others.

- **Contractors and Exporters**—OPIC's insurance coverage for contractors and exporters protects the U.S. company from wrongful calling of bid, performance, or advance payment guarantees and from customs bonds; loss of physical assets and bank accounts due to host country confiscation or political violence, as well as inconvertibility of proceeds from the sale of equipment used at the site; and losses due to unresolved contractual disputes with the foreign buyer. This insurance can protect U.S. companies acting as contractors in international construction, sales, or service contracts and exporters of heavy machinery and other goods. Coverage under this program is issued when the U.S. company has a contract with a foreign government buyer.

LEASE INSURANCE OPIC offers political risk insurance coverage for cross-border operating and capital-lease transactions with terms of at least 36 months. OPIC's insurance for assets leased under an operating lease provides coverage for the original cost of the leased assets (including duties, freight, and installation) incurred by the lessor. Insurance for capital leases covers the stream of payments due under the lease agreement. OPIC's insurance provides coverage against the following:

- Currency inconvertibility—deterioration of the investor's ability to convert profits, debt service, and other remittances from local currency into U.S. dollars
- Expropriation—loss of an investment due to expropriation, nationalization, or confiscation by a foreign government
- Political violence—loss of assets or income due to war, revolution, insurrection, or politically motivated civil strife, terrorism, and sabotage

Coverage is also available for equity investments in and loans to offshore leasing companies for management and maintenance agreements involving leasing companies and for consigned inventory. OPIC also insures against host government actions that prevent lessors from enforcing their rights to repossess, reexport, and deregister leased equipment.

SMALL BUSINESS CENTER POLITICAL RISK INSURANCE OPIC protects small business overseas investments against political uncertainties. It provides insurance against loss or damage resulting from political violence such as terrorism or war, nationalization or expropriation by a foreign government, or the inability to convert local currency and repatriate profits. One value-added function of this product is that applications will be processed within a 60-day period. Interest rates are fixed and based on the nature of the risk. Terms extend up to 20 years and generally offer up to USD 15 million in coverage. Any U.S. small business with annual revenues less than USD 35 million is eligible for coverage.

A small business was able to expand its optical components manufacturing facility in Russia with $777,000 in political risk insurance from OPIC. OPIC's insurance will enable International Scientific Products Corporation (ISP) of New York to increase production and quality control at ISP's operation in St. Petersburg. The Russian enterprise, ISP Optics Sankt Petersburg, produces optical components such as lenses, domes, prisms, polarizers and wave plates that are sold to markets in the United States and worldwide. This project is expected to generate 20 local jobs as well as tax revenue for the country. Additionally, ISP has ensured that senior management of the enterprise will receive MBA coursework and that its opticians will receive professional training in the United States.

Source: OPIC News, April 2003

COVERAGE OPIC insures investments in new and existing enterprises for a term up to 20 years. With the exception of principal and interest from loans and leases from financial institutions to unrelated third parties, OPIC covers up to 90 percent of an investment (OPIC's statutes require that investors bear the risk of loss of at least 10 percent), not to exceed USD 200 million per project. Furthermore, OPIC typically issues insurance commitments equal to 270 percent of the initial investment—90 percent representing the original investment and 180 percent covering future earnings.

ELIGIBILITY OPIC may insure an investment by an eligible investor in a project controlled by foreign interests, but only the eligible investor's share is insured, not the entire project. Eligible investors are U.S. citizens, corporations, partnerships, or other associations substantially owned by U.S. citizens or created under the laws of the United States or of any state or territory of the United

States. Eligible foreign businesses must be at least 95 percent owned by investors eligible under the preceding criteria.

APPLICATION Prior to applying for political risk insurance coverage, investors are required to register their projects with OPIC's Insurance Department before an investment will be made or irrevocably committed. Project registration is free, and all information is treated as confidential. A registration is valid for two years and may be renewed in one-year increments. To process the application, OPIC will charge the investor a retainer fee used to reimburse OPIC's out-of-pocket expenses associated with the review process. In the event that OPIC offers insurance coverage for an investment and the investor accepts, any unused portion of the retainer fee is refunded. Similarly, when OPIC is not able to offer insurance, any unused portion of the fee is returned. However, if the investor declines the offered coverage, the fee is nonrefundable.

Insurance Department
Overseas Private Investment Corporation
1100 New York Avenue, NW
Washington, DC 20527
Tel: 202-336-8799
Fax: 202-408-9859
E-mail: info@opic.gov
Web: www.opic.gov

U.S. Agency for International Development (USAID)

USAID offers financing to private entities through its Development Credit Agency (DCA). This agency permits USAID to issue loans, guarantees, and grants in industries and sectors that need this type of assistance to encourage sustainable growth in the developing world.

LOANS AND GUARANTEES The purpose of DCA is to enhance credit options to the private sector. DCA guarantees require true private sector risk sharing, and USAID's share of a lender's risk cannot exceed 50 percent (except as otherwise approved by the Credit Review Board). DCA offers a mixture of grant and credit assistance in settings where USAID is seeking more disciplined and sustainable assistance relationships. Two types of fees are involved: a one-time Commitment Fee of 0.25 to 2.00 percent of the guaranteed amount and a semi-annual Utilization Fee paid on the outstanding guaranteed amount ranging from 0.25 to 2.00 percent.

Office of Development Credit
1300 Pennsylvania Avenue, Room 210
Washington, DC 20523
Tel: 202-712-4265
Fax: 202-216-3593
E-mail: odc@usaid.gov

World Bank

World Bank guarantees are provided to private lenders and are typically associated with financing infrastructure projects where the demand for funding is large and political, sovereign risks are significant, and long-maturity financing is critical to a project's viability. By covering risks that the market is not able to adequately bear or evaluate, guarantees can attract new sources of financing, reduce financing costs, and extend maturities. The Bank's guarantee may be for specified risks (partial risk guarantee) or for all credit risks during a specified part of the financing term (partial credit guarantee).

PARTIAL RISK GUARANTEES These guarantees cover specific government obligations spelled out in agreements with the project entity and ensure payment in the case of debt service default resulting from the nonperformance of contractual obligations undertaken by governments or their agencies in private sector projects. Typical government contractual obligations include:

- Maintaining the agreed-upon regulatory framework, including tariff formulas.
- Delivering inputs, such as fuel supplied to a private power company.
- Paying for outputs, such as power purchased by a government utility from a private power company or bulk water purchased by a local public distribution company.
- Compensating for project delays or interruptions caused by government actions or political events.

Coverage under the Partial Risk Guarantee protects against the performance of government-owned entities, including payment obligations of a utility, obligations to supply fuel, and obligations to provide foreign exchanges. It also protects against changes in law, political events in the host country, and certain natural events relating to the government entities.

The World Bank's Executive Board approved a proposal to provide a partial risk guarantee for an amount equivalent to $30.3 million in support of the Azito Power Project, operated by CINERGY (owned by Asea Brown Boveri Limited, ABB, and its partners, Industrial Promotion Services and Electricité de France), in Côte d'Ivoire. The total project cost is estimated at $223 million and consists of a power plant and a transmission component. The IDA Partial Risk Guarantee will secure financing for the associated transmission line.

Source: World Bank Press Release, May 1998

PARTIAL CREDIT GUARANTEES These guarantees cover debt service defaults on a specified portion of a loan or bond. Such guarantees allow public sector projects to extend maturities and lower spreads. The types of risks covered by these guarantees include breach of contract, availability and convertibility of foreign exchange, changes in law, and expropriation and nationalization.

The World Bank, through IBRD, granted a $180 million partial credit guarantee to complete the financing plan of the Gas Sector Development Project—Bolivia-Brazil Gas Pipeline. The pipeline is a joint undertaking of the Brazilian Petroleum Company Petrobras and major international players in the gas sector, promoted by the governments of Bolivia and Brazil. It is comprised of a natural gas pipeline 3,150 kilometers long that extends from Rio Grande, Bolivia, through the Brazilian States of Mato Grosso do Sul, Sao Paulo, Parana, Santa Catarina and Rio Grande do Sul. Gas transported by the pipeline will be supplied to industrial and residential users in Brazil's principal cities, including Campo Grande, Sao Paulo, Rio de Janeiro, Curitiba and Porto Alegre.

Source: World Bank DevNews Media Center, December 20, 2000

PARTIAL CREDIT GUARANTEES FOR LONGER MATURITIES These guarantees cover all events of nonpayment for a designated part of a financing and encourage extension of maturity by covering a part of a financing, usually the later maturities. The need for such guarantees arises if short-term financing (for the construction period, for example) is available but the prospects of rolling over such financing are uncertain.

The Bank charges a standby fee and a guarantee fee. The standby fee is applied during the period when the guarantee is in force but not callable. The standby fee is currently 25 basis points per annum on the Bank's guarantee exposure. The guarantee fee, applied during the period when the guarantee is callable, is currently in the range of 40 to 100 basis points per annum on outstanding debt covered by the guarantee, which consists of a base fee of 25 basis points plus a premium ranging from 15 to 75 basis points.

Projects that benefit from a Bank guarantee are required to meet standard Bank appraisal criteria, including technical, financial, economic, and environmental aspects, regardless of whether the guarantee is undertaken in conjunction with an investment loan from the Bank or on a stand-alone basis (i.e., without an accompanying Bank investment loan for the same project). For stand-alone operations, the Bank may substantially base its own appraisal on studies or analyses undertaken by other multilateral financial agencies, private lenders, or sponsors.

The private sponsor chooses the lead manager in a manner suitable to its objectives and the circumstances of the project. For project finance transactions, once the project documentation has been substantially negotiated and the guarantee structure and coverage has been broadly agreed upon, the lead manager for the financing prepares an information memorandum to attract financial institutions to participate in the loan financing guaranteed by the Bank.

Manager, Project Finance and Guarantees Division
The World Bank
1818 H Street, NW, Room Q5131
Washington, DC 20433
Tel: 202-473-1650
Fax: 202-477-0218
Web: www.worldbank.org

Guarantees Contact
Tel: 202-473-7878
Fax: 202-477-0218
Web: www.worldbank.org/guarantees

Appendix A:
Department of Commerce (DOC), Department of State, and U.S. Agency for International Development (USAID) Country Desk Officers

Business Counseling Contacts at the Department of Commerce:
Former Soviet Union Countries: 202-482-4655
Central and Eastern Europe: 202-482-2645
Rest of the World: 800-872-8723

Business Counseling Contacts at the Department of State and U.S. Agency for International Development (all telephone numbers are in area code 202):

A

COUNTRY	DOC OFFICER	DOC	STATE	USAID
Afghanistan	Timothy Gilman	482-2954	647-9552	712-1861
Albania			647-3747	712-0262
Algeria	Christopher Cerone	482-1860	647-4680	712-4111
Andorra			647-1412	
Angola	Finn Holm-Olsen	482-4228	647-9858	712-1187
Antigua	Michelle Brooks	482-2527	647-4384	712-1644
Argentina	Randy Mye	482-1548	647-2401	
Armenia		482-4655	647-6758	712-4843
Australia			647-7828	
Austria	Philip Combs	482-2920	647-2448	
Azerbaijan		482-4655	647-6048	712-5017

B

COUNTRY	DOC OFFICER	DOC	STATE	USAID
Bahamas	Mark Siegelman	482-5680	647-2621	
Bahrain	Christopher Cerone	482-1860	647-6571	
Baltic States			647-3187	
Bangladesh	John Simmons	482-2954	647-9552	712-5366
Barbados	Michelle Brooks	482-2527	647-2620	
Belarus		482-4655	736-4443	712-0141
Belgium	Simon Bensimon	482-5401	647-6592	
Belize	Michelle Brooks	482-2527	647-3727	712-1768
Benin	Debra Henke	482-5149	647-1596	712-5441
Bermuda			647-6591	
Bhutan	Timothy Gilman	482-2954	647-2141	
Bolivia	Rebecca Hunt	482-2521	647-3076	712-1664
Bosnia-Herzegovina			647-4195	712-5913
Botswana	Finn Holm-Olsen	482-4228	647-9856	712-1963
Brazil	Horace Jennings	482-3871	647-2407	712-1664
British Indian Ocean Territory			647-5684	
Brunei	Edward Oliver	482-4958	647-3276	
Bulgaria		482-2645	647-4850	712-1116
Burkina Faso	Philip Michelini	482-4388	647-1658	
Burma (Myanmar)	Gary Bouck	482-4958	647-3132	712-1577
Burundi	Philip Michelini	482-4388	647-4966	712-4723

C

COUNTRY	DOC OFFICER	DOC	STATE	USAID
Cambodia	Gary Bouck	482-4958	647-3095	712-1577
Cameroon	Debra Henke	482-5149	647-3138	712-4544
Canada	Kathy Keim	482-3103	647-2170	
Cape Verde	Philip Michelini	482-4388	647-0252	712-4128
Cayman Islands	Mark Siegelman	482-5680		
Central African Republic	Philip Michelini	482-4388	647-2973	712-0585
Chad	Philip Michelini	482-4388	647-2973	712-4153
Chile	Roger Turner	482-1495	647-2296	712-4740
China			647-6803	
Colombia	Paul Moore	482-1659	647-3023	712-1527
Comoros	Chandra Watkins	482-4564	736-4644	
Congo, Republic of Kinshasa	Debra Henke	482-5149	647-2216	712-4723
Congo, Democratic Republic of (Brazzaville)	Debra Henke	482-5149	647-1637	712-4723
Cook Islands			647-4745	
Costa Rica	Mark Siegelman	482-5680	647-3518	712-1768
Côte d'Ivoire			647-1540	712-4153
Croatia			647-1739	712-4029
Cuba	Mark Siegelman	482-5680	647-9272	

| Cyprus | Ann Corro | 482-3945 | 647-6112 | 712-1601 |
| Czech Republic | | 482-2645 | 647-1457 | 712-0782 |

D

COUNTRY	DOC OFFICER	DOC	STATE	USAID
Denmark	James Devlin	482-3254	647-8431	
Djibouti	Chandra Watkins	482-4564	647-8913	712-1518
Dominica	Michelle Brooks	482-2527	647-4384	
Dominican Republic	Mark Siegelman	482-3680	736-4322	712-1618

E

COUNTRY	DOC OFFICER	DOC	STATE	USAID
East Timor			647-1221	712-0324
Ecuador	Paul Moore	482-1659	647-3338	712-4957
Egypt	Thomas Sams	482-5506	647-4259	712-1335
El Salvador	Helen Lee	482-2528	647-3505	712-1187
Equatorial Guinea	Philip Michelini	482-4388	647-3138	712-4544
Eritrea	Chandra Watkins	482-4564	736-4644	712-5779
Estonia			647-8908	712-0782
Ethiopia	Chandra Watkins	482-4564	736-4679	712-5779

F

COUNTRY	DOC OFFICER	DOC	STATE	USAID
Fiji			736-4683	
Finland	James Devlin	482-3254	647-8431	
France	Elena Mikalis	482-6008	647-3072	
French Antilles			647-2620	
French Polynesia			736-4683	

G

COUNTRY	DOC OFFICER	DOC	STATE	USAID
Gabon			647-1637	712-5441
Gambia	Philip Michelini	482-4388	647-3407	712-4153
Gaza Strip				712-5731
Georgia		482-4655	647-6795	712-5017
Germany	Brenda Fisher	482-2435	647-2005	
Ghana	Debra Henke	482-5149	647-1596	712-4544
Gibraltar			647-8027	
Greece	Ann Corro	482-3945	647-6113	
Greenland			647-5669	
Grenada	Michelle Brooks	482-2527	647-2621	
Guadeloupe			647-2620	

Guatemala	Helen Lee	482-2328	647-3559	712-1743
Guinea	Philip Michelini	482-4388	647-1658	712-4153
Guinea-Bissau	Philip Michelini	482-4388	647-1540	712-4153
Guyana	Michelle Brooks	482-2527	647-2621	712-1618

H

COUNTRY	DOC OFFICER	DOC	STATE	USAID
Haiti	Mark Siegelman	482-5680	736-4707	712-5601
Honduras	Helen Lee	482-2328	647-0087	712-0319
Hong Kong	Sheila Baker	482-3932	647-6300	
Hungary		482-2645	647-3238	712-0782

I

COUNTRY	DOC OFFICER	DOC	STATE	USAID
Iceland	James Devlin	482-3254	647-8378	
India	Timothy Gilman	482-2954	647-2141	712-4721
Indonesia	Edward Oliver	482-3877	647-1221	712-0581
Iran	Paul Thanos	482-1860	647-6111	
Iraq	Thomas Sams	482-1860	647-5692	
Ireland	Boyce Fitzpatrick	482-2177	647-8027	712-0782
Israel	Paul Thanos	482-1860	647-3672	712-1189
Italy	Boyce Fitzpatrick	482-2177	647-3746	
Ivory Coast	Philip Michelini	482-4388		

J

COUNTRY	DOC OFFICER	DOC	STATE	USAID
Jamaica	Mark Siegelman	482-5680	647-2620	712-1641
Japan	Ed Leslie	482-2425	647-3152	
Jordan	Paul Thanos	482-1860	647-1022	712-1189

K

COUNTRY	DOC OFFICER	DOC	STATE	USAID
Kazakhstan		482-4655	647-6859	712-1669
Kenya	Chandra Watkins	482-4564	647-6473	712-1518
Kiribati			647-4712	
Korea, North	William Golike	482-4390	647-7717	712-4632
Korea, South	Dan Duvall	482-4390	647-7717	712-4632
Kosovo				712-5577
Kuwait	Thomas Sams	482-5506	647-6571	
Kyrgystan		482-4655	647-6740	712-1669

L

COUNTRY	DOC OFFICER	DOC	STATE	USAID
Laos	Gary Bouck	482-4958	647-2036	712-1577
Latvia		482-2645	647-8908	712-0782
Lebanon	Corey Wright	482-5506	647-1030	712-1189
Lesotho	Finn Holm-Olsen	482-4228	647-9855	712-0902
Liberia	Philip Michelini	482-4388	647-0252	712-0638
Libya	Claude Clement	482-5545	647-4674	
Liechtenstein			647-0425	
Lithuania		482-2645	647-8378	712-0782
Luxembourg	Simon Bensimon	482-5401	647-6557	

M

COUNTRY	DOC OFFICER	DOC	STATE	USAID
Macao	Sheila Baker	482-3932	647-6300	
Macedonia			647-2542	712-5954
Madagascar	Chandra Watkins	482-4564	647-6453	712-5779
Malawi	Finn Holm-Olsen	482-4228	647-9838	712-1959
Malaysia	Edward Oliver	482-4958	647-3276	
Maldives	John Simmons	482-2954	647-2351	
Mali	Philip Michelini	482-4388	647-1658	712-0585
Malta	Robert McLaughlin	482-3748	647-3746	
Marshall Islands			647-4712	
Martinique			647-2620	
Mauritania	Philip Michelini	482-4388	647-3407	712-4153
Mauritius	Chandra Watkins	482-4564	647-4644	712-0035
Mexico	Shawn Ricks	482-0300	647-9894	712-1743
Micronesia			647-4712	
Moldova		482-4655	647-6733	712-0141
Monaco			647-3072	
Mongolia	Sheila Baker	482-3932	647-6803	712-1002
Montserrat	Michelle Brooks	482-2527		
Morocco	Claude Clement	482-5545	647-1724	712-4386
Mozambique	Finn Holm-Olsen	482-4228	647-9857	712-0302

N

COUNTRY	DOC OFFICER	DOC	STATE	USAID
Namibia	Finn Holm-Olsen	482-4228	647-9855	712-0839
Nauru			736-4683	
Nepal	Timothy Gilman	482-2954	647-1450	712-5366
Netherlands	Simon Bensimon	482-5401	647-6557	
Netherlands Antilles	Michelle Brooks	482-2527	647-2620	
New Caledonia			736-4683	
New Zealand	Gary Bouck	482-4958	736-4745	
Nicaragua	Mark Siegelman	482-5680	647-1510	712-0954

Niger	Philip Michelini	482-4388	647-1596	712-0585
Nigeria	Debra Henke	482-5149	647-3469	712-0769
Norway	James Devlin	482-4414	647-6582	

O

COUNTRY	DOC OFFICER	DOC	STATE	USAID
Oman	Paul Thanos	482-1860	647-6558	712-4111

P

COUNTRY	DOC OFFICER	DOC	STATE	USAID
Pacific Islands	Gary Bouck	482-4958	647-4741	
Pakistan	Timothy Gilman	482-2954	647-9823	712-0161
Palau			647-5239	
Panama	Helen Lee	482-2528	647-4161	712-1648
Papua New Guinea			647-5239	
Paraguay	Randolph Mye	482-1548	647-2296	712-4957
Peru	Rebecca Hunt	482-2521	647-4177	712-0482
Philippines	Edward Oliver	482-4958	647-3276	712-1002
Poland		482-2645	647-4139	712-0782
Portugal	Mary Beth Double	482-4508	647-3746	
Puerto Rico	Mark Siegelman	482-5680		

Q

COUNTRY	DOC OFFICER	DOC	STATE	USAID
Qatar	Paul Thanos	482-1860	647-6572	

R

COUNTRY	DOC OFFICER	DOC	STATE	USAID
Reunion			647-3072	
Romania		482-2645	647-4272	712-0262
Russia		482-4655	647-9806	712-5608
Rwanda	Philip Michelini	482-4388	647-2973	712-4723

S

COUNTRY	DOC OFFICER	DOC	STATE	USAID
St. Barthlemy	Michelle Brooks	482-2527		
St. Kitts-Nevis	Michelle Brooks	482-2527	647-2130	
St. Lucia	Michelle Brooks	482-2527	647-2130	
St. Vincent-Grenadines	Michelle Brooks	482-2527	647-2130	

Samoa			736-4745	
San Marino			647-3072	
Sao Tome and Principe	Philip Michelini	482-4388	647-1637	712-5441
Saudi Arabia	Claude Clement	482-1860	647-7550	
Senegal	Philip Michelini	482-4388	647-1540	712-4128
Serbia and Montenegro				712-0825
Sierra Leone	Philip Michelini	482-4388	647-2214	712-0638
Singapore	Edward Oliver	482-4958	647-3276	
Slovakia		482-2645	647-3191	712-0782
Slovenia			736-7152	712-0782
Soloman Islands			736-4745	
Somalia	Chandra Watkins	482-4564	647-8913	712-0251
South Africa	Emily Solomon	482-5148	647-9862	712-5883
Spain	Mary Beth Double	482-4508	647-3746	
Sri Lanka	John Simmons	482-2954	647-2351	712-5366
Sudan	Chandra Watkins	482-4564	647-4084	712-5509
Suriname	Michelle Brooks	482-2527	647-2620	
Swaziland	Finn Holm-Olsen	482-4228	647-8434	712-0902
Sweden	James Devlin	482-4414	647-8431	
Switzerland	Philip Combs	482-2920	647-0425	
Syria	Thomas Sams	482-5506	647-1131	

T

COUNTRY	DOC OFFICER	DOC	STATE	USAID
Taiwan	Robert Chu	482-4390	647-7711	
Tajikistan		482-4655	647-6757	712-1669
Tanzania	Finn Holm-Olsen	482-4228	647-8284	712-5779
Thailand	Edward Oliver	482-4958	647-3132	712-1577
Togo	Debra Henke	482-5149	647-2214	712-5441
Tonga			736-4683	
Trinidad and Tobago	Michelle Brooks	482-2527	647-2621	
Tunisia	Corey Wright	482-5506	647-4371	712-4111
Turkey	Anne Corro	482-3945	647-6113	712-1601
Turkmenistan		482-4655	647-6859	712-1669
Tuvala			736-4683	

U

COUNTRY	DOC OFFICER	DOC	STATE	USAID
Uganda	Chandra Watkins	482-4564	647-6453	712-5779
Ukraine		482-4655	647-8671	712-0141
United Arab Emirates	Claude Clement	483-5545	647-6572	
United Kingdom	Robert McLaughlin	482-3748	647-8027	
Uruguay	Roger Turner	482-1495	647-2407	
Uzbekistan		482-4655	647-6765	712-1669

V

COUNTRY	DOC OFFICER	DOC	STATE	USAID
Vatican			647-3746	
Venezuela	Laura Zeiger-Hatfield	482-4303	647-3338	712-4957
Vietnam	Gary Bouck	482-4958	647-3132	712-1577
Virgin Islands	Michelle Brooks	482-2527		

W

COUNTRY	DOC OFFICER	DOC	STATE	USAID
West Bank				712-5731
Western Sahara			647-2214	

Y

COUNTRY	DOC OFFICER	DOC	STATE	USAID
Yemen	Paul Thanos	482-1860	647-6558	712-4111
Yugoslavia (Kosovo)			647-4277	
Yugoslavia (Montenegro)			647-0310	
Yugoslavia (Serbia)			736-7479	

Z

COUNTRY	DOC OFFICER	DOC	STATE	USAID
Zaire	Philip Michelini	482-4388		
Zambia	Finn Holm-Olsen	482-4228	647-9857	712-1515
Zimbabwe	Finn Holm-Olsen	482-4228	647-9852	712-1818

Appendix B:
U.S. Department of
Commerce (DOC)
District Offices

(* denotes an Export Assistance Center)

ALABAMA
Birmingham
Tel: 205-731-1331
Fax: 205-731-0076

ALASKA
Anchorage
Tel: 907-271-6237
Fax: 907-271-6242

ARIZONA
Phoenix
Tel: 602-640-2513
Fax: 602-640-2518

Tucson
Tel: 520-670-5540
Fax: 520-791-5413

ARKANSAS
Little Rock
Tel: 501-324-5794
Fax: 501-324-7380

CALIFORNIA
Bakersfield
Tel: 661-637-0136
Fax: 661-637-0156

Fresno
Tel: 559-227-6582
Fax: 559-227-6509

Indio
Tel: 760-342-4455
Fax: 760-342-3535

Los Angeles (Downtown)
Tel: 213-894-8784
Fax: 213-894-8789

Los Angeles (West)
Tel: 310-235-7206
Fax: 310-235-7220

Monterey
Tel: 831-641-9850
Fax: 831-641-9849

Newport Beach
Tel: 949-660-1688
Fax: 949-660-1338

Novato
Tel: 415-492-4548
Fax: 415-492-4549

Oakland			*Ontario*	
Tel:	510-273-7350		Tel:	909-466-4134
Fax:	510-251-7352		Fax:	909-466-4140
Sacramento			*San Diego*	
Tel:	916-498-5155		Tel:	619-557-5395
Fax:	916-498-5923		Fax:	619-557-6176
San Francisco			*San Jose*	
Tel:	415-705-2300		Tel:	408-271-7300
Fax:	415-705-2297		Fax:	408-271-7307
Ventura				
Tel:	805-676-1573			
Fax:	805-981-1892			

COLORADO
Denver

Tel:	303-844-6001
Fax:	303-844-5651

CONNECTICUT
Middletown

Tel:	860-638-6950
Fax:	860-638-6970

DELAWARE
Served by the Philadelphia EAC

FLORIDA

Clearwater			*Fort Lauderdale*	
Tel:	727-893-3738		Tel:	954-356-6640
Fax:	813-449-2889		Fax:	954-356-6644
Miami			*Orlando*	
Tel:	305-526-7425		Tel:	407-648-6235
Fax:	305-526-7434		Fax:	407-648-6756
Tallahassee				
Tel:	850-942-9635			
Fax:	904-921-5395			

GEORGIA

Atlanta			*Savannah*	
Tel:	404-657-1900		Tel:	912-652-4204
Fax:	404-657-1970		Fax:	912-652-4241

HAWAII
Honolulu

Tel:	808-522-8040
Fax:	808-541-3435

ILLINOIS
*Chicago

Tel:	312-353-4798
Fax:	312-353-8098

Peoria

Tel:	309-671-7815
Fax:	309-671-7818

INDIANA
Carmel

Tel:	317-582-2300
Fax:	317-582-2301

KANSAS
Wichita

Tel:	316-263-4067
Fax:	316-683-7326

KENTUCKY
Lexington

Tel:	859-225-7001
Fax:	859-225-6501

Somerset

Tel:	606-677-6160
Fax:	606-678-2267

LOUISIANA
*New Orleans

Tel:	504-589-6546
Fax:	504-589-2337

MAINE
Portland

Tel:	207-541-7400
Fax:	207-541-7420

IDAHO
Boise

Tel:	208-334-3857
Fax:	208-334-2783

Libertyville

Tel:	847-327-9082
Fax:	847-247-0423

Rockford

Tel:	815-987-8123
Fax:	815-963-7943

IOWA
Des Moines

Tel:	515-288-8614
Fax:	515-284-4021

Louisville

Tel:	502-582-5066
Fax:	502-582-6573

Shreveport

Tel:	318-676-3064
Fax:	318-676-3063

MARYLAND
*Baltimore

Tel:	410-962-4539
Fax:	410-962-4529

MASSACHUSETTS
Boston
Tel: 617-424-5990
Fax: 617-424-5992

MICHIGAN
Detroit
Tel: 313-226-3650
Fax: 313-226-3657

Grand Rapids
Tel: 616-458-3564
Fax: 616-458-3872

Pontiac
Tel: 248-975-9600
Fax: 248-975-9606

MINNESOTA
Minneapolis
Tel: 612-348-1638
Fax: 612-348-1650

MISSISSIPPI
Jackson
Tel: 601-965-4130
Fax: 601-965-5386

MISSOURI
Kansas City
Tel: 816-410-9201
Fax: 816-426-3140

St. Louis
Tel: 314-425-3302
Fax: 314-425-3381

MONTANA
*Served by the Boise
District Office*

NEBRASKA
Omaha
Tel: 402-597-0193
Fax: 402-221-3668

NEVADA
Las Vegas
Tel: 702-229-1157
Fax: 702-366-0688

Reno
Tel: 775-784-5203
Fax: 775-784-5343

NEW HAMPSHIRE
Portsmouth
Tel: 603-334-6074
Fax: 603-334-6110

NEW JERSEY
Newark
Tel: 973-645-4682
Fax: 973-645-4783

Trenton
Tel: 609-989-2100
Fax: 609-989-2395

NEW MEXICO
Santa Fe
Tel: 505-827-0350
Fax: 505-827-0263

NEW YORK
Buffalo
Tel: 716-551-4191
Fax: 716-551-5290

Long Island
Tel: 516-739-1765
Fax: 516-571-4161

Rochester
Tel: 716-263-6480
Fax: 716-325-6505

Harlem
Tel: 212-860-6200
Fax: 212-860-6203

*New York
Tel: 212-809-2642
Fax: 212-264-1356

Westchester
Tel: 914-682-6712
Fax: 914-682-6698

NORTH CAROLINA
*Charlotte
Tel: 704-333-4886
Fax: 704-332-2681

Raleigh
Tel: 919-715-7373
Fax: 919-715-7777

Greensboro
Tel: 336-333-5345
Fax: 336-333-5158

NORTH DAKOTA
Served by the
Minneapolis EAC

OHIO
Cincinnati
Tel: 513-684-2944
Fax: 513-684-3227

Columbus
Tel: 614-365-9510
Fax: 614-365-9598

*Cleveland
Tel: 216-522-4750
Fax: 216-522-2235

Toledo
Tel: 419-241-0683
Fax: 419-241-0684

OKLAHOMA
Oklahoma City
Tel: 405-608-5302
Fax: 405-231-4211

Tulsa
Tel: 918-581-7650
Fax: 918-581-2844

OREGON
Eugene
Tel: 541-242-2384
Fax: 541-465-6704

*Portland
Tel: 503-326-3001
Fax: 503-326-6351

PENNSYLVANIA
Harrisburg
| Tel: | 717-221-4510 |
| Fax: | 717-221-4505 |

Pittsburgh
| Tel: | 412-395-5050 |
| Fax: | 412-395-4875 |

*Philadelphia
| Tel: | 215-597-6101 |
| Fax: | 215-597-6123 |

PUERTO RICO
San Juan (Hato Rey)
| Tel: | 787-766-5555 |
| Fax: | 787-766-5692 |

RHODE ISLAND
Providence
| Tel: | 401-528-5104 |
| Fax: | 401-528-5067 |

SOUTH CAROLINA
Charleston
| Tel: | 803-760-3794 |
| Fax: | 803-727-4052 |

Columbia
| Tel: | 803-765-5345 |
| Fax: | 803-253-3614 |

SOUTH DAKOTA

Greenville
| Tel: | 864-271-1976 |
| Fax: | 864-271-4171 |

Sioux Falls
| Tel: | 605-330-4264 |
| Fax: | 605-330-4266 |

TENNESSEE
Knoxville
| Tel: | 865-545-4637 |
| Fax: | 865-545-4435 |

Memphis
| Tel: | 901-323-1543 |
| Fax: | 901-544-3646 |

Nashville
| Tel: | 615-259-6060 |
| Fax: | 615-736-2454 |

TEXAS
Arlington
| Tel: | 817-277-1313 |
| Fax: | 817-299-9601 |

Austin
| Tel: | 512-916-5939 |
| Fax: | 512-482-5940 |

Fort Worth
| Tel: | 817-212-2673 |
| Fax: | 817-871-6031 |

Houston
| Tel: | 713-718-3063 |
| Fax: | 713-229-2203 |

San Antonio
| Tel: | 210-228-9878 |
| Fax: | 210-228-9874 |

UTAH
  Salt Lake City
    Tel: 801-524-5116
    Fax: 801-524-5886

VERMONT
  Montpelier
    Tel: 802-828-4508
    Fax: 802-828-3258

VIRGINIA
  Arlington
    Tel: 703-524-2885
    Fax: 703-524-2649

  Richmond
    Tel: 804-771-2246
    Fax: 804-771-2390

WASHINGTON
  *Seattle
    Tel: 206-553-5615
    Fax: 206-553-7253

  Spokane
    Tel: 509-353-2625
    Fax: 509-353-2449

WEST VIRGINIA
  Charleston
    Tel: 304-347-5123
    Fax: 304-347-5408

  Wheeling
    Tel: 304-243-5493
    Fax: 304-233-7492

WISCONSIN
  Milwaukee
    Tel: 414-297-3473
    Fax: 414-297-3470

WYOMING
  Served by the
    Denver EAC

REGIONAL OFFICES
  Office of Africa and the Middle East
    Department of Commerce
    Room 2329
    1401 Constitution Avenue, NW
    Washington, DC 20230
    Tel: 202-482-4651
    Fax: 202-482-0224

  Office of Asia and the Pacific
    Department of Commerce
    Room 2036
    1401 Constitution Avenue, NW
    Washington, DC 20230
    Tel: 202-482-4527
    Fax: 202-482-4760

Office of Europe, Russia, and the Independent States
Department of Commerce
Room 3863
1401 Constitution Avenue, NW
Washington, DC 20230
Tel: 202-482-5638
Fax: 202-482-6038

Office of the Western Hemisphere
Department of Commerce
Room 3826
1401 Constitution Avenue, NW
Washington, DC 20230
Tel: 202-482-5324
Fax: 202-482-4736

Appendix C:
State International
Trade Offices

Alabama
Development Office Division
401 Adams Avenue, Suite 690
Montgomery, AL 36130
Tel: 334-242-0400
Fax: 334-242-0486

Alaska
Department of Community and Economic Development
550 West Seventh Street, Suite 1770
Anchorage, AK 99501
Tel: 907-269-8110
Fax: 907-269-8125

Arizona
International Trade and Investment Division
3800 N. Central, Suite 1500
Phoenix, AZ 85012
Tel: 602-280-1371
Fax: 602-280-1378

Arkansas
Department of Economic Development
One Capitol Mall
Little Rock, AR 72201
Tel: 501-682-5196
Fax: 501-324-9856

California
Global Economic Development Division
1102 Q Street, Suite 6000
Sacramento, CA 95814
Tel: 916-324-5511
Fax: 916-324-5791

Colorado

International Trade Office
    1625 Broadway, Suite 1700
    Denver, CO 80202
    Tel: 303-892-3850
    Fax: 303-892-3820

Connecticut

Industry Clusters & International Division
    505 Hudson Street
    Hartford, CT 06106
    Tel: 860-270-8067
    Fax: 860-270-8070

Delaware

Economic Development Office
    820 N. French Street
    Wilmington, DE 19801
    Tel: 302-577-8464
    Fax: 302-577-8499

District of Columbia

Office of International Affairs
    1350 Pennsylvania Avenue, NW
    Suite 317
    Washington, DC 20004
    Tel: 202-442-4400
    Fax: 202-727-6703

Florida

State Trade Office
    Office of Tourism, Trade & Economic Development
    The Capital, Suite 2001
    Tallahassee, FL 32399
    Tel: 850-487-2568
    Fax: 850-487-3014

Georgia

Department of Industry, Trade and Tourism
    285 Peachtree Center Avenue, NE
    Suite 1100
    Atlanta, GA 30303
    Tel: 404-656-3571
    Fax: 404-651-6506

Hawaii
Department of Business, Economic Development & Tourism
250 South Hotel Street, 4th Floor
Honolulu, HI 96804
Tel: 808-587-2584
Fax: 808-587-3388

Idaho
Department of Commerce
700 W. State Street
P.O. Box 83720
Boise, ID 83720
Tel: 208-334-2470
Fax: 208-334-2631

Illinois
Department of Commerce
100 West Randolph, Suite 3-400
Chicago, IL 60601
Tel: 312-814-7164
Fax: 312-814-6581

Indiana
Department of Commerce
One North Capitol, Suite 700
Indianapolis, IN 46204
Tel: 317-233-3762
Fax: 317-233-1680

Iowa
Department of Economic Development
200 East Grand Avenue
Des Moines, IA 50309
Tel: 515-242-4743
Tel: 515-242-4918

Kansas
Department of Commerce
1000 SW Jackson, Suite 100
Topeka, KS 66612
Tel: 785-296-4027
Fax: 785-296-5263

Kentucky
Cabinet for Economic Development
2300 Capitol Plaza Tower
500 Mero Street
Frankfort, KY 40601
Tel: 502-564-7140
Fax: 502-564-3256

Louisiana
Department of Economic Development
International Trade Division
1051 N. 3rd Street
P.O. Box 94185
Baton Rouge, LA 70804
Tel: 225-342-4323
Fax: 225-342-5389

Maine
International Trade Center
511 Congress Street
Portland, ME 04101
Tel: 207-541-7400
Fax: 207-541-7420

Maryland
International Trade Department of Business & Economic Development
217 East Redwood Street, Suite 1300
Baltimore, MD 21202
Tel: 410-767-0690
Fax: 410-333-4302

Massachusetts
Trade Office
10 Park Plaza, Suite 3720
Boston, MA 02116
Tel: 617-973-8650
Fax: 617-277-3488

Michigan
Economic Development Corporation
300 N. Washington Square
Lansing, MI 48913
Tel: 517-373-9808
Fax: 517-241-3683

Minnesota
Trade Office
1000 Minnesota World Trade Center
30th East 7th Street
St. Paul, MN 55101
Tel: 651-297-4222
Fax: 651-296-3555

Mississippi
Development Authority, International Division
6000 Woolfolk Building
501 North West Street
Jackson, MS 39201
Tel: 601-359-6672
Fax: 601-359-3605

Missouri
Economic Development Programs
301 W. High Street
P.O. Box 118
Jefferson City, MO 65102
Tel: 573-751-4855
Fax: 573-526-1567

Montana
Department of Commerce Business Resource Division
301 South Park
P.O. Box 200501
Helena, MT 59620
Tel: 406-841-2752
Fax: 406-841-2701

Nebraska
Department of Economic Development
301 Centennial Mall South
P.O. Box 94666
Lincoln, NE 68509
Tel: 402-471-4668
Fax: 402-471-3365

Nevada
Economic Development
555 East Washington, Suite 5400
Las Vegas, NV 89101
Tel: 702-486-2700
Fax: 702-486-2701

New Hampshire
New Hampshire International Trade
Resource Center
17 New Hampshire Avenue
Portsmouth, NH 03801
Tel: 603-334-6074
Fax: 603-334-6110

New Jersey
Department of Commerce and Economic Development
20 West State Street
P.O. Box 820
Trenton, NJ 08625
Tel: 609-633-3606
Fax: 609-633-3672

New Mexico
Economic Development and Tourism Department
1100 St. Francis Drive
Santa Fe, NM 87505
Tel: 505-827-0307
Fax: 505-827-0263

New York
State Trade Office
633 Third Avenue
New York, NY 10017
Tel: 212-803-2352
Fax: 212-803-2399

North Carolina
Department of Commerce
International Trade
301 North Wilmington Street
4320 Mail Service Center
Raleigh, NC 27699

Tel: 919-733-7193
Fax: 919-733-0110

North Dakota
Economic Development and Finance
1600 E. Century Avenue, Suite 2
Bismarck, ND 58503
Tel: 701-328-5300
Fax: 701-328-5320

Ohio
Department of Development, International Trade
77 South High Street, 29th Floor
Columbus, OH 43215
Tel: 614-466-5017
Fax: 614-463-1540

Oklahoma
Department of Commerce
900 North Stiles
P.O. Box 26980
Oklahoma City, OK 73104
Tel: 800-879-6552
Fax: 405-815-5245

Oregon
Economic Development Department, International Division
121 Southwest Salmon Street
Suite 205
Portland, OR 97204
Tel: 503-229-5625
Fax: 503-222-5050

Pennsylvania
Office of International Business Development
Commonwealth Keystone Building
400 North Street, 4th Floor
Harrisburg, PA 17120
Tel: 717-787-7190
Fax: 717-772-5106

Puerto Rico

Department of Commerce
420 Ponce De Leon Avenue
Midtown 10th Floor
San Juan, Puerto Rico 00918
Tel: 787-766-5555
Fax: 787-766-6569

Rhode Island

Department of Economic Development
One West Exchange Street
Providence, RI 02903
Tel: 401-222-2601
Fax: 401-222-2102

South Carolina

International Trade Development
1201 Main Street, Suite 1700
P.O. Box 927
Columbia, SC 29202
Tel: 803-737-0400
Fax: 803-737-0418

South Dakota

International Business Institute
1200 South Jay Street
P.O. Box 864
Aberdeen, SD 57401
Tel: 605-626-3149
Fax: 605-626-3004

Tennessee

Office of International Affairs
312 8th Avenue North
Nashville, TN 37243
Tel: 615-741-1888
Fax: 615-741-7306

Texas
Office of Trade and International Relations
1700 North Congress Avenue
P.O. Box 12728-2728
Austin, TX 78711
Tel: 512-936-0249
Fax: 512-936-0445

Utah
International Business and Economic Development
324 South State Street, Suite 500
Salt Lake City, UT 84111
Tel: 801-538-8737
Fax: 801-538-8889

Vermont
Department of Economic Development
National Life Building, Drawer 20
Montpelier, VT 05620
Tel: 802-828-3211
Fax: 802-828-3258

Virgin Islands
Department of Economic Development
1050 Norre Gade, Suite 5
St. Thomas, Virgin Islands 00802
Tel: 340-714-1700
Fax: 340-714-8106

Virginia
Division of International Trade Development
901 Easy Byrd Street
P.O. Box 798
Richmond, VA 23218
Tel: 804-371-0198
Fax: 804-371-8860

Washington
International Trade Office
2001 6th Avenue, Suite 2600
Seattle, WA 98121
Tel: 206-256-6100
Fax: 206-256-6158

West Virginia

Development Office, International Division
1900 Kanawha Boulevard East
Charleston, WV 25305
Tel: 304-558-2234
Fax: 304-558-1957

Wisconsin

Division of International Development
201 West Washington Avenue
P.O. Box 7970
Madison, WI 53707
Tel: 608-266-6675
Fax: 608-266-5551

Wyoming

International Division
300 South Wolcott, Suite 200
Casper, WY 82601
Tel: 307-237-4692
Fax: 307-237-4699

Appendix D:
United States Department of Agriculture (USDA) Agricultural Trade Offices Abroad

LOCAL OFFICE	U.S. MAILING ADDRESS

Brazil

Edificio Suárez Trade
Alameda Santos 2224
Conjunto 11
01418-200 Sao Paulo
Brazil
Tel: (011-55-11) 282-3528
Fax: (011-55-11) 883-7535
E-mail: atosp@unisys.com.br

Agricultural Trade Office
American Consulate Sao Paulo
UNIT 3502
APO AA 34030-3502

Caribbean Basin

U.S. Agricultural Trade Office
909 SE First Avenue, Suite 720
Miami, FL 33131
United States
Tel: 305-536-5300
Fax: 305-536-7577
E-mail: cbato@cbato.net
Web: www.cbato.fas.usda.gov

Agricultural Trade Office
American Consulate Shanghai
PSC 461, Box 200
FPO AP 96521-0002

LOCAL OFFICE	U.S. MAILING ADDRESS

China

Guangzhou
China Hotel, Office Tower
12th Floor, Room 12-59-61
Liu Hua Lu
Guangzhou 510015
China
Tel: (011-86-20) 8667-7553 or
        8666-3388 ext. 1291
Fax: (011-86-20) 8666-0703
E-mail: ato@gitic.com.cn

Agricultural Trade Office
American Consulate Guangzhou
Department of State
Washington, DC 20521-4090

Hong Kong
Foreign Agricultural Service
18th Floor, St. John's Building
33 Garden Road, Central
Hong Kong
China
Tel: (011-852) 2841-2350
Fax: (011-852) 2845-0943
E-mail: 106122.2744@compuserv.com

Agricultural Trade Office
U.S. Consulate Hong Kong
PSC 464, Box 30
FPO AP 96522-0002

Shanghai
American International PSC
Center
AT Shanghai Center
1376 Nanjing Road West
Shanghai 200040
China
Tel: (011-86-21) 6279-8622
Fax: (011-86-21) 6279-8336
E-mail: atos@public.sta.net.cn

Agricultural Trade Office
American Consulate Shanghai
Department of State
Washington, DC 20521-4100

Germany

Agricultural Trade Office
Alsterufer 28
20354 Hamburg
Germany
Tel: (011-49-40) 41-46-07-0
Fax: (011-49-40) 41-46-07-20
E-mail: 104520.264@CompuServe.com

Agricultural Trade Office
U.S. Consulate Hamburg
Department of State
Washington DC 20521-5180

LOCAL OFFICE	U.S. MAILING ADDRESS

Indonesia

Wisma Metropolitan II, 3rd Floor
Jl, Jendral Sudirman Kav. 29-31
Jakarta 12920
Indonesia
Tel: (011-62-21) 526-2850, ext. 4001
Fax: (011-62-21) 571-1251
E-mail: atojkt@rad.net.id

Agricultural Trade Office
Box 1, UNIT 8129
APO AP 96520-0001

Italy

U.S. Agricultural Trade Office
Via Principe Amedeo 2/10
20121 Milano
Italy
Tel: (011-39-2) 290-351-59
Fax: (011-39-2) 659-9641
E-mail: agmilan@fas.usda.gov
Web: www.usis.it

American Embassy/AGR
PSC 59, Box 100 M
APO AE 09624

Japan

Osaka
2-11-5 Nishi Tenma
Kita-ku
Osaka 530, Japan
Tel: (011-81-6) 6315-5904
Fax: (011-81-6) 6315-5906
E-mail: atoosaka@ppp.bekkoame.ne.jp

Agricultural Trade Office
U.S. Consulate Osaka-Kobe
UNIT 45004, Box 239
APO AP 96337-5004

Tokyo
Tokyu Tameike Building
8th Floor
1-1-14, Akasaka
Minato-ku, Tokyo 107
Japan
Tel: (011-81-3) 3224-5115/3505-6050
Fax: (011-81-3) 3582-6429
E-mail: agtokyo@ppp.bekkoame.or.jp

Agricultural Trade Office
U.S. Embassy Tokyo
UNIT 45004, Box 226
APO AP 96337-5004

LOCAL OFFICE	U.S. MAILING ADDRESS

Korea

U.S. Agricultural Trade Office
Room 303, Leema Building
146-1 Susong-dong
Chongro-ku Seoul 110-140
South Korea
Tel: (011-82-2) 397-4188
Fax: (011-82-2) 720-7921
E-mail: atoseoul@uriel.net

Agricultural Trade Office
American Embassy Seoul
UNIT 15550-0001
APO AP 96205-0001

Mexico

Mexico City
Jaime Balmes No. 8-201
Col. Los Morales Polanco
11510 Mexico City, D.F.
Mexico
Tel: (011-52-5) 280-5291/5277
Fax: (011-52-5) 281-6093
E-mail: ato@intmex.com

Agricultural Trade Office
P.O. Box 3087
Laredo, TX 78044-3087

Nuevo Laredo
Tamps, Calle Allende 3330
Col. Jardin
88260 Nuevo Laredo, Tamps
Mexico
Tel: (011-52-87) 191-603/604
Fax: (011-52-87) 191-605
E-mail: agrnl@nld.bravo.net

Agricultural Trade Office
Drawer 3089
Laredo, TX 78044-3087

Russia

19/23 Novinskiy Bul'var
121099 Moscow
Russia
Tel: (011-7095) 956-4103
Fax: (011-7095) 255-9951
E-mail: atoffice@corbina.ru

Agricultural Trade Office
American Embassy Moscow
PSC 77 AGR
APO AE 09721

LOCAL OFFICE	U.S. MAILING ADDRESS

Saudi Arabia

Riyadh
American Embassy
P.O. Box 9041
Riyadh 11413
Saudi Arabia
Tel: (011-966-1) 488-3800, ext. 1560
Fax: (011-966-1) 482-4364
E-mail: usda_riyadh@hotmail.com

Agricultural Trade Office
American Embassy Riyadh
UNIT 61307
APO AE 09803-1307

Jeddah
Foreign Agricultural Service
U.S. Consulate
Palestine Road, Ruwais
P.O. Box 149
Jeddah 21411, Saudi Arabia
Tel: (011-966-2) 661-2408
         or 667-0080, ext. 299
Fax: (011-966-2) 667-6196
E-mail: atojeddah@usda1.sprint.com

Agricultural Trade Office
U.S. Consulate Jeddah
UNIT 62122
APO AE 09811-2112

Singapore *(including Brunei and Papua New Guinea)*

U.S. Agricultural Trade Office
541 Orchard Road, #08-03
Liat Towers
Singapore 0923
Tel: (011-65) 737-1233/1729
Fax: (011-65) 732-8307
E-mail: ato_sing@pacific.net.sg

Agricultural Trade Office
U.S. Embassy Singapore
PSC 470 (AGRICULTURE)
FPO AP 96534-0001

Taiwan

American Institute in Taiwan
54 Nan Hai Road
Taipei
Taiwan
Tel: (011-82-22) 2337-6525
Fax: (011-82-22) 2305-7073
E-mail: mailto:ato@mail.ait.org.orw

Agricultural Trade Office
U.S. Consulate Taipei
Department of State
Washington, DC 20521-4170

LOCAL OFFICE	U.S. MAILING ADDRESS

United Arab Emirates *(including Bahrain, Kuwait, Qatar, and the Sultanate of Oman)*

U.S. Agricultural Trade Office
P.O. Box 9343
Dubai, UAE
Tel: (011-971-4) 313-612/314-063
Fax: (011-971-4) 314-998
E-mail: atodubai@emirates.net.ae

Agricultural Trade Office
U.S. Consulate Dubai
Washington, DC 20250-6000

United Kingdom *(including Ireland)*

U.S. Department of Agriculture
24 Grosvenor Square
Box 48
London, WlA 1AE
United Kingdom
Tel: +44 (0) 20 7894 0464
Fax: +44 (0) 20 7894 0031
E-mail: AgLondon@fas.usda.gov

U.S. Agricultural Trade Office
American Embassy London
PSC 801, Box 48
FPO AE 09498-4048

Appendix E:
Foreign Embassies in the United States

(Online Directory at www.embassy.org)

Afghanistan
2341 Wyoming Avenue, NW
Washington, DC 20008
Tel: 202-234-3770
Fax: 202-328-3516

Albania
2100 S Street, NW
Washington, DC 20008
Tel: 202-223-4942
Fax: 202-628-7342

Algeria
2137 Wyoming Avenue, NW
Washington, DC 20008
Tel: 202-265-2800
Fax: 202-667-2174

Andora
Two United Nations Plaza, 25th Floor
New York, NY 10017
Tel: 212-750-8064
Fax: 212-750-6630

Angola
2100-2108 16th Street, NW
Washington, DC 20009
Tel: 202-785-1156
Fax: 202-785-1258

Antigua and Barbuda

32 New Mexico Avenue, NW
Washington, DC 20016
Tel: 202-362-5122
Fax: 202-362-5225

Argentina

1600 New Hampshire Avenue, NW
Washington, DC 20009
Tel: 202-238-6400
Fax: 202-332-3171

Armenia

2225 R Street, NW
Washington, DC 20008
Tel: 202-319-1976
Fax: 202-319-2982

Australia

1601 Massachusetts Avenue, NW
Washington, DC 20036
Tel: 202-797-3000
Fax: 202-797-3168

Austria

3524 International Court, NW
Washington, DC 20008
Tel: 202-895-6775
Fax: 202-895-6772

Azerbaijan

2741 34th Street, NW
Washington, DC 20008
Tel: 202-337-3500
Fax: 202-337-5911

Bahamas

2220 Massachusetts Avenue, NW
Washington, DC 20008
Tel: 202-319-2660
Fax: 202-319-2668

Bahrain

3502 International Drive, NW
Washington, DC 20008
Tel: 202-342-1111
Fax: 202-362-2192

Bangladesh

3510 International Drive, NW
Washington, DC 20008
Tel: 202-244-0183
Fax: 202-244-5366

Barbados

2144 Wyoming Avenue, NW
Washington, DC 20008
Tel: 202-939-9200
Fax: 202-332-7467

Belarus

1619 New Hampshire, NW
Washington, DC 20009
Tel: 202-986-1606
Fax: 202-986-1805

Belgium

3330 Garfield Street, NW
Washington, DC 20008
Tel: 202-333-6900
Fax: 202-333-3079

Belize

2535 Massachusetts Avenue, NW
Washington, DC 20008
Tel: 202-332-9636
Fax: 202-332-6888

Benin

2124 Kalorama Road, NW
Washington, DC 20008
Tel: 202-232-6656/57/58
Fax: 202-265-1996

Bolivia

    3014 Massachusetts Avenue, NW

    Washington, DC 20008

    Tel: 202-483-4410

    Fax: 202-328-3712

Bosnia and Herzegovina

    2109 E Street, NW

    Washington, DC 20037

    Tel: 202-337-1500

    Fax: 202-337-1502

Botswana

    1531-1533 New Hampshire Ave., NW

    Washington, DC 20036

    Tel: 202-244-4990

    Fax: 202-244-4164

Brazil

    3006 Massachusetts Avenue, NW

    Washington, DC 20008

    Tel: 202-238-2700

    Fax: 202-238-2827

Brunei

    3520 International Court, NW

    Washington, DC 20008

    Tel: 202-237-1838

    Fax: 202-885-0560

Bulgaria

    1621 22nd Street, NW

    Washington, DC 20008

    Tel: 202-387-0174

    Fax: 202-234-7973

Burkina Faso

    2340 Massachusetts Avenue, NW

    Washington, DC 20008

    Tel: 202-332-5577

    Fax: 202-667-1882

Burma
>2300 S Street, NW
>Washington, DC 20008
>Tel: 202-332-9044
>Fax: 202-332-9046

Burundi
>2233 Wisconsin Avenue, NW
>Suite 212
>Washington, DC 20007
>Tel: 202-342-2574
>Fax: 202-342-2578

Cambodia
>4530 16th Street, NW
>Washington, DC 20011
>Tel: 202-726-7742
>Fax: 202-726-8381

Cameroon
>2349 Massachusetts Avenue, NW
>Washington, DC 20008
>Tel: 202-265-8790
>Fax: 202-387-3826

Canada
>501 Pennsylvania Avenue, NW
>Washington, DC 20001
>Tel: 202-682-1740
>Fax: 202-682-7701

Cape Verde
>3415 Massachusetts Avenue, NW
>Washington, DC 20007
>Tel: 202-965-6820
>Fax: 202-965-1207

Central African Republic
>1618 22nd Street, NW
>Washington, DC 20008
>Tel: 202-483-7800
>Fax: 202-332-9893

Chad

2002 R Street, NW
Washington, DC 20009
Tel: 202-462-4009
Fax: 202-265-1937

Chile

1732 Massachusetts Avenue, NW
Washington, DC 20036
Tel: 202-785-1746
Fax: 202-887-5579

China, People's Republic

2300 Connecticut Avenue, NW
Washington, DC 20008
Tel: 202-328-2500
Fax: 202-588-0032

Colombia

2118 LeRoy Place, NW
Washington, DC 20008
Tel: 202-387-8338
Fax: 202-232-8643

Comoros

420 East 50th Street
New York, NY 10022
Tel: 212-972-8010
Fax: 212-983-4712

Congo, Democratic Republic of (formerly Zaire)

1800 New Hampshire Avenue, NW
Washington, DC 20009
Tel: 202-234-7690
Fax: 202-237-0748

Costa Rica

2114 S Street, NW
Washington, DC 20008
Tel: 202-234-2945
Fax: 202-265-4795

Côte d'Ivoire

2424 Massachusetts Avenue, NW
Washington, DC 20008
Tel: 202-797-0300
Fax: 202-462-9444

Croatia

2343 Massachusetts Avenue, NW
Washington, DC 20008
Tel: 202-588-5899
Fax: 202-588-8936

Cyprus

2211 R Street, NW
Washington, DC 20008
Tel: 202-462-5772
Fax: 202-483-6710

Czech Republic

3900 Spring of Freedom Street, NW
Washington, DC 20008
Tel: 202-274-9100
Fax: 202-966-8540

Denmark

3200 Whitehaven Street, NW
Washington, DC 20008
Tel: 202-234-4300
Fax: 202-328-1470

Djibouti

1156 15th Street, NW, Suite 515
Washington, DC 20005
Tel: 202-331-0270
Fax: 202-331-0302

Dominican Republic

1715 22nd Street, NW
Washington, DC 20008
Tel: 202-332-6280
Fax: 202-265-8057

Ecuador

2535 15th Street, NW
Washington, DC 20009
Tel: 202-234-7200
Fax: 202-667-3482

Egypt

3521 International Court, NW
Washington, DC 20008
Tel: 202-895-5400
Fax: 202-244-4319/5131

El Salvador

2308 California Street, NW
Washington, DC 20008
Tel: 202-265-9671
Fax: 202-234-3834

Equatorial Guinea

1712 I Street, NW, Suite 410
Washington, DC 20006
Tel: 202-296-4174
Fax: 202-296-4195

Eritrea

1708 New Hampshire Avenue, NW
Washington, DC 20009
Tel: 202-319-1991
Fax: 202-319-1304

Estonia

1730 M Street NW, Suite 503
Washington, DC 20036
Tel: 202-588-0101
Fax: 202-588-0108

Ethiopia

3506 International Drive, NW
Washington, DC 20008
Tel: 202-364-1200
Fax: 202-686-9551

Fiji

2233 Wisconsin Avenue, NW
Suite 240
Washington, DC 20007
Tel: 202-337-8320
Fax: 202-337-1996

Finland

3301 Massachusetts Avenue, NW
Washington, DC 20008
Tel: 202-298-5800
Fax: 202-298-6030

France

4101 Reservoir Road, NW
Washington, DC 20007
Tel: 202-944-6000
Fax: 202-944-6166

Gabon

2034 20th Street, NW
Washington, DC 20009
Tel: 202-797-1000
Fax: 202-332-0668

Gambia

1156 15th Street, NW
Suite 905
Washington, DC 20005
Tel: 202-785-1399
Fax: 202-785-1430

Georgia

1615 New Hampshire Avenue, NW
Suite 300
Washington, DC 20009
Tel: 202-387-2390
Fax: 202-393-4537

Germany

4645 Reservoir Road, NW
Washington, DC 20007
Tel: 202-298-4000
Fax: 202-298-4249

Ghana

3512 International Drive, NW
Washington, DC 20008
Tel: 202-686-4520
Fax: 202-686-4527

Greece

2221 Massachusetts Avenue, NW
Washington, DC 20008
Tel: 202-939-1300
Fax: 202-939-1324

Grenada

1701 New Hampshire Avenue, NW
Washington, DC 20009
Tel: 202-265-2561
Fax: 202-265-2468

Guatemala

2220 R Street, NW
Washington, DC 20008
Tel: 202-745-4952
Fax: 202-745-1908

Guinea

2112 Leroy Place, NW
Washington, DC 20008
Tel: 202-483-9420
Fax: 202-483-8688

Guinea-Bissau, Republic of

15929 Yunkon Lane
Rockville, MD 20855
Tel: 301-947-3958
Fax: 202-347-3954

Guyana

2490 Tracy Place, NW
Washington, DC 20008
Tel: 202-265-6900
Fax: 202-232-1297

Haiti

2311 Massachusetts Avenue, NW
Washington, DC 20008
Tel: 202-332-4090
Fax: 202-745-7215

Honduras

3007 Tilden Street, NW, Suite 4M
Washington, DC 20008
Tel: 202-966-7702
Fax: 202-966-9751

Hungary

3910 Shoemaker Street, NW
Washington, DC 20008
Tel: 202-362-6730
Fax: 202-966-8135

Iceland

1156 15th Street, NW, Suite 1200
Washington, DC 20005
Tel: 202-265-6653
Fax: 202-265-6656

India

2107 Massachusetts Avenue, NW
Washington, DC 20008
Tel: 202-939-7000
Fax: 202-265-4351

Indonesia

2020 Massachusetts Avenue, NW
Washington, DC 20036
Tel: 202-775-5200
Fax: 202-775-5365

Iran

2209 Wisconsin Avenue, NW
2nd Floor
Washington, DC 20007
Tel: 202-965-4990
Fax: 202-965-1073

Ireland

2234 Massachusetts Avenue, NW
Washington, DC 20008
Tel: 202-462-3939
Fax: 202-232-5993

Israel

3514 International Drive, NW
Washington, DC 20008
Tel: 202-364-5500
Fax: 202-364-5560

Italy

3000 Whitehaven Street, NW
Washington, DC 20008
Tel: 202-612-4400
Fax: 202-518-2154

Jamaica

1520 New Hampshire Avenue, NW
Washington, DC 20036
Tel: 202-452-0660
Fax: 202-452-0081

Japan

2520 Massachusetts Avenue, NW
Washington, DC 20008
Tel: 202-238-6700
Fax: 202-328-2187

Jordan

3504 International Drive, NW
Washington, DC 20008
Tel: 202-966-2664
Fax: 202-966-3110

Kazakhstan

1401 16th Street, NW
Washington, DC 20036
Tel: 202-232-5488
Fax: 202-232-5845

Kenya
> 2249 R Street, NW
> Washington, DC 20008
> Tel: 202-387-6101
> Fax: 202-462-3829

Korea (South)
> 2320 Massachusetts Avenue, NW
> Washington, DC 20008
> Tel: 202-939-5600
> Fax: 202-797-0595

Kuwait
> 2600 Virginia Avenue, NW
> Washington, DC 20037
> Tel: 202-338-0211
> Fax: 202-338-0957

Kyrgyzstan
> 1732 Wisconsin Avenue, NW
> Washington, DC 20007
> Tel: 202-338-5141
> Fax: 202-338-5139

Laos
> 2222 S Street, NW
> Washington, DC 20008
> Tel: 202-332-6416
> Fax: 202-332-4923

Latvia
> 4325 17th Street, NW
> Washington, DC 20011
> Tel: 202-726-8213
> Fax: 202-726-6785

Lebanon
> 2560 28th Street, NW
> Washington, DC 20008
> Tel: 202-939-6300
> Fax: 202-939-6324

Lesotho

2511 Massachusetts Avenue, NW
Washington, DC 20008
Tel: 202-797-5533
Fax: 202-234-6815

Liberia

5201 16th Street, NW
Washington, DC 20011
Tel: 202-723-0437
Fax: 202-723-0436

Lithuania

2622 16th Street, NW
Washington, DC 20009
Tel: 202-234-5860
Fax: 202-328-0466

Luxembourg

2200 Massachusetts Avenue, NW
Washington, DC 20008
Tel: 202-265-4171
Fax: 202-328-8270

Macedonia Fyr

3050 K Street, NW
Washington, DC 20007
Tel: 202-337-3063
Fax: 202-337-3093

Madagascar

2374 Massachusetts Avenue, NW
Washington, DC 20008
Tel: 202-265-5525
Fax: 202-265-3034

Malawi

1400 20th Street, NW
Washington, DC 20036
Tel: 202-223-4814
Fax: 202-265-0976

Malaysia

2401 Massachusetts Avenue, NW
Washington, DC 20008
Tel: 202-328-2700
Fax: 202-483-7661

Mali

2130 R Street, NW
Washington, DC 20009
Tel: 202-332-2249
Fax: 202-332-6603

Malta

2017 Connecticut Avenue, NW
Washington, DC 20008
Tel: 202-462-3611
Fax: 202-387-5470

Marshall Islands

2433 Massachusetts Avenue, NW
Washington, DC 20008
Tel: 202-234-5414
Fax: 202-232-3236

Mauritania

2129 Leroy Place, NW
Washington, DC 20008
Tel: 202-232-5700
Fax: 202-319-2623

Mauritius

4301 Connecticut Avenue, NW
Suite 441
Washington, DC 20008
Tel: 202-244-1491
Fax: 202-966-0983

Mexico

1911 Pennsylvania Avenue, NW
Washington, DC 20006
Tel: 202-728-1700
Fax: 202-728-1698

Micronesia
> 1725 N Street, NW
> Washington, DC 20036
> Tel: 202-223-4383
> Fax: 202-223-4391

Moldova
> 2101 S Street, NW
> Washington, DC 20008
> Tel: 202-667-1130
> Fax: 202-667-1204

Mongolia
> 2833 M Street, NW
> Washington, DC 20007
> Tel: 202-298-7117
> Fax: 202-298-9227

Morocco
> 1601 21st Street, NW
> Washington, DC 20009
> Tel: 202-462-7979
> Fax: 202-462-7643

Mozambique
> 1990 M Street, Suite 570 NW
> Washington, DC 20036
> Tel: 202-293-7146
> Fax: 202-835-0245

Namibia
> 1605 New Hampshire Avenue, NW
> Washington, DC 20009
> Tel: 202-986-0540
> Fax: 202-986-0443

Nepal
> 2131 Leroy Place, NW
> Washington, DC 20008
> Tel: 202-667-4550
> Fax: 202-667-5534

Netherlands, The
4200 Linnean Avenue, NW
Washington, DC 20008
Tel: 202-244-5300
Fax: 202-362-3430

New Zealand
37 Observatory Circle, NW
Washington, DC 20008
Tel: 202-328-4800
Fax: 202-667-5227

Nicaragua
1627 New Hampshire Avenue, NW
Washington, DC 20009
Tel: 202-939-6570
Fax: 202-939-6542

Niger
2204 R Street, NW
Washington, DC 20008
Tel: 202-483-4224
Fax: 202-483-3169

Nigeria
1333 16th Street, NW
Washington, DC 20036
Tel: 202-986-8400
Fax: 202-775-1385

Norway
2720 34th Street, NW
Washington, DC 20008
Tel: 202-333-6000
Fax: 202-337-0870

Oman
2535 Belmont Road, NW
Washington, DC 20008
Tel: 202-387-1980
Fax: 202-745-4933

Pakistan
2315 Massachusetts Avenue, NW
Washington, DC 20008
Tel: 202-939-6200
Fax: 202-387-0484

Palau
1150 18th Street, NW, Suite 750
Washington, DC 20036
Tel: 202-452-6814
Fax: 202-452-6281

Panama
2862 McGill Terrace, NW
Washington, DC 20008
Tel: 202-483-1407
Fax: 202-483-8416

Papua New Guinea
1779 Massachusetts Avenue, NW
Suite 805
Washington, DC 20036
Tel: 202-745-3680
Fax: 202-745-3679

Paraguay
2400 Massachusetts Avenue, NW
Washington, DC 20008
Tel: 202-483-6960
Fax: 202-234-4508

Peru
1700 Massachusetts Avenue, NW
Washington, DC 20036
Tel: 202-833-9860
Fax: 202-659-8124

Philippines
1600 Massachusetts Avenue, NW
Washington, DC 20036
Tel: 202-467-9300
Fax: 202-467-9417

Poland

2640 16th Street, NW
Washington, DC 20009
Tel: 202-234-3800
Fax: 202-328-6271

Portugal

2125 Kalorama Road, NW
Washington, DC 20008
Tel: 202-328-8610
Fax: 202-462-3726

Qatar

4200 Wisconsin Avenue, NW
Suite 200
Washington, DC 20016
Tel: 202-274-1600
Fax: 202-237-0061

Romania

1607 23rd Street, NW
Washington, DC 20008
Tel: 202-332-2879
Fax: 202-232-4748

Russia

2650 Wisconsin Avenue, NW
Washington, DC 20007
Tel: 202-298-5700
Fax: 202-298-5735

Rwanda

1714 New Hampshire Avenue, NW
Washington, DC 20009
Tel: 202-232-2882
Fax: 202-232-4544

St. Kitts & Nevis

3216 New Mexico Avenue, NW
Washington, DC 20016
Tel: 202-686-2636
Fax: 202-686-5740

St. Lucia
3216 New Mexico Avenue, NW
Washington, DC 20016
Tel: 202-364-6792
Fax: 202-364-6728

St. Vincent & Grenadines
3216 New Mexico Avenue, NW
Washington, DC 20016
Tel: 202-364-6730
Fax: 202-364-6736

Saudi Arabia
601 New Hampshire Avenue, NW
Washington, DC 20037
Tel: 202-337-4076
Fax: 202-944-5983

Senegal
2112 Wyoming Avenue, NW
Washington, DC 20008
Tel: 202-234-0540
Fax: 202-332-6315

Seychelles
800 Second Avenue, Suite 400C
New York, NY 10017
Tel: 212-687-9766
Fax: 212-972-1786

Sierra Leone
1701 19th Street, NW
Washington, DC 20009
Tel: 202-939-9261
Fax: 202-483-1793

Singapore
3501 International Place, NW
Washington, DC 20008
Tel: 202-537-3100
Fax: 202-537-0876

Slovak Republic
3523 International Court, NW
Washington, DC 20008
Tel: 202-237-1054
Fax: 202-237-6438

Slovenia
1525 New Hampshire Avenue, NW
Washington, DC 20036
Tel: 202-667-5363
Fax: 202-667-4563

Solomon Islands
820 Second Avenue, Suite 400 L
New York, NY 10017
Tel: 212-599-6193
Fax: 212-661-8925

South Africa
3051 Massachusetts Avenue, NW
Washington, DC 20008
Tel: 202-232-4400
Fax: 202-265-1607

Spain
2375 Pennsylvania Avenue, NW
Washington, DC 20037
Tel: 202-728-2330
Fax: 202-728-2302

Sri Lanka, Republic of
2148 Wyoming Avenue, NW
Washington, DC 20008
Tel: 202-483-4026
Fax: 202-232-7181

Sudan
2210 Massachusetts Avenue, NW
Washington, DC 20008
Tel: 202-338-8565
Fax: 202-667-2406

Suriname

4301 Connecticut Avenue, NW
Suite 460
Washington, DC 20008
Tel: 202-244-7488
Fax: 202-244-5878

Swaziland

3400 International Drive, NW
Suite 3M
Washington, DC 20008
Tel: 202-362-6683
Fax: 202-244-8059

Sweden

1501 M Street, NW
Washington, DC 20005
Tel: 202-467-2600
Fax: 202-467-2656

Switzerland

2900 Cathedral Avenue, NW
Washington, DC 20008
Tel: 202-745-7900
Fax: 202-387-2564

Syria

2215 Wyoming Avenue, NW
Washington, DC 20008
Tel: 202-232-6313
Fax: 202-234-9548

Tanzania

2139 R Street, NW
Washington, DC 20008
Tel: 202-884-1080
Fax: 202-797-7408

Thailand

1024 Wisconsin Avenue, NW
Washington, DC 20007
Tel: 202-944-3600
Fax: 202-944-3611

Togo

2208 Massachusetts Avenue, NW
Washington, DC 20008
Tel: 202-234-4212
Fax: 202-232-3190

Trinidad and Tobago

1708 Massachusetts Avenue, NW
Washington, DC 20036
Tel: 202-467-6490
Fax: 202-785-3130

Tunisia

1515 Massachusetts Avenue, NW
Washington, DC 20005
Tel: 202-862-1850
Fax: 202-862-1858

Turkey

1714 Massachusetts Avenue, NW
Washington, DC 20036
Tel: 202-612-6700
Fax: 202-612-6744

Turkmenistan

2207 Massachusetts Avenue, NW
Washington, DC 20008
Tel: 202-588-1500
Fax: 202-588-0697

Uganda

5911 16th Street, NW
Washington, DC 20011
Tel: 202-726-7100
Fax: 202-726-1727

Ukraine

3350 M Street, NW
Washington, DC 20007
Tel: 202-333-0606
Fax: 202-333-0817

United Arab Emirates
3522 International Court, NW
Suite 300
Washington, DC 20008
Tel: 202-328-4536
Fax: 202-337-7029

United Kingdom
3100 Massachusetts Avenue, NW
Washington, DC 20008
Tel: 202-588-6500
Fax: 202-588-7870

Uruguay
2715 M Street, NW, 3rd Floor
Washington, DC 20007
Tel: 202-331-1313
Fax: 202-331-8142

Uzbekistan
1746 Massachusetts Avenue, NW
Washington, DC 20036
Tel: 202-887-5300
Fax: 202-293-6804

Venezuela
1099 30th Street, NW
Washington, DC 20007
Tel: 202-342-2214
Fax: 202-342-6820

Vietman
1233 20th Street, NW, Suite 400
Washington, DC 20036
Tel: 202-861-0737
Fax: 202-861-0917

Western Samoa
800 Second Avenue, Suite 400D
New York, NY 10017
Tel: 212-599-6196
Fax: 212-599-0797

Yemen

2600 Virginia Avenue, NW, Suite 705
Washington, DC 20037
Tel: 202-965-4760
Fax: 202-337-2017

Yugoslavia

2134 Kalorama Road, NW
Washington, DC 20008
Tel: 202-332-0333
Fax: 202-332-3933

Zambia

2419 Massachusetts Avenue, NW
Washington, DC 20008
Tel: 202-265-9717
Fax: 202-332-0826

Zimbabwe

1608 New Hampshire Avenue, NW
Washington, DC 20009
Tel: 202-332-7100
Fax: 202-483-9326

Appendix F: United States Embassies Abroad

Albania
Tirana Rruga E. Labinoti 103
PSC 59, Box 100 (A)
Tirana, Albania
Tel: 355-42-47285
Fax: 355-42-32222

Algeria
4 Chemin Cheikh Bachir El-Ibrahimi
B.P. Box 549 16000
Algiers, Algeria
Tel: 213-2-69-12-55
Fax: 213-2-69-39-79

Angola
Rua Boumedienne No. 32
Mirimar
Luanda, Angola
Tel: 244-2-445-481/447-028
Fax: 244-2-446-924

Argentina
4300 Avenida Colombia
1425 MN Buenos Aires
Buenos Aires, Argentina
Tel: 541-1-5777-4533
Fax: 541-1-5777-4240

Armenia
18 Gbaghramyan Ave
Yerevan 375019, Armenia
Tel: 3741-520-791
Fax: 3741-520-800

Australia
MLC Center, Level 59
19-29 Martin Place
Sydney NSW 2000, Australia
Tel: 612-9373-9200
Fax: 61-9373-9184

Austria
Boltzmanngasse 16, A-1090
Vienna, Austria
Tel: 431-313-390
Fax: 431-310-06820

Azerbaijan
Azadlig Prospect 83
Baku, Azerbaijan 370007
Tel: 9-9412-98-03-35
Fax: 9-9412-98-37-55

Bahamas
P.O. Box N-8197
Nassau, Bahamas
Tel: 242-322-1181
Fax: 242-356-0222

Bahrain
Building No. 979, Road 3119, Block 321
Zinj District
Bahrain
Tel: 973-273-300
Fax: 973-256-717

Bangladesh
Madani Avenue, Baridhara
Dhaka 1212, Bangladesh
Tel: 880-2-882-4700
Fax: 880-2-882-3744

Barbados
Canadian Imperial Bank of Commerce Building
Broad Street
P.O. Box 302
Bridgetown, Barbados
Tel: 246-436-4950
Fax: 246-429-5246

Belarus
Starovilenskaya #46-220002
Minsk, Belarus
Tel: 375-172-10-12-83
Fax: 375-172-26-16-01

Belgium
27 Boulevard du Regent
B-1000 Brussels
Brussels, Belgium
Tel: 32-2-508-2111
Fax: 32-2-511-2725

Belize
29 Gabourel Lane and Hutson St.
P.O. Box 286, Unit 7401
APO AA 34025
Belize City, Belize
Tel: 501-2-277161
Fax: 501-2-230802

Benin
Rue Caporal Bernard Anani
B.P. 2012
Cotonou, Benin
Tel: 229-30-06-50
Fax: 229-30-06-70

Bermuda
Crown Hill, 16 Middle Rd, Devonshire
P.O. Box HM325
Hamilton, Bermuda
Tel: 441-295-1342
Fax: 441-295-1592

Bolivia

Ave. Arce No. 2780
P.O. Box 425
La Paz, Bolivia
Tel: 591-2-430120
Fax: 591-2-433900

Bosnia-Herzegovina

43 Alipaslina
Sarajevo, Bosnia-Herzegovina
Tel: 387-33-445-700
Fax: 387-33-659-722

Botswana

P.O. Box 90
Gaborone, Botswana
Tel: 267-395-3982
Fax: 267-391-2782

Brazil

R Padre Joao Manoel, 933
Cerqueira Cesar
01411-001 Sao Paulo-SP, Brazil
Tel: 11-3081-6511
Fax: 11-3062-5154

Barunei

Third Floor-Teck Guan Plaza,
Jalan Sultan,
Bandar Seri Begawan BS8811, Brunei
Tel: 673-2-220-384
Fax: 673-2-225-293

Bulgaria

1 Saborna Street, Unit 1335
APO AE 09213-1335
Sofia, Bulgaria
Tel: 359-2-937-5100
Fax: 359-2-963-2022

Burkina Faso
    01 B.P. 35
    Ougadougou, Burkina Faso
    Tel: 226-30-67-23
    Fax: 226-30-38-90

Burma
    581 Merchant St.
    GPO 521, Box B
    APO AP 96546
    Tel: 95-1-379880
    Fax: 95-1-256018

Burundi
    B.P. 3H, 1720
    Bujumbura, Burundi
    Tel: 257-22-34-54
    Fax: 257-22-29-26

Cambodia
    16, Street 228 (btw. 51 & 63)
    Phnom Penh Cambodia
    Tel: 855-23-216-436
    Fax: 855-23-216-437

Cameroon
    Rue Nachtigal
    B.P. 817
    Yaounde, Cameroon
    Tel: 237-223-05-12
    Fax: 237-223-07-53

Canada
    490 Sussex Drive
    Ottawa, Ontario K1NIG8
    Canada
    Tel: 613-238-5335
    Fax: 613-238-4470

Republic of Cape Verde
Rua Abilio Macedo 81
C.P. 201
Praia, Republic of Cape Verde
Tel: 238-61-56-16
Fax: 238-61-13-55

Central African Republic
Avenue David Dacko
B.P. 924
Bangui, Central African Republic
Tel: 236-61-02-00
Fax: 236-61-44-94

Chad
Ave. Felix Eboue
B.P. 413
N'Djamena, Chad
Tel: 235-51-70-09
Fax: 235-51-56-54

Chile
Ave. Andres Bello 2800
APO AA 34033
Santiago, Chile
Tel: 56-2-232-2600
Fax: 56-2-330-3710

China
12-21 China World Trade Center
No.1 Jianguomeriwai Ave.
Beijing, China
Tel: 86-10-6532-3831
Fax: 86-10-6505-4574

Columbia
Carrera 45 #22D-45
Bogota, Columbia
Tel: 57-1-315-0811
Fax: 57-1-315-2197

Comoros
(See Mauritius)

Congo, Republic of the
310 Ave. des Aviateurs
Kinshasa-Gombe
Republic of Congo
Tel: 243-81-225-5872
Fax: 243-88-43467

Costa Rica
Calle 120 Avedina 0
Pavas, San Jose, Costa Rica
Tel: 506-220-3939
Fax: 506-220-2305

Côte d'Iviore
5 Rue Jesse Owens
Abidjan, Cote D-Iviore
Tel: 225-2021-0979
Fax: 225-2022-3259

Croatia
Andrije Hebranga 2
Unit 1345
Zagreb 10000, Croatia
Tel: 385-1-661-2200
Fax: 385-1-661-2373

Cuba
Calzada between L & M St.
Havana, Cuba
Tel: 537-333-551/59
Fax: 537-33-1084

Cyprus
Metochiou and Ploutarchou Street
Engomi – 2407 Nicosia
Cyprus
Tel: 357-2277-6400
Fax: 357-2278-0944

Czech Republic
Trziste 15
11801 Prague 1,
Prague, Czech Republic
Tel: 420-257-530-663
Fax: 420-257-531-165

Denmark
Dag Hammarskjolds Alle 24
2100 Copenhagen
PSC 73
Tel: 45-35-55-3144
Fax: 45-35-43-0223

Djiouti, Republic of
Plateau du Serpent
Blvd. Marechal Joffre & Calle
Leopoldo Navarro,
B.P. 185, Djibouti
Tel: 253-353995
Fax: 253-353940

Dominican Republic
Corner of Calle Cesar Nicolas Penson
Unit 5500
APO Miami 34041-0008
Santo, Dominican Republic
Tel: 809-221-2171
Fax: 809-686-7437

Ecuador
Avenida 12 de Octubre y Avenida Patria
APO AA 34039
Quito Ecuador
Tel: 593-2-562890
Fax: 593-2-502052

Egypt
American Embassy Cario-5
Latin America St. Garden City
Cairo, Egypt
Tel: 20-2797-3300
Fax: 20-2797-3200

El Salvador
>Blvd. Santa Elena
>Urbanizacion Santa Elena
>Antiguo, Custcatlan,
>La Libertad, El Salvador
>Tel: 503-278-4444
>Fax: 503-278-6011

Eritea
>Franklin D. Roosevelt St.
>P.O. Box 211
>Asmira, Eritea
>Tel: 291-112-0004
>Fax: 291-112-7584

Estonia
>Kentmanni 20
>15099
>Tallinn, Estonia
>Tel: 372-668-8100
>Fax: 372-668-8134

Ethiopia
>Entoto Street
>P.O. Box 1014
>Addis Ababa, Ethiopia
>Tel: 2511-550666
>Fax: 2511-551328

Fiji
>31 Loftus Street
>P.O. Box 218
>Suva, Fiji
>Tel: 679-314466
>Fax: 679-300-081

Finland
>Itainen Puistotie 14B
>Helsinki, Finland
>Tel: 358-917-1931
>Fax: 358-963-5332

France
    2 Avenue Gabriel
    75008 Paris
    Paris, France
    Tel: 331-4312-2222
    Fax: 331-4266-9783

Gabon
    Boulevard de la Mer
    B.P. 4000
    Libreville, Gabon
    Tel: 241-762003/4
    Fax: 241-745-507

Gambia
    Fajara, Kairaba Ave
    P.M.B. No. 19
    Banjul, The Gambia
    Tel: 220-392-856
    Fax: 220-392-475

Georgia
    25 Antoneli Str.
    Tbilisi 380026, Georgia
    Tel: 011-995-32-989-967
    Fax: 011-995-32-933-759

Germany
    Neustadtische Kirchstr 4-5
    10117 Berlin, Germany
    Tel: 030-8305-0
    Fax: 030-831-4926

Ghana
    Ring Road East
    P.O. Box 194
    Accra, Ghana
    Tel: 233-217-75348
    Fax: 233-217-76008

Greece
> 91 Vasillissis Sophias Ave.
> 10160 Athens
> Athens, Greece
> Tel: 30-210-721-2951
> Fax: 301-645-6282

Grenada
> Ross Point Inn
> P.O. Box 54
> St. George's, Grenada
> Tel: 809-440-1173/8
> Fax: 809-444-4820

Guatemala
> 7-01 Avenida de la Reforma
> Zone 10
> APO AA 34024
> 01010 Guatemala City
> Tel: 502-331-1541
> Fax: 502-332-0065

Guinea
> Rue KA 038
> B.P. 603, Conakry, Guinea
> Tel: 244-41520/21/23
> Fax: 244-41522

Guinea-Bissau
> Bairro de Penha
> C.P. 297, 1067 Codex
> Bissau, Guinea-Bissau
> Tel: 245-25-2273/6
> Fax: 245-20-2282

Guyana
> 99-100 Young and Duke Streets
> P.O. Box 10507
> Kingstown, Georgetown
> Tel: 592-225-4900-9
> Fax: 592-225-8497

Haiti

> 5 Harry Truman Boulevard
> P.O. Box 1761
> Port-Au-Prince, Haiti
> Tel: 509-222-0200
> Fax: 509-223-9038

The Holy Sea

> Villa Domiziana
> Via Delle Terme Deciane 26
> APO AE 09624
> Vatican City, Rome, Italy
> Tel: 396-46741
> Fax: 396-575-8346

Honduras

> Avenida La Paz
> Apdo. Postal 3453
> Tegucigalpa, Honduras
> Tel: 504-236-9320
> Fax: 504-236-9037

Hong Kong

> 26 Garden Rd.
> PSC 464 , Box 30
> FPO AP 96522-0002
> Hong Kong
> Tel: 852-2523-9011
> Fax: 852-2845-0943

Hungary

> V. 1054 Szabadsag Ter 12
> H 1054 Budapest, Hungary
> Tel: 361-475-4400
> Fax: 361-475-4764

Iceland

> Laufasvegur 21
> 101 Reykjavik, Iceland
> Tel: 354-562-9100
> Fax: 354-562-9123

India

    Shantipath Chanakyapuri
    New Delhi 110021,
    New Delhi, India
    Tel: 91-11-688-9033
    Fax: 91-11-687-2028

Indonesia

    Jl. Medan Merdeka Selatan 4-5
    Jakarta 10110, Indonesia
    Tel: 62-21-3435-9000
    Fax: 62-21-3857-189

Iraq

    Opp. For Ministry Club
    Masbah Quarter
    P.O. Box 2447
    Alwiyah, Baghdad, Iraq
    Tel: 964-1-719-6138/9
    Fax: 964-1-718-9297

Ireland

    42 Elgin Road
    Ballsbridge
    Dublin 4, Ireland
    Tel: 353-1-668-8777
    Fax: 353-1-668-9946

Israel

    71 Hayarkon Street
    Tel Aviv
    Tel Aviv, Israel
    Tel: 972-03519-7457
    Fax: 972-03516-4390

Italy

    Via Veneto 119/A
    00187-Rome
    Rome, Italy
    Tel: 39-06-46741
    Fax: 39-06-4882-672

Jamaica

2 Oxford Road,
Kingston, 5 Jamaica, W.I.
Tel: 876-935-6053/4
Fax: 876-929-3637

Japan

1-10-5, Alasaka
Minato-ku
Tokyo, Japan 107-8420
Tel: 81-3224-5000
Fax: 81-3505-1862

Jordan

P.O. Box 354
Amman 11118, Jordan
APO AE 09892-0200
Amman, Jordan
Tel: 962-6-592-0101
Fax: 962-6-592-0121

Kazakhstan

99/97 Furmanova St.
Almaty, Kazakhstan 480012
Tel: 7-3272-63-3905
Fax: 7-3272-63-3883

Kenya

Barclay's Plaza
Loita St.
P.O. Box 30143
Nairobi, Kenya
Tel: 254-2-240-290
Fax: 254-2-216511

Korea

U.S. Embassy Consular Section
32 Sejongno, Jongo-gu
Chongro-ku, Unit 15550
Seoul, 110-710 Korea
APO AP 96205-0001
Tel: 82-2-397-4114
Fax: 82-2-397-4101

Kuwait

Unit 69000
1-3001, P.O. Box 77 SAFAT
Kuwait
Tel: 965-539-5307
Fax: 965-538-0281

Kyrgyz Republic

171 Prospect Mira
Bishkek 720016, Kyrgyz Republic
Tel: 966-312-551-241
Fax: 966-312-551-264

Laos

19-Rue Bartholonie
Vientinne, Lao P.D.R.
Vientinne, Lao
Tel: 856-212-12581
Fax: 856-212-13045

Latvia

Raina Boulevard 7
LV-1510
Latvia
Tel: 371-7036-200
Fax: 371-7820-047

Lebanon

P.O. Box 70-840, Antelias
Beirut, Lebanon
Tel: 04-542-600
Fax: 04-544-136

Lesotho

P.O. Box 333
Maseru 100, Lesotho
Tel: 266-312-666
Fax: 266-310-441

Liberia

111 United Nations Drive
P.O. Box 10-0098
Mamba Point, Monrovia
Tel: 231-226-370/380
Fax: 231-226-148

Lithuania

Akmenu 6, 2600
Vilnius, Lithuania
Tel: 370-5-266-5500
Fax: 370-5-266-5510

Luxembourg

22 Blvd. Emmanuel-Servais
2535 Luxembourg
Tel: 352-460123
Fax: 352-461401

Macedonia

Bul Llinden BB
9100 Skopje
Skopje, Macedonia
Tel: 389-92-116-180
Fax: 389-92-117-103

Madagascar

14 and 16 Rue Rainitovo
Antsahavola, B.P. 620
Antananarivo 101, Madagascar
Tel: 261-20-22-212-57
Fax: 261-20-22-345-39

Malawi

P.O. Box 30016
Lilongwe 3, Malawi
Tel: 265-1-773-166
Fax: 265-1-770-471

Malaysia
376 Jalan Tun Razak
50400 Kuala Lumpur
P.O. Box No. 10035
Kuala Lumpur, Malaysia
Tel: 603-2168-5000
Fax: 603-2142-2207

Mali
Rue Rochester
B.P. 34
Bamako, Mali
Tel: 223-222-5663
Fax: 223-222-3712

Malta
Development House, 3rd Floor
St. Anne St.
P.O. Box 535
Valletta, Malta
Tel: 011-356-2561-4000
Fax: 011-356-243-229

Marshall Islands
P.O. Box 1379
Majuro, Marshall Islands 96960
Tel: 692-247-4011
Fax: 692-247-4012

Mauritania
B.P. 222
Nouakchott, Mauritania
Tel: 222-2-526-60
Fax: 222-2-515-92

Mauritius
Rogers House, 4th Floor
John Kennedy Ave.
Port Louis, Mauritius
Tel: 230-202-4400
Fax: 230-208-9534

Mexico
Embajada de Estados Unidos
Paseo de la Reforma 305
Col. Cauhtemoc
06500 Mexico, D.F.
Tel: 525-5-5080-2000
Fax: 525-5-5511-9980

Micronesia
P.O. Box 1286,
Kolonia, Pohnpei 96941 FSM
Micronesia
Tel: 691-320-2187
Fax: 691-320-2186

Moldova
#103 Mateevici Street
Chisinau, Moldova 2009
Tel: 373-223-3772
Fax: 373-223-3044

Mongolia
P.O. Box 1021
Ulaanbaatar 13, Mongolia
Tel: 976-11-329-095
Fax: 976-11-320-776

Morocco
2 Avenue De Mohammad El Fassi
Rabat, Morocco
Tel: 212-3776-2265
Fax: 212-3776-5661

Mozambique
Ave. Mao Tse Tung 542
P.O. Box 783, Maputo
Maputo, Mozambique
Tel: 258-1-491-916
Fax: 258-1-491-918

Namibia

Ausplan Building
14 Lossen St, Private Bag 12029
Windhoek, Nambia
Tel: 264-61-221-601
Fax: 264-61-229-792

Nepal

Panipokhari
P.O. Box 295
Kathmandu, Nepal
Tel: 977-1-44-111-79
Fax: 977-1-44-199-63

Netherlands

Lange Voorhout 102
2514 EJ The Hague
The Hague, Netherlands
Tel: 31-70-310-9209
Fax: 31-70-361-4688

Netherlands Antilles

J.B. Gorsiraweg #1
P.O. Box 158
Williemstad, Curacao
Tel: 599-9-613-066
Fax: 599-9-616-489

New Zealand

29 Fitzherbert Terrace, Thorndon
P.O. Box 1190
Wellington, New Zealand
Tel: 011-644-462-6000
Fax: 011-644-499-0490

Nicaragua

Km. 4-1/2 Carretera Sur.
P.O. Box 327
Managua, Nicaragua
Tel: 505-2-66-010
Fax: 505-2-669-056

Niger

Rue de Ambassades
B.P. 11201
Niamey, Niger
Tel: 227-722-661
Fax: 227-733-167

Nigeria

7 Mambilla Street
Off Aso Drive Maitama District
Abuja, Nigeria
Tel: 234-9-523-0916
Fax: 234-9-523-0353

Norway

Drammensveien 18
0244 Oslo
Oslo, Norway
Tel: 47-22-44-8550
Fax: 47-22-56-2751

Oman

P.O. Box 202
PC 115 Madinat Al Sultan Qaboos
Sultanate of Oman
Tel: 968-698-989
Fax: 968-699-771

Pakistan

Ramna 5, Diplomatic Enclave
Islamabad, Pakistan
Tel: 92-51-208-0000
Fax: 92-51-227-6427

Republic of Palau

P.O. Box 6028
Koror, Republic of Palau 96940
Tel: 680-488-2920/2990
Fax: 680-488-2911

Panama
    P.O. Box 6959
    Panama 5
    Panama
    Tel: 507-207-7000
    Fax: 507-227-1964

Papua New Guinea
    Douglas St.
    P.O. Box 1492
    Port Moresby, Papua New Guinea
    Tel: 675-321-1455
    Fax: 675-321-3423

Paraguay
    1776 Mariscal Lopez Ave.
    Asuncion, Paraguay
    Tel: 595-21-213-715
    Fax: 595-21-213-728

Peru
    Avenida Enclada, Cdra 17 s/a
    Surco Lima 33, Peru
    Tel: 51-1-434-3000
    Fax: 51-1-618-2397

Philippines
    1201 Roxas Boulevard
    Ermita 1000
    Manila, Philippines
    Tel: 63-2-523-1001
    Fax: 63-2-522-4361

Poland
    Aleje Ujazdowskie 29/31
    00-540 Warsaw, Poland
    Tel: 48-22-628-3041
    Fax: 48-22-628-8298

Portugal
Av das Forcas Armadas
1600-081 Lisboa
Lisbon, Portugal
Tel: 351-21-727-3300
Fax: 351-21-727-9109

Qatar
P.O. Box 2399
Doha, Qatar
Tel: 974-488-4101
Fax: 974-488-4298

Romania
Tudor Arghezi 7-9
Bucharest, Romania
Tel: 40-21-210-4042
Fax: 40-21-210-0395

Russia
Bolshoy Deviatinsky Pereulok, 8
Moscow, 121099
Russian Federation
Tel: 095-728-5084
Fax: 095-728-5577

Rwanda
377 Blvd. de la Revolution
B.P. 28
Kigali, Rwanda
Tel: 250-75601
Fax: 250-72128

Saudi Arabia
P.O. Box 94309
Riyadh 11693
Saudi Arabia
Tel: 966-1-488-3800
Fax: 966-1-488-7360

Senegal
> B.P. 49, Ave Jean XXIII
> Dakar, Senegal
> Tel: 221-823-4296
> Fax: 221-822-2991

Serbia-Montenegro
> Kneza Milosa-50
> 11000Belgrade,
> Serbia-Montenegro
> Tel: 381-11-361-9344
> Fax: 381-11-361-8684

Sierra Leone
> Corner of Walpole
> and Siaka Stevens Streets
> Freetown, Sierra Leone
> Tel: 232-22-226-481
> Fax: 232-22-225-471

Singapore
> 27 Napier Road
> Singapore 258-508
> Tel: 65-6476-9100
> Fax: 65-6476-9340

Slovak Republic
> Hviezdoslavovo Namestie 4
> 81102 Bratislava, Slovak Republic
> Tel: 011-42-5330861
> Fax: 011-42-5334711

Slovenia
> Presernova 31
> 1000 Ljubljana
> Slovenia
> Tel: 011-386-1-200-5500
> Fax: 011-386-1-200-5535

South Africa
877 Pretorius St
Arcadia 0083
P.O. Box 9536
Pretoria, South Africa
Tel: 27-12-342-1048
Fax: 27-12-342-2244

Spain
Serrano 75
28006 Madrid,
Spain
Tel: 91-587-2200
Fax: 91-587-2303

Sri Lanka
210 Galle Road
Colombo 3, Sri Lanka
Tel: 94-1-448007
Fax: 94-1-437345

Sudan
Sharia Ali Abdul Latif
P.O. Box 699
APO AE 09829
Khartoum, Sudan
Tel: 249-11-774611
Fax: 249-11-774137

Suriname
Dr. Sophie Redmondstraat 129
P.O. Box 1821
Paramaribo, Suriname
Tel: 597-472-900
Fax: 597-479-829

Swaziland
Embassy House
Allister Miller Street
Mbabane, Swaziland
Tel: 268-404-0677
Fax: 268-404-5846

Sweden
Dag Hammarskjolds Vag 31
S-115 89 Stockholm, Sweden
Tel: 08-783-5300
Fax: 08-661-1964

Switzerland
Jubilaeumstrasse 93
3001 Bern, Switzerland
Tel: 031-357-7011
Fax: 031-357-7344

Syria
Abou Roumaneh
Al Mansur Street, No. 2
P.O. Box 29
Damascus, Syria
Tel: 963-11-333-1342
Fax: 963-11-224-7938

Taiwan
7 Lane 134
Hsin Yi Road, Section 3
Taipei, Taiwan
Tel: 886-2-709-2000
Fax: 886-2-702-7675

Tajikistan
10 Pavlov Street
Dushanbe, Tajikistan 734003
Tel: 992-372-21-0348
Fax: 992-372-51-0028

Tanzania
686 Old Bagnoyo Road
P.O. Box 9123
Dar Es Salaam, Tanzania
Tel: 255-222-66-8001
Fax: 255-222-66-8238

Thailand

95 Wireless Road
Bangkok 10330 Thailand
Tel: 66-2-205-4005
Fax: 66-2-254-1171

Togo

Angle Rue Kovenout Rue 15 Beniglato
& Rue Vauban B.P. 852
Lome, Togo
Tel: 228-221-2294
Fax: 228-221-7952

Trinidad and Tobago

15 Queens Park West
P.O. Box 752
Port-of-Spain, Trinidad and Tobago
Tel: 868-622-6371
Fax: 868-628-5462

Tunisia

Zone Nord Est. de Burges
Du Lac Nord de Tunis
2045 La Goulette
Tunis, Tunisia
Tel: 216-71-107-000
Fax: 216-71-962-115

Turkey

110 Ataturk Boulevard
Kauaklidere, 06100
Ankara, Turkey
Tel: 90-312-455-5555
Fax: 90-312-468-0019

Turkmenistan

9 Pushkin St.
Ashgabat, Turkmenistan 744000
Tel: 9-9312-35-00-45
Fax: 9-9312-39-26-14

Uganda

Plot 1577 Ggaba Road
P.O. Box 7007
Kampala, Uganda
Tel: 041-233231
Fax: 041-259794

Ukraine

10 Yuria Kotsubynskoho
4053 Kiev, Ukraine
Tel: 380-44-490-4000
Fax: 380-44-490-4085

United Arab Emirates

Al-Sudan Street
P.O. Box 4009
Abu Dhabi, United Arab Emirates
Tel: 971-2-443-6691
Fax: 971-2-443-5786

United Kingdom

24 Grosvenor Square
London, W. 1A 1AE, England
Tel: 44-0207-499-9000
Fax: 44-0207-491-2485

United States

U.S. Mission to the United Nations
799 United Nations Plaza
New York, NY 10017
Tel: 212-415-4000
Fax: 212-415-4443

Uruguay

Lauro Muller 1776
Montevideo 11200, Uruguay
APO AA 34035
Tel: 598-2-418-7777
Fax: 598-2-418-8611

Uzbekistan

    82 Chilanzarskaya
    Tashkent, Uzbekistan
    Tel: 7-3712-77-14-07
    Fax: 7-3712-89-13-35

Venezuela

    Calle F con Calle Suapure
    Urb. Colinas de Valle Arriba
    Caracas 1080, Venezuela
    Tel: 0212-975-7831
    Fax: 0212-975-8991

Vietnam

    7 Lang Ha Street
    Ba Dinh District
    Hanoi, Vietnam
    Tel: 844-772-1500
    Fax: 844-772-1510

Republic of Yemen

    Dhahr Himyar Zone
    Sheraton Hotel District
    P.O. Box 22347
    Sanaa, Republic of Yemen
    Tel: 967-1-303-115
    Fax: 967-1-303-117

Zambia

    Corner of Independence and
    United Nations Avenues
    P.O. Box 31617
    Lusaka, Zambia
    Tel: 260-1-250-955
    Fax: 260-1-252-225

Zimbabwe

    172 Herbert Chitapo Ave
    P.O. Box 3340
    Harare, Zimbabwe
    Tel: 263-4-250593
    Fax: 263-4-796488

Appendix G: Small Business Administration (SBA) District Offices

ALABAMA
Birmingham
205-290-7101

ALASKA
Anchorage
907-271-4022

ARIZONA
Phoenix
602-745-7200

ARKANSAS
Little Rock
501-324-5871

CALIFORNIA
Fresno
559-487-5791

Glendale
818-552-3210

Sacramento
916-930-3700

San Diego
619-557-7250

San Francisco
415-744-6820

Santa Ana
714-550-7420

COLORADO
Denver
303-844-2607

CONNECTICUT
Hartford
860-240-4700

DELAWARE
Wilmington
302-573-6060

DISTRICT OF COLUMBIA
202-606-4000

FLORIDA
Jacksonville
904-443-1900

Miami
305-536-5521

GEORGIA
Atlanta
404-331-0100

HAWAII
Honolulu
808-541-2990

IDAHO
Boise
208-334-1696

ILLINOIS
Chicago
312-353-4528

INDIANA
Indianapolis
317-226-7272

IOWA
Cedar Rapids
319-362-6405

Des Moines
515-284-4422

KANSAS
Wichita
316-269-6616

KENTUCKY
Louisville
502-582-5761

LOUISIANA
New Orleans
504-589-6685

MAINE
Augusta
207-622-8274

MARYLAND
Baltimore
410-962-4392

MASSACHUSETTS
Boston
617-565-5590

MICHIGAN
Detroit
313-226-6075

MINNESOTA
Minneapolis
612-370-2324

MISSISSIPPI
Jackson
601-965-4378

MISSOURI
Kansas City
816-374-6708

St. Louis
314-539-6600

MONTANA
Helena
406-441-1081

NEBRASKA
Omaha
402-221-4691

NEVADA
Las Vegas
702-388-6611

NEW HAMPSHIRE
Concord
603-225-1400

NEW JERSEY
Newark
973-645-2434

NEW MEXICO
Albuquerque
505-346-6764

NEW YORK
Buffalo
716-551-4301

New York City
212-264-4354

Syracuse
315-471-9393

NORTH CAROLINA
Charlotte
704-344-6563

NORTH DAKOTA
Fargo
701-239-5131

OHIO
Cleveland
216-522-4180

Columbus
614-469-6860

OKLAHOMA
Oklahoma City
405-231-5521

OREGON
Portland
503-326-2682

PENNSYLVANIA
Philadelphia
215-580-2722

Pittsburgh
412-395-6560

RHODE ISLAND
Providence
401-528-4562

SOUTH CAROLINA
Columbia
803-765-5377

SOUTH DAKOTA
Sioux Falls
605-367-4891

TENNESSEE
Nashville
615-963-7253

TEXAS
Dallas/Fort Worth
817-684-5500

Harligen
956-427-8533

San Antonio
210-403-5900

El Paso
915-633-7001

Houston
713-773-6500

UTAH
Salt Lake City
801-746-2269

VERMONT
Montpelier
802-828-4422

VIRGINIA
Richmond
804-771-2400

WASHINGTON
Spokane
509-353-2800

WEST VIRGINIA
Clarksburg
304-623-5631

WISCONSIN
Madison
608-441-5263

WYOMING
Casper
307-261-6500

Appendix H:
Small Business
Development Centers

ALABAMA

SBDC, University of Alabama
    901 South 15th Street, Suite 201
    Birmingham, AL 35294
    Tel: 205-934-6760
    Fax: 205-934-0538

ALASKA

SBDC, Anchorage
    430 West 7th Avenue, Suite 110
    Anchorage, AK 99501
    Tel: 907-274-7232
    Fax: 907-274-9524

ARIZONA

SBDC, Maricopa County Community Colleges
    2411 West 14th Street, Suite 114
    Tempe, AZ 85281
    Tel: 480-784-0590
    Fax: 602-230-7989

ARKANSAS

SBDC, University of Arkansas
    Little Rock Technology Center Building
    100 South Main, Suite 401
    Little Rock, AR 72201
    Tel: 501-324-9043
    Fax: 501-324-9049

CALIFORNIA
SBDC, California Trade and Commerce Agency
1102 Q Street, Suite 6000
Sacramento, CA 95814
Tel: 916-324-5068
Fax: 916-322-5084

COLORADO
SBDC, Office of Business Development
1625 Broadway, Suite 1700
Denver, CO 80202
Tel: 303-892-3840
Fax: 303-892-3848

CONNECTICUT
SBDC, University of Connecticut
2100 Hillside Road, 2 Bourn Place
Storrs, CT 06269
Tel: 203-486-4135
Fax: 203-486-1576

DELAWARE
SBDC, University of Delaware
One Innovation Way, Suite 301
Delaware Technology Park
Newark, DE 19711
Tel: 302-831-1555
Fax: 302-831-1423

DISTRICT OF COLUMBIA
SBDC, Howard University
2600 6th Street, NW, Room 128
Washington, DC 20059
Tel: 202-806-1550
Fax: 202-806-1777

FLORIDA
SBDC, University of West Florida
19 West Garden Street, 3rd Floor
Pensacola, FL 32501
Tel: 850-595-6060
Fax: 850-595-6070

GEORGIA
SBDC, University of Georgia
Chicopee Complex, Room 2007
1180 East Broad Street
Athens, GA 30602
Tel: 706-542-6762
Fax: 706-542-6803

HAWAII
SBDC, University of Hawaii at Hilo
100 Pauahi Street, Suite 109
Hilo, HI 96720
Tel: 808-969-1814
Fax: 808-969-7669

IDAHO
SBDC, Boise State University
College of Business
1910 University Drive
Boise, ID 83725
Tel: 208-426-1640
Fax: 208-426-3877

ILLINOIS
SBDC, Lincoln Land Community College
1300 South 9th Street
Springfield, IL 62703
Tel: 217-789-1017
Fax: 217-522-3512

INDIANA
SBDC, Indianapolis
429 North Pennsylvania Street, Suite 100
Indianapolis, IN 46204
Tel: 317-226-7264
Fax: 317-226-7259

IOWA
SBDC, Iowa State University
137 Lynn Avenue
Ames, IA 50014
Tel: 515-292-6351
Fax: 515-292-0020

KANSAS

SBDC Topeka Lead Center
Fort Hays State University
214 SW 6th Avenue, Suite 301
Topeka, KS 66603
Tel: 785-296-6514
Fax: 785-291-3261

KENTUCKY

SBDC, University of Kentucky/Lexington
4th Floor Central Library Building
140 East Main Street
Lexington, KY 40507
Tel: 606-257-7666
Fax: 606-257-1751

LOUISIANA

SBDC, Northeast Louisiana University
College of Business Administration
700 University Avenue, Room 2-57
Monroe, LA 71209
Tel: 318-342-5506
Fax: 318-342-5510

MAINE

SBDC, University of Southern Maine
15 Surrenden Street
P.O. Box 9300
Portland, ME 04104
Tel: 207-780-4949
Fax: 207-780-4810

MARYLAND

SBDC, Baltimore—Central Region
Towson University
8000 York Road
Towson, MD 21252
Tel: 410-830-5001
Fax: 410-830-5009

MASSACHUSETTS
SBDC, University of Massachusetts
School of Management
Room 205
Amherst, MA 01003
Tel: 413-545-6301
Fax: 413-545-1273

MICHIGAN
Wayne State University
School of Business Administration
2727 Second Avenue
Suite 107
Detroit, MI 48201
Tel: 313-964-1798
Fax: 313-964-3648

MINNESOTA
St. Paul, SBDC—Lead Center
500 Metro Square
121 Seventh Place East
St. Paul, MN 55101
Tel: 612-297-5773
Fax: 612-296-1290

MISSISSIPPI
SBDC, University of Mississippi
P.O. Box 1848 B-19
Track Drive
University, MS 38677
Tel: 601-232-5001
Fax: 601-232-5650

MISSOURI
SBDC, University of Missouri, Columbia
1205 University Avenue, Suite 300
Columbia, MO 65211
Tel: 573-882-0344
Fax: 573-884-4297

MONTANA
SBDC, Montana Department of Commerce
1015 Poplar Avenue
Helena, MT 59601
Tel: 406-447-1512
Fax: 406-447-1514

NEBRASKA
SBDC, University of Nebraska, Omaha
60th & Dodge Streets
CBA Room 407
Omaha, NE 68182-0248
Tel: 402-554-2521
Fax: 402-554-3473

NEVADA
SBDC, University of Nevada in Reno
College of Business Administration
Business Building, Room 411
Reno, NV 89557
Tel: 775-784 1717
Fax: 775-784-4337

NEW HAMPSHIRE
SBDC, University of New Hampshire
108 McConnell Hall
Durham, NH 03824
Tel: 603-862-2200
Fax: 603-862-4876

NEW JERSEY
SBDC, Rutgers University
49 Bleeker Street
Third Floor, Ackerson Hall
Newark, NJ 07102
Tel: 973-353-5950
Fax: 973-353-1110

NEW MEXICO
SBDC, Santa Fe Community College
6401 Richards Avenue
Santa Fe, NM 87508
Tel: 505-438-1343
Fax: 505-428-1469

NEW YORK
SBDC, State University of New York
SUNY Plaza 41 State Street
Albany, NY 12246
Tel: 518-443-5398
Fax: 518-465-4992

NORTH CAROLINA
SBDC, University of North Carolina
5 West Hargett, Suite 600
Raleigh, NC 27601
Tel: 919-715-7272
Fax: 919-715-7777

NORTH DAKOTA
SBDC, University of North Dakota
188 Gramble Hall
P.O. Box 7308
Grand Forks, ND 58202
Tel: 701-777-3700
Fax: 701-777-3225

OHIO
SBDC, Department of Development
77 South High Street, 28th Floor
Columbus, OH 43215
Tel: 614-466-2711
Fax: 614-466-0829

OKLAHOMA
SBDC, Southeast Oklahoma State University
517 University
Station A, Box 2584
Durant, OK 74701
Tel: 580-745-7577
Fax: 580-745-7471

OREGON
SBDC, Lane Community College
1445 Willamette Street, Suite 1
Eugene, OR 97401
Tel: 541-463-5255
Fax: 541-687-0627

PENNSYLVANIA
SBDC, University of Pennsylvania
The Wharton School
3733 Spruce Street, 409 Vance Hall
Philadelphia, PA 19104
Tel: 215-898-4861
Fax: 215-898-1063

PUERTO RICO
SBDC
Union Plaza Building, 10th Floor
416 Ponce de Leon Avenue
Hato Rey, PR 00918
Tel: 787-763-6811
Fax: 787-763-6875

RHODE ISLAND
SBDC, Bryant College
1150 Douglas Pike
Smithfield, RI 02917
Tel: 401-232-6111
Fax: 401-232-6933

SOUTH CAROLINA
SBDC, University of South Carolina
College of Business Administration
Hipp Building
1710 College Street
Columbia, SC 29208
Tel: 803-777-4907
Fax: 803-777-4403

SOUTH DAKOTA

SBDC, University of South Dakota
School of Business
414 East Clark Street
Vermillion, SD 57069
Tel: 605-677-5287
Fax: 605-677-5427

TENNESSEE

SBDC, Memphis State University
South Campus
Getwell Road, Building #1
Memphis, TN 38152
Tel: 901-678-2500
Fax: 901-678-4072

TEXAS

SBDC, Dallas (North Texas)
1402 Corinth Street
Dallas, TX 75215
Tel: 214-860-5835
Fax: 214-860-5813

UTAH

SBDC, Salt Lake Community College
1623 South State Street
Salt Lake City, UT 84115
Tel: 801-957-3480
Fax: 801-957-3489

VERMONT

SBDC, Vermont Technical College
P.O. Box 188
Randolph Center, VT 05061
Tel: 802-728-9101
Fax: 802-728-3026

VIRGINIA

SBDC, Department of Business Administration
707 East Main Street, Suite 300
Richmond, VA 23219
Tel: 804-371-8106
Fax: 804-371-8185

VIRGIN ISLANDS

SBDC, St. Thomas
Nisky Center, Suite 202
Charlotte Amalie
St. Thomas, Virgin Islands 0080
Tel:　　340-776-3206
Fax:　　340-775-3756

WASHINGTON

SBDC, Washington State University
College of Business and Economics
501 Johnson Tower
Pullman, WA 99164
Tel:　　509-335-8045
Fax:　　509-335-0949

WEST VIRGINIA

SBDC, Charleston—Lead Center
State Capitol Complex, Building 6, Room 652
1900 Kanawha Boulevard East
Charleston, WV 25305
Tel:　　304-558-2960
Fax:　　304-558-0127

WISCONSIN

SBDC, University of Wisconsin
432 North Lake Street, Room 423
Madison, WI 53706
Tel:　　608-263-7794
Fax:　　608-263-7830

WYOMING

Wyoming SBDC
University of Wyoming
P.O. Box 3922
Laramie, WY 82071
Tel:　　307-766-3505
Fax:　　307-766-3406

Appendix I: Small Business Administration Export Assistance Centers

STATE	REGIONAL OFFICE	PHONE	REGIONAL MANAGER
Alabama	Atlanta, GA	404-657-1961	Ray Gibeau
Alaska	Seattle, WA	206-553-0051	Pru Balatero
Arizona	Los Angeles, CA	310-235-7203	Sandra Edwards
Arkansas	Dallas, TX	817-277-0767	Rick Schulze
California (Northern)	San Francisco, CA	415-744-8474	Mark Quinn
California (Southern)	Los Angeles, CA	310-235-7203	Sandra Edwards
Colorado	Denver, CO	303-844-6622	Dennis Chrisbaum
Connecticut	Boston, MA	617-424-5953	John Joyce
Delaware	Philadelphia, PA	215-597-6101	Robert Elsas
District of Columbia	Baltimore, MD	410-962-4582	Deborah Conrad
Florida	Miami, FL	305-536-5521	Mary Hernandez
Georgia	Atlanta, GA	404-657-1961	Ray Gibeau
Hawaii	Los Angeles, CA	310-235-7203	Sandra Edwards
Idaho (Northern)	Seattle, WA	206-553-0051	Pru Balatero
Idaho (Southern)	Portland, OR	503-326-5498	Inge McNeese
Illinois	Chicago, IL	312-353-8065	John Nevell
Indiana	Chicago, IL	312-353-8065	John Nevell
Iowa	St. Louis, MO	314-425-3304	John Blum
Kansas	St. Louis, MO	314-425-3304	John Blum
Kentucky	Atlanta, GA	404-657-1961	Ray Gibeau
Louisiana	Dallas, TX	817-277-0767	Rick Schulze
Maine	Boston, MA	617-424-5953	John Joyce
Maryland	Baltimore, MD	410-962-4582	Deborah Conrad
Massachusetts	Boston, MA	617-424-5953	John Joyce

STATE	REGIONAL OFFICE	PHONE	REGIONAL MANAGER
Michigan	Detroit, MI	313-226-3670	John O'Gara
Minnesota	Minneapolis, MN	612-348-1642	Nancy Libersky
Mississippi	Atlanta, GA	404-657-1961	Ray Gibeau
Missouri	St. Louis, MO	314-425-3304	John Blum
Montana	Portland, OR	503-326-5498	Inge McNeese
Nebraska	St. Louis, MO	314-425-3304	John Blum
Nevada	Los Angeles, CA	310-235-7203	Sandra Edwards
New Hampshire	Boston, MA	617-424-5953	John Joyce
New Jersey	Philadelphia, PA	215-597-6101	Robert Elsas
New Mexico	Denver, CO	303-844-6622	Dennis Chrisbaum
New York	Cleveland, OH	216-522-4731	Patrick Hayes
North Carolina	Charlotte, NC	704-333-2130	Dan Holt
North Dakota	Minneapolis, MN	612-348-1642	Nancy Libersky
Ohio	Cleveland, OH	216-522-4731	Patrick Hayes
Oklahoma	Dallas, TX	817-277-0767	Rick Schulze
Oregon	Portland, OR	503-326-5498	Inge McNeese
Pennsylvania (Eastern)	Philadelphia, PA	215-597-6101	Robert Elsas
Pennsylvania (Western)	Cleveland, OH	216-522-4731	Patrick Hayes
Rhode Island	Boston, MA	617-424-5953	John Joyce
South Carolina	Charlotte, NC	704-333-2130	Dan Holt
South Dakota	St. Louis, MO	314-425-3304	John Blum
Tennessee	Atlanta, GA	404-657-1961	Ray Gibeau
Texas	Dallas, TX	817-277-0767	Rick Schulze
Utah	Denver, CO	303-844-6622	Dennis Chrisbaum
Vermont	Boston, MA	617-424-5953	John Joyce
Virginia	Baltimore, MD	410-962-4582	Deborah Conrad
Washington (Northern)	Seattle, WA	206-553-0051	Pru Balatero
Washington (Southern)	Portland, OR	503-326-5498	Inge McNeese
West Virginia	Baltimore, MD	410-962-4582	Deborah Conrad
Wisconsin	Chicago, IL	312-353-8065	John Nevell
Wyoming	Denver, CO	303-844-6622	Dennis Chrisbaum

Appendix J:
Selected Development Finance Institutions

ORGANIZATION	COUNTRY	ADDRESS	PHONE
African Development Bank (AfDB)	Côte d'Ivoire	Rue Joseph Anoma 01 BP 1387 Abdijan 01	(225) 20-20-44-44
Agence Francaise de Developpement (AFD)	France	5, rue Roland Barthes 75598 Paris Cedex 12	33 1 53-44-31-31
Agricultural Bank	Libya	P.O. Box 1100 Tripoli	(00218) 21
Agricultural Bank of Iran	Iran	P.O. Box 14155/6395 Tehran 14454	(0098 21) 825 2246
Agricultural Bank of Sudan	Sudan	P.O. Box 1363 Karthoum	(00249 11) 777432
Agricultural Cooperative Bank	Syria	P.O. Box 4325 Damascus	(00936 11) 215132
Agricultural Credit Corporation	Jordan	P.O. Box 77 Amman Jordan	(00962 6) 661105
Agricultural Development Bank	Ghana	Cedi-House, Liberia Road, POB 4191, Accra	661118
Agricultural Development Bank Nepal	Nepal	Ramshah Path Kathmandu	977-1-262885
Agricultural Development Bank of Pakistan	Pakistan	P.O. Box 1400 Islamabad	(0092 51) 202 009
Algerian Bank for Development	Algeria	12 Bd du Colonel Amirouche Algiers, 16000	213-263-88-95
Antigua and Barbuda Development Bank	Antigua and Barbuda	27 St. Mary's Street, Box 1279, St. John's	(268) 462 0838
Arab Bank for Economic Development in Africa (BADEA)	Sudan	P.O. Box 2640 Khartoum	249-11-773646

WEB/E-MAIL

WEB/E-MAIL	Year	Government Owned	Loans & Guarantees	Equity	Insurance	Technical Assistance	Institution Type
Web: www.afdb.org E-mail: afdb@afdb.org	1964		X	X			Regional
Web: www.afd.fr E-mail: com@afd.fr	1941	X	X	X		X	Global Bilateral
	1957	X	X				National
Web: www.agri-bank.com E-mail: info@agri-bank.com	1980	X	X				National
E-mail: agric-bank@yahoo.com	1957	X	X				National
	1888	X	X				National
	1959	X	X			X	National
Web: www.adbghana.com E-mail: adbweb@africaonline.com.gh	1965	51%	X				National
Web: www.adbn.gov.np/introduction.html E-mail: info@adbn.gov.np	1967	X	X			X	National
Web: www.adbp.org.pk E-mail: adbp@isb.paknet.com.pk	1961	X	X				National
							National
							National
Web: www.badea.org E-mail: badea@badea.org	1975		X			X	Region to Region

ORGANIZATION	COUNTRY	ADDRESS	PHONE
Arab Fund for Economic & Social Development	Kuwait	P.O. Box 21923 Safat 13080	(965) 48 44 500
Armenian Development Bank	Armenian	21/1 Paronyan Str., 375015 Yerevan	(374 1) 538930
Asian Development Bank (ADB)	Philippines	6 ADB Avenue Mandaluyong City 0401 Metro Manila	632 632 4444
Bahamas Development Bank	Bahamas	Cable Beach, West Bay Street P.O. Box N-3034 Nassau, Bahamas	242 327-5780-6
Banca de Desarrollo Agropecuario	Panama	Av. 4 de Julio y Calle L Apartado Postal 5282 Zona 5	(00507) 2620140
Banco Latinoamericano de Exportaciones (BLADEX)	Panama	Apdo. 6-1497, El Dorado	(507) 210 8500
Banco Nacional de Desarrollo Agricola	Honduras	Apartado Postal 212 Tegucigalpa	(00504) 2373790
BANCOMEXT	Mexico	Camino a Sta. Teresa 1679, Delegación Alvaro Obregón 01900	55-5481-60-00
Bangladesh Krishi Bank	Bangladesh	83-85 Motijheel Commercial Area, Dhaka, Bangladesh	880-2-9560031-5
Bank Mandiri	Indonesia	Plaza Mandiri 22nd Floor Jl. Jend. Gatot Subroto Kav. 36-38 Jakarta 12190	(62-21) 524 5577
Bank of Agriculture and Rural Development	Algeria	17, Bd Colonel Amirouche Algiers	213-2-743273
Bank of Maldives	Maldives		

WEB/E-MAIL	Year	Government Owned	Loans & Guarantees	Equity	Insurance	Technical Assistance	Institution Type
Web: www.arabfund.org E-mail: hq@arabfund.org	1974		X			X	Regional
Web: www.armdb.com E-mail: info@armdb.com	1990		X				National
Web: www.adb.org E-mail: information@adb.org	1966		X	X		X	Regional
Web: www.bahamasdevelopmentbank.com E-mail: grodgers@bahamasdevelopmentbank.com	1974	X	X			X	National
	1973	X	X				National
Web: www.blx.com E-mail: webmaster@blx.com	1977		X			X	Regional
E-mail: vpresid@netsys.hn	1980	X	X				National
Web: www.bancomext.com E-mail: privatesector@adb.org	1937	X	X	X		X	National
E-mail: bkb@citechco.net	1973		X				National
Web: www.bankmandiri.com	1997	X	X	X			National
							National
Web: www.bankofmaldives.com.mv	1982	X	X				National

279

ORGANIZATION	COUNTRY	ADDRESS	PHONE
Banque Nationale de Developpement Agricole	Mali	Immeuble CCA, Quartier de Fleuve Bamako	(00223) 226464
Banque Ouest Africaine de Developpement (BOAD)	Togo	P.O. Box 1172 Lome	(228) 221-59-06
Belgian Corporation for International Investment (BMI-SBI)	Belgium	Avenue de Tevurenlaan 168/b.9 1150 Brussels	32 2 776 01 00
Black Sea Trade & Development Bank (BSTDB)	Greece	1 Komninon str. 54624 Thessaloniki	(30) 310-290-400
Brazilian Development Bank	Brazil	Av. República do Chile, 100 - Centro 20031-917 - Rio de Janeiro - RJ	(21) 2277-7447
BRE Bank	Poland	Ul. Senatorska 18 00-950 Warszawa	(0 22) 829 00 00
Business Development Bank of Canada	Canada	BDC Building 5 Place Ville Marie, Suite 400 Montreal (Quebec) H3B 5E7	1 877 232-2269
Caisse Nationale de Credit Agricole	Morocco	12 avenue d'Alger B.P. 49 Rabat	(00212 7) 725920
Caribbean Development Bank (CDB)	Barbados	P.O. Box 408 Wildey, St. Michael	246431 1600
CDC Capital Partners	England	One Bessborough Gardens London SW1V 2JQ	44 (0)20 7828 4488
Centenary Rural Development Bank Ltd.	Uganda	Plot 7, Entebbe Road, P.O. Box 1892, Kampala	(00256 41) 251276
Central American Bank for Economic Integration (CABEI)	Honduras	Apartado Postal 772 Tegucigalpa, MDC	(502) 331-1260

WEB/E-MAIL	Year	Government Owned	Loans & Guarantees	Equity	Insurance	Technical Assistance	Institution Type
	1981	X	X				National
Web: www.boad.org E-mail: boadsiege@boad.org	1973		X	X		X	Regional
Web: www.bmi-sbi.be E-mail: info@bmi-sbi.be	1971		X	X		X	Bilateral
Web: www.bstdb.gr E-mail: info@bstdb.org	1998		X	X		X	Regional
Web: www.bndes.gov.br	1952	X	X	X		X	National
Web: www.brebank.com.pl E-mail: redakcjaportalu@brebank.com.pl	1986		X	X			National
Web: www.bdc.ca E-mail: info@bdc.ca	1944		X	X			National
	1961	X	X				National
Web: www.caribank.org E-mail: info@caribank.org	1969		X	X		X	Regional
Web: www.cdcgroup.com E-mail: info@cdcgroup.com	1948		X	X			Global Bilateral
	1983		X				National
Web: www.bcie.org E-mail: webmail-gt@bcie.org	1961		X				Regional

ORGANIZATION	COUNTRY	ADDRESS	PHONE
Central Bank of Swaziland	Swaziland	P.O. Box 546 Mbabane	268 404 3221/5
China Development Bank	China	Rm 3307-08 One International Finance Ctr, I Harbour View St Central Hong Kong	(852) 2801 6218
Compania Espanola de Financiacion del Desarrollo	Spain	Príncipe de Vergara, n° 132, planta 12 28002 Madrid	91 7454480
Corporacion Andina de Fomento (CAF)	Venezuela	P.O. Box Carmelitas 5086 Ave. Luis Roche, Torre CAF, Altamira, Caracas	(58212) 209-2111
The Cyprus Development Bank	Cyprus	P.O. Box 21415, CY-1508 Nicosia	357-22846500
Czech-Moravian Guarantee and Development Bank	Czech Republic	Jeruzalémská 964/4, 110 00 Praha 1	420 255 721 111
The Danish International Investment Funds	Denmark	Bremerholm 4 DK-1069 Copenhagen K	453-363-7500
Ducroire/Delcredere	Belgium	Square de Meeus 40-1000	32 2 509 42 11
Deutsche Gesellschaft (DEG)	Germany	Dag-Hammarskjold-Weg 1 – 5 P.O. Box 5180 65726 Eschborn	496196/790
Development Bank of Ethiopia	Ethiopia	Josip Broz Tito Str., P.O. Box 1900, Addis Ababa	(00251 1) 511188
Development Bank of Japan	Japan	9-1, Otemachi 1-chome, Chiyoda-ku, Tokyo, Japan 100-0004	03-3244-1900
Development Bank of Kazakhstan	Kazakhstan	Samal 12, Astana Tower, 16-18 Floors, Astana 473000	7 (3172) 580260

WEB/E-MAIL	Year	Government Owned	Loans & Guarantees	Equity	Insurance	Technical Assistance	Institution Type
Web: www.centralbank.org.sz E-mail: info@centralbank.org.sz	1974		X				National
Web: www.cdb.com.cn	1994		X			X	National
Web: www.cofides.es E-mail: cofides@cofides.es	1988		X	X		X	Bilateral
Web: www.caf.com E-mail: infocaf@caf.com	1966		X	X			Regional
Web: www.cdb.com.cy E-mail: info@cdb.com.cy	1963		X	X			National
Web: www.cmzrb.cz E-mail: info@cmzrb.cz	1992		X	X		X	National
Web: www.ifu.dk E-mail: ifu@ifu.dk	1967	X	X	X			Bilateral
Web: www.ondd.be	1921		X		X		Bilateral
Web: www.gtz.de E-mail: international.services@gtz.de	1975	X	X			X	Global Bilateral
	1970	X	X				National
Web: www.dbj.go.jp	1999		X			X	National
Web: www.kdb.kz E-mail: info@kdb.kz	2000	X	X				National

ORGANIZATION	COUNTRY	ADDRESS	PHONE
Development Bank of Mauritius	Mauritius	Port-Louis (Head Office) Chaussée	(230) 208 0241
Development Bank of Samoa	Samoa	P.O. Box 1232, Apia	(685) 22 861
Development Bank of Seychelles	Seychelles	P.O. Box 217 Victoria	(248) 224 471
Development Bank of Singapore (DBS)	Singapore	6 Shenton Way, DBS Building Singapore 068809	65 6327 2265
Development Bank of Solomon Islands	Solomon Islands	P.O. Box 911 Honiara	(00677) 21595
Development Bank of Southern Africa	South Africa	1258 Lever Road, Headway Hill, Mirand	011-313-3911
Development Bank of the Philippines	Philippines	Sen. Gil J. Puyat Avenue corner Makati Avenue, Makati City	(632) 815-0904
Development Bank of Turkey	Turkey	Izmir cad. No. 35 Kizilay – Ankara	90 312 418 1515
Eastern and Southern African Trade and Development Bank (PTA)	Kenya	22nd and 23rd Floors, NSSF Building, Bishops Road, Nairobi	254 2 2712250
European Bank for Reconstruction and Development (EBRD)	England	One Exchange Square London EC2A 2JN	442-073-386-372
European Investment Bank (EIB)	England	100, boulevard Konrad Adenauer L - 2950 Luxembourg	30 (2) 235-0070
Export Development Canada (EDC)	Canada	151 O'Connor Ottawa, Canada KIA 1K3	613 598 2500
Farmers Bank for Investment and Rural Development	Sudan	P.O. Box 11984 Khartoum	(00249 11) 774960
Fiji Development Bank	Fiji	Kings Road, P.O. Box 317, Nausori	679 347 7277

WEB/E-MAIL	Year	Government Owned	Loans & Guarantees	Equity	Insurance	Technical Assistance	Institution Type
Web: www.dbm-ltd.com E-mail: dbm@intnet.mu	1964		X				National
Web: www.dbsamoa.ws E-mail: falefal@dbsamoa.ws	1974		X	X		X	National
Web: www.dbs.sc E-mail: dbsmd@seychelles.net	1977	50%	X				National
Web: www.dbs.com E-mail: corpbank@dbs.com	1968		X	X			Quasi
E-mail: dbsi@welkam.solomon.com.sb	1978	X	X	X		X	National
Web: www.dbsa.org	1983		X	X	X		National
Web: www.devbankphil.com.ph E-mail: info@devbankphil.com.ph	1947		X				National
Web: www.tkb.com.tr E-mail: tkbhaberlesme@tkb.com.tr	1975	X	X			X	National
Web: www.ptabank.org E-mail: official@ptabank.org	1985		X	X		X	Regional
Web: www.ebrd.com E-mail: generalenquiries@ebrd.com	1991		X	X			Regional
Web: www.eib.org E-mail: info@eib.org	2000		X	X			Regional
Web: www.edc.ca E-mail: export@edc.ca	1995		X	X	X		Bilateral
	1998		X				National
Web: www.fijidevelopmentbank.com E-mail: isoa@fdb.com.fj	1967		X				National

ORGANIZATION	COUNTRY	ADDRESS	PHONE
Finanzierungsgarantie - Gesellschaft (FGG)	Austria	Gasometer A, Guglgasse 6, 1110 Vienna	43-1-501 75-0
Finnfund	Finland	P.O. Box 391 FIN-00121 Helsinki	358 (9) 348-434
Gabonese Bank of Development	Gabon	Alfred Marche Street Box 05, Libreville	241 76 24 89
German Investment and Development Company (DEG)	Germany	Belvederestrasse 40 D-50933 Koln	(02 21) 49 86-0
Government Development Bank for Puerto Rico	Puerto Rico	P.O. Box 42001, San Juan, PR 00940-2001	(787) 722-2525
Hungarian Development Bank	Hungary	1051 Budapest, Nádor u. 31., Levélcím: 1365 Budapest, 5. PF. 678	428-1400, 428-1500
Industrial Development Bank	Israel	Asia House. 4 Weizman St., Tel-Aviv 61334	972-3-6972772
Industrial Development Bank of India	India	IDBI Tower Cuffe Parade Bombay 400 005	(91 22) 218-9111
Industrial Development Bank of Turkey	Turkey	Meclisi Mebusan Caddesi No:161, 80040 Findikli-Istanbul	(212) 334 50 50
Industrial Development Corporation (IDC)	South Africa	19 Fredman Drive Sandown 2196	27 (0) 11 269-3000
Industrial Investment Bank of India	India	19, Netaji Subhas Road Calcutta – 700001	220-9941
Inter-American Development Bank	United States	1300 New York Avenue, NW Washington, DC 20577	202-623-1000
Inter-American Investment Corporation	United States	1300 New York Avenue, NW Washington, DC 20577	202-623-3900

WEB/E-MAIL	Year	Government Owned	Loans & Guarantees	Equity	Insurance	Technical Assistance	Institution Type
Web: www.fgg.at E-mail: fgg@fgg.at	1969		X			X	Bilateral
Web: www.finnfund.fi E-mail: finnfund@finnfund.fi	1980		X	X			Bilateral
Web: www.bgd-gabon.com E-mail: infos@bgd-gabon.com	1960		X				National
Web: www.deginvest.de E-mail: businessrelations@deginvest.de	1962		X	X	X	X	Global Bilateral
Web: www.gdb-pur.com E-mail: gdbcomm@bgf.gobierno.pr		X	X				National
Web: www.mfb.hu E-mail: bank@mfb.hu	1991						National
Web: www.dbank.co.il	1957	X	X				National
Web: www.idbi.com	1964	51%	X	X		X	National
Web: www.tskb.com.tr E-mail: info@tskb.com.tr	1950		X				National
Email: callcentre@idc.com.za	1940		X				Regional
Web: www.iibiltd.com E-mail: iibiho@vsnl.com	1956	X	X	X		X	National
Web: www.iadb.org E-mail: webmaster@iadb.com	1959		X	X			Regional
Web: www.iadb.org/iic E-mail: iicmail@iadb.org	1996		X	X			Regional

ORGANIZATION	COUNTRY	ADDRESS	PHONE
International Bank for Reconstruction and Development (IBRD)	United States	1818 H Street, NW Washington, DC 20433	202-473-1000
International Finance Corporation (IFC)	United States	2121 Pennsylvania Avenue, NW Washington, DC 20433	202-477-1234
Islamic Development Bank	Saudi Arabia	P.O. Box 5925 Jeddah 21432	(9662) 6361400
Japan Bank for International Cooperation (JBIC)	Japan	4-1 Ohtemachi 1 –chome, Chiyoda-ku Tokyo 100-8144	86-10-6505-8989
The Korea Development Bank	Korea	16-3, Youido-dong, Yongdeungpo-ku, Seoul 150-973	82-2-787-7407
Kreditanstalt fur Wiederaufbau	Germany	Postfach 11 11 41 D-60046 Frankfurt	49 (69) 74 310
Local Development Bank	Algeria	5 Rue Gaci Amar Staoueli, 42000 W. Tipaza	213-239-28-06
Nacional Financiera	Mexico	Av. Insurgentes Sur 1971 Col. Guadelupe Inn 01020	01 55 53 25 64 00
National Commercial Bank of Dominica	Dominica	NCB Head Office 64 Hillsborough Street Roseau	1 767 448 4401
National Development Bank of Botswana	Botswana	Development House, Plot 1123 The Mall, Gabarone	09 267 352801
National Development Bank	Sri Lanka	40 Navam Mawatha Colombo 2	94 1 437701
Netherlands Development Finance Company (FMO)	Netherlands	Koningskade 40 2596 AA The Hague	31 070 314 96 54
Nigerian Agricultural and Cooperative Bank Ltd.	Nigeria	Yakubu Gowon Way PMB 2155 Kaduna	(00234 62) 234957

WEB/E-MAIL	Year	Government Owned	Loans & Guarantees	Equity	Insurance	Technical Assistance	Institution Type
Web: www.worldbank.org	1946		X	X	X	X	Global Multilateral
Web: www.ifc.org E-mail: info@ifc.org	1956		X	X			Global Multilateral
Web: www.isdb.org E-mail: idbarchives@isdb.org.sa	1975		X			X	Region to Region
Web: www.jbic.go.jp	1999		X				Bilateral
Web: www.kdb.co.kr	1954	X	X	X		X	National
Web: www.kfw.de E-mail: kfw.asa@kfw.de	1948		X	X			Bilateral
							National
Web: www.nafin.com E-mail: info@nafin.gob.mx	1934	X	X	X		X	National
Web: www.ncbdominica.com E-mail: chairman@ncb.dm	1978		X				National
Web: www.ndb.bw							National
E-mail: info@ndb.org	1979	X	X	X	X		National
Web: www.fmo.nl E-mail: info@fmo.nl	1970	51%	X	X		X	Global Bilateral
	1973	X	X				National

ORGANIZATION	COUNTRY	ADDRESS	PHONE
Nordic Development Fund (NDF)	Finland	Fabianinkatu 34 P.O. Box 185, FIN-00171 Helsinki	358 9 1800451
Nordic Environment Finance Corporation	Finland	Fabianinkatu 34 P.O. Box 249 FIN-00171 Helsinki	358 9 18001
Nordic Investment Bank (NIB)	Finland	Fabianinkatu 34 P.O. Box 249 FIN-00171 Helsinki	358 9 18001
NORDSAD	Zambia	Anglo American Building, 6th Floor 74 Independence Avenue P.O. Box 35577 10101 Lusaka	260 1 255663
North American Development Bank	United States	203 South St. Mary's, Suite 300 San Antonio, TX 78205	210-231-8000
Oman Development Bank	Oman	P.O. Box 309 Muscat	(968) 738021
Overseas Private Investment Corporation (OPIC)	United States	1100 New York Avenue, NW Washington, DC 20527	202-336-8799
Portuguese Agency of Support for Development (APAD)	Portugal	Tivoli Forum Av. of the Freedom, n° 180-A 1250-146 Lisbon	21 317 73 00
Principal Bank for Development and Agricultural Credit	Egypt	110 Qasr Al-Aini Street Cairo	(0020 2) 3563873
Romania Development Bank	Romania		
Russian Regional Development Bank	Russia	129594 Moscow, Sushchevsky Val, 65	095-933-03-43
Small Industries Development Bank of India	India	10/10 Madan Mohan Malviya Marg Luckno – 226 001	2209517-21

WEB/E-MAIL	Year	Government Owned	Loans & Guarantees	Equity	Insurance	Technical Assistance	Institution Type
Web: www.ndf.fi E-mail: info@ndf.fi	1989		X	X			Bilateral
Web: www.nefco.org E-mail: info@nefco.fi	1990		X	X			Region to Region
Web: www.nibank.org	1976		X				Bilateral
Web: www.norsad.org E-mail: norsad@norsad.org	1991		X				Region to Region
Web: www.nadb.org E-mail: webmaster@nadb.org	1993		X				Regional
							National
Web: www.opic.gov E-mail: info@opic.gov	1971	X	X	X	X		Bilateral
E-mail: apad@apad.pt	2000		X	X	X	X	Bilateral
	1931	X	X				National
Web: www.brd.ro							National
Web: www.vbrr.ru E-mail: bank@vbrr.ru	1996	X	X	X			National
Web: www.sidbi.com	1990		X	X		X	National

ORGANIZATION	COUNTRY	ADDRESS	PHONE
Societa Italiana per le Imprese all'Estero (SIMEST)	Italy	Corso Vittorio Emanuele II, n. 323 00186 Rome	3906 686351
Societe Internationale Financiere pour les Investissements et le Developpement en Afrique (SIFIDA)	Switzerland	22 rue François-Perréard, POB 310, 1225 Chêne-Bourg / Geneva	(41) 22 869 20 00
Swedfund International	Sweden	Sveavägen 24-26 Stockholm	46 8 725 94 00
Trade and Development Bank of Mongolia	Mongolia	Khudaldaany gudamj-7, Ulaanbaatar-11	(976-1)-321171
United Nations Development Programme	United States	One United Nations Plaza New York, NY 10017	212-906-5558
United States Agency for International Development (USAID)	United States	Ronald Reagan Building Washington, DC 20523	202-712-4810
Yemen Bank for Reconstruction & Development	Yemen	P.O. Box 541, Sana'a	967 1 270483

WEB/E-MAIL	Year	Government Owned	Loans & Guarantees	Equity	Insurance	Technical Assistance	Institution Type
Web: www.simest.it E-mail: info@simest.it	1991		X	X			Bilateral
Web: www.sifida.com E-mail: headoffice@sifida.com	1970		X	X			Quasi
Web: www.swedfund.se E-mail: info@swedfund.se		X	X	X			Bilateral
Web: www.tdbm.mn E-mail: tdbank@tdbm.mn	1990	70%	X				National
Web: www.undp.org E-mail: enquiries@undp.org			X	X		X	Global Multilateral
Web: www.usaid.gov E-mail: AandAOmbudsman@usaid.gov	1961	X	X		X		Bilateral
Web: www.ybrd.com.ye E-mail: info@ybrd.com.ye	1962	52%	X				National

Appendix K:
Selected Government-Backed Equity Funds

AGEN.	FUND	FUND MANAGER	ADDRESS
OPIC	Africa Growth Fund	Equator Overseas Services Limited	45 Glastonbury Boulevard Glastonbury, CT 06033 Tel: 860-633-9999
OPIC	Africa Millennium Fund	Savage Holdings LLC	1414 Avenue of the Americas Suite 1804 New York, NY 10019 Tel: 212-750-7400 fsavage@savageholdings.com
OPIC	Agribusiness Partners International	Agribusiness Management Company, LLC	America First Companies 11004 Farnam Street Omaha, NE 68102 Tel: 402-930-3060 bpetyon@am1st.com
OPIC	AIG Brunswick Millennium Fund	American International Group/Brunswick Capital Mgm	175 Water Street 24th Floor New York, NY 10038 Tel: 212-458-2156
OPIC	Allied Small Business Fund	Allied Capital Corp.	1919 Pennsylvania Ave. NW Washington, DC 20006 Tel: 202-973-6319
OPIC	Aqua International Partners Fund	Texas Pacific Group	345 California Street Suite 3300 San Francisco, CA 94104 Tel: 415-743-1570 jsylvia@texpac.com
OPIC	Asia Development Partners	Olympus Capital Holdings (Asia)	153 East 53rd Street 43rd Floor New York, NY 10022 Tel: 212-292-6531 dmintz@zbi.com
OPIC	Asia Pacific Growth Fund	Hambrecht & Quist Asia Pacific	156 University Ave Palo Alto, CA 94104 Tel: 650-838-8098

GEOGRAPHY	SIZE (Million USD)	SHORT DESCRIPTION
Sub-Saharan Africa	25	Mining, manufacturing, and financial services
Sub-Saharan Africa	350	Equity or quasi-equity securities of companies that work in the Infrastructure Sector and that operate in countries eligible for investment in sub-Saharan Africa
NIS/Baltics	95	Agriculture, food firms, infrastructure projects, privatizations, food storage, and distribution facilities
Russia, NIS and Baltics	288.5	Large infrastructure projects, Including power, transportation, natural resource development, and related industries
All OPIC countries	20	Basic manufacturing and service industries sponsored by qualifying U.S. small business
All OPIC countries	237.75	Operating and special-purpose companies involved in the treatment, bulk supply, and distribution of water in emerging market countries
Southeastern Asia	150	Telecommunications, consumer products, and financial services
Southeastern Asia	75.25	Light manufacturing, financial, construction, high-tech, and telecom services

AGEN.	FUND	FUND MANAGER	ADDRESS
OPIC	Bancroft Eastern Europe Fund	Bancroft UK, Ltd.	7/11 Kensington High Street London W8 5NP Tel: 44-20-7368-3347 martin@bancroftgroup.com
OPIC	Emerging Europe Fund	TDA Capital Partners, Inc.	15 Valley Drive Greenwich, CT 06831 Tel: 203-625-4525 jhapler@templeton.com
OPIC	Global Environment Emerging Markets Fund I	GEF Management	1225 Eye Street NW Suite 900 Washington, DC 20005 Tel: 202-789-4500
OPIC	Global Environment Emerging Markets Fund II	GEF Management	1226 Eye Street NW Suite 900 Washington, DC 20005 Tel: 202-789-4500
OPIC	The Great Circle Fund, L.P.	Great Circle Capital, LLC	2039 Palmer Avenue Larchmont, NY 10538 Tel: 914-834-7000 Rburke@GreatCircleCapital.com
OPIC	India Private Equity Fund	Indocean Capital Advisers	Oppenheimer Tower, World Financial Center New York, NY 10281 Tel: 212-667-8190 michele.buchignani@ us.cibc.com
OPIC	Inter-Arab Investment Fund	InterArab Management, Inc.	National Securities Building, P.O. Box 941430, Amman 11194, Jordan Tel: 962-6-566-2481
OPIC	Modern Africa Growth And Investment Fund	Modern Africa Fund Managers LLC	1100 Connecticut Avenue, NW Suite 500 Washington, DC 20036 Tel: 202-887-1772 SDCASHIN@aol.com
OPIC	New Century Capital Partners	NCH Advisers	712 Fifth Avenue 46th Floor New York, NY 10019 Tel: 212-641-3229
OPIC	Newbridge Andean Partners	ACON Investments, LLC	1133 Connecticut Avenue, NW Suite 700 Washington, DC 20036 Tel: 202-861-6060 ext 103

GEOGRAPHY	SIZE (Million USD)	SHORT DESCRIPTION
Central Europe/ Baltic republics	90.8525	Distribution networks, basic manufacturing, consumer goods, and related service networks
Central and Eastern Europe	60	Sustainable development industries
All OPIC countries	66.7	Environment-oriented sectors relating to the developing, financing, operating, or supplying of infrastructure relating to clean energy and water
All OPIC countries	120	Environment-oriented sectors relating to the developing, financing, operating, or supplying of infrastructure relating to clean energy and water
All OPIC countries	200	Equity and quasi-equity investments in companies operating in the maritime transportation, logistics, and services industries that are new, expanding, or in the process of being restructured or privatized
India	140	Consumer goods, basic manufacturing, banking, computer, and related industries
Jordan, West Bank/ Gaza, Oman	45	Basic industries that create intra- and inter-regional synergies
Sub-Saharan Africa	117	Focus on manufacturing, telecommunications, and natural resources
Former Soviet Countries	250	Diversified manufacturing, consumer products, and financial and service industries
South America	160	Diversified manufacturing and financial and service industries

AGEN.	FUND	FUND MANAGER	ADDRESS
OPIC	Poland Partners	Landon Butler & Company	700 Thirteenth Street, NW Suite 1150 Washington, DC 20005 Tel: 202-737-7300
OPIC	Russia Partners A	Sigular Guff & Co.	630 Fifth Avenue, 16th Floor New York, NY 10111 Tel: 212-332-5108
OPIC	Russia Partners B	Sigular Guff & Co.	631 Fifth Avenue, 16th Floor New York, NY 10111 Tel: 212-332-5108
OPIC	Soros Investment Capital Ltd.	Soros Private Funds Management LLC	Tel: 212-333-9727
OPIC	South America Private Equity Growth	Baring Latin America Partners LLC	230 Park Avenue New York, NY 10169 Tel: 212-309-1795
OPIC	ZM Africa Investment Fund	Zephyr Management LP	320 Park Avenue New York, NY 10022 Tel: 212-508-9410
IFC	Advent Central and Eastern Europe II	Advent International Corporation	75 State Street Boston, MA 02109 Tel: 617-951-9788 wbalz@adventinternational.com
IFC	Advent Latin American Private Equity Fund II	Advent International	75 State Street Boston, MA 02109 Tel: 617-951-9788 wbalz@adventinternational.com
IFC	AfriCap	AfriCap MicroVentures, Ltd	365 Bay Street, Suite 600 Toronto, Ontario, Canada M5H 2V1 Tel: (416) 362-9670 sharpe@calmeadow.com
IFC	Africa Infrastructure Fund	Emerging Markets Partnsherhip	Paul V. Applegarth 2001 Pennsylvania Avenue, NW Suite 1100 Washington, DC 20006 Tel: 202-331-9051
IFC	The AIG Emerging Europe Infrastructure Fund	Emerging Markets Partnership (EMP)	43-45 Portman Square London W1H 9TH 44-(0)207-886-3600

GEOGRAPHY	SIZE (Million USD)	SHORT DESCRIPTION
Poland	63.5	Manufacturing, consumer goods, distribution networks, merchandising, and related service networks
Russia	105	Natural resource-related companies, telecommunications, light manufacturing, and consumer products and services
Russia	50	Natural resource-related companies, telecommunications, light manufacturing, and consumer products and services
Balkans	200	Provide equity capital to Southeast Europe as part of the international recovery effort
South America	180	Diversified manufacturing and financial and service industries
South Africa	120	Diversified manufacturing and financial and service industries
Central and Eastern Europe	150	Medium-sized enterprises in the region
Latin America	250	Later-stage businesses with limited exposure to fast-growing telecommunications
Africa	15	Make investments in the form of equity and quasi-equity in about ten well-performing MFIs in Africa
Africa	500	Infrastructure projects and infrastructure-related industries
Central and Eastern Europe	1,000	Infrastructure-related industries

AGEN.	FUND	FUND MANAGER	ADDRESS
IFC	All Asia Growth Ventures - I	Asian Venture Capital Managers and All AsiaCapital Managers	7th Floor, All AsiaCapital Center 105 Paseo De Roxas Makati City 1200, Philippines Tel: (63-2) 818-3211
IFC	Bancroft II	Bancroft Group L.P.	251 Brompton Road London SW3 2EP United Kingdom Tel: (44) 207 823 9222 martin@bancroftgroup.com
IFC	Baring Mexico Private Equity Fund	Baring Private Equity Partners	Homero No. 440 9 Piso Desp. 901-901 Col. Polanco 11560 Mexico, DF Tel: +(5255) 52 54 32 80
IFC	Baring Vostok Private Equity Fund	Baring Vostok Capital Partners	10 Uspenski Pereolok Moscow, Russia 103006
IFC	Black Sea Fund	Global Finance	14 Filikis Eterias Square, 10673 Athens, Greece Tel +30-210 7208 900
IFC	Brazilian Corporate Governance Fund	Bradesco Templeton Asset Management	Av. Brig. Faria Lima, 1461-10 Andar 01 481-900 Sao Paolo, Brazil Tel: 55 11 3039 3721 stephen@bradescotempleton .com.br
IFC	Capital Alliance Private Equity Fund	Africa Capital Alliance	P.O. Box 55955 Northlands 2116, South Africa Tel: (011) 27-11-268-6911
IFC	Central America Growth Fund	Provident Group	Armando Gonzalez Tel: 212-601-2400 agonzalez@provident-group. com
IFC	China Private Equity Fund	China International Capital Corporation	28/F, China World Trade Tower 2 1 Jian-guo-men-wai Avenue Beijing, China Tel: (86) 10 6505 8165
IFC	Colombia Capital Growth Fund	TCW/Latin America Partners, LLC	LSilva@ifc.org

GEOGRAPHY	SIZE (Million USD)	SHORT DESCRIPTION
Phillipines	70	Investments in early development companies and those with fairly clear prospects of going public in the short term
Central and Eastern Europe	Euro 250	Diversifies companies with focus on later-stage business
Mexico	50-60	Minority equity stakes in unlisted Mexican middle-market enterprises
Primarily in Russia	150	Investment in private sector infrastructure and natural resource development
CIS	50	Medium-sized enterprises in the Black Sea region
Brazil	100	Mid-sized Brazilian companies committed to implementing the highest international standards of corporate governance
Nigeria	30-40	Joint venture investments with foreign companies seeking to establish or reestablish operations in Nigeria
Central America	50	Target medium-sized enterprises with long-term growth and capital appreciation potential
China	100	Established companies with substantial operations in China
Colombia	225	Investments in Colombian middle-market companies that are strategically placed and in need of risk capital

AGEN.	FUND	FUND MANAGER	ADDRESS
IFC	Croatia Capital Partnership	CCP Ventures Ltd.	Mr. Ante Cicin-Sain Pantovcak 104c 10000 Zagreb, Croatia Tel/Fax: (385)1-48-22-304
IFC	Darby-BBVA Latin American Private Equity Fund	Darby Overseas Investments	1133 Connecticut Avenue, NW Suite 400 Washington DC 20036 Tel: 202-872-0500
IFC	Futuregrowth Empowerment Fund	Futuregrowth Asset Management (Pty) Limited	Tel: (27-21) 659-5418 jdebruyn@futuregrowth.co.za
IFC	Hambrecht & Quist Korea Growth and Restructuring Fund	H&Q Asia Pacific	156 University Avenue Palo Alto, CA 94301 Tel: 650-838-8088
IFC	Icatu Equity Partners	Banco Icatu	Av. Presidente Wilson, 231 10. Andar Rio de Janeiro 20030-021 Tel: (21) 3804 8500
IFC	IndAsia Fund	IndAsia Fund Advisers AMP Asset Management	3, Scheherazade, Justice Vyas Road, Colaba Mumbai - 400 005 India
IFC	Korea Corporate Governance Fund	Zurich Scudder Investments, Inc.	345 Park Avenue 16th Floor New York, NY 10154
IFC	Macedonia SEAF	Small Enterprise Assistance Fund	Vladimir Pesevski Metropolit Teodosij Gologanov 28 1000 Skopje, Macedonia Tel: 389 2 137 178
IFC	Maghreb Invest Fund	Maghreb Invest Gestion	Tel: 202-473-7711 Fax: 202-974-4384
IFC	Mexico Partners Trust	Grupo Financiero Inbursa and Lazard Freres & Co	
IFC	Patagonia Fund	Merchant Bankers, Asociados S.A. (MBA), and Elektra Fleming	c/o Patterson Belknap Webb & Tyler LLP New York, NY 10036 Tel: 212-336-2000
IFC	The Private Equity/ Venture Cap Fund	Quadriga Capital Russia	Tel: 202 473-0696 sandrews2@ifc.org

GEOGRAPHY	SIZE (Million USD)	SHORT DESCRIPTION
Croatia	25-30	SMEs
Latin America	250	Export/cross-border oriented companies and domestic market/consolidation-oriented companies
South Africa	54	Targeted at black empowerment and developmental investment opportunities in South Africa
Korea	140	SMEs, with a focus on technology-related firms
Brazil	200	Influential minority equity positions in Brazilian mid-sized enterprises
India	100	Companies that have developed under the protected domestic environment and now need help to adapt to the more liberalized environment
Korea	150	Medium-sized Korean companies seeking to implement the highest standards of corporate governance
Macedonia	12.5	Support viable SME equity investments
Morocco	30	Small- and medium-sized companies to support expansion and diversification, including restructuring
Mexico	250	Help Mexican middle-market enterprises restructure
Argentina	55	Mid-sized Argentine companies
Primarily Russia	140	Diversified manufacturing and financial and service industries

AGEN.	FUND	FUND MANAGER	ADDRESS
IFC	Proa Fondo de Inversion de Desarrollo de Empresas	Moneda Asset Management S.A.	Av. Isidora Goyenechea 3621, Piso 8 Santiago 6760412, Chile Tel: (56-2) 337 7900
IFC	Renewable Energy and Efficiency Fund	Energy Investors Funds, Environmental Enterprises Assistance Fund, and E & Co	K. R. Locklin 727 15th Street, NW, 11th Floor Washington, DC 20005 Tel: 202-783-4419
IFC	Scudder Latin American Power Fund	Scudder, Stevens and Clark	
IFC	SEAF Trans-Balkan Fund	Small Enterprise Assistance Fund	20-22 Zlaten Rog St., Floor 5th kv. Lozents Sofia 1407, Bulgaria Tel: (359-2) 917 4950
IFC	SEF Central Asian Small Equity Investment Fund	Small Enterprise Assistance Fund	1100 17th Street, NW Suite 1101 Washington, DC 20036 Fax: 202-737-5536
IFC	South Africa Junior Mining Fund	Decorum Capital Partners	Tel: 27 11 644-2458
IFC	South Africa Private Equity Fund, L.P.	Brait Capital Partners Limited	Private Bag X1 Northlands 2116 Johannesburg, South Africa Tel: +27(11) 507-1000
IFC	TCW/ICICI India Private Equity Fund	TCW/ICICI Investment Partners, L.L.C.	Raheja Plaza, 4th Floor, 17 Commissariat Road, D'Souza Circle, Bangalore - 560 025 India
IFC	TCW LA Fund	TCW/Latin American Partners LLC	Gary Ritelny Tel: 212-707-1216
IFC	Terra Capital Fund	Dynamo Administracao de Recursos Ltda.	
IFC	Thai Equity Fund	Lombard/Pacific Partners	600 Montgomery Street 36th Floor San Francisco, CA 94111 Tel: 415-397-5900
IFC	Tuninvest Private Equity Fund	SIPAREX	139, rue de Vendome 69477 Lyon, France Tel +(33) 04 72 83 23 23

GEOGRAPHY	SIZE (Million USD)	SHORT DESCRIPTION
Chile	50	Medium-sized unlisted Chilean companies
Global	110 Equity, 100 Debt	Renewable energy (both grid-connected and off-grid) and energy efficiency projects in developing countries
Latin America	150-250	Private sector power projects located in several countries
Balkans	25	SMEs with demonstrated growth potential in the Balkan region
Central Asia	20	Specifically at SMEs, strong focus on agribusiness and agricultural processing
Southern and Central Africa	250	Invest in prefeasibility stage (after the resource has been identified), feasibility study stage, and early stages of production in junior mining projects
South Africa	350	Growth companies
India	125	Unlisted equity or equity-related securities issued by medium-sized, later-stage, and some early-stage companies
Latin America	100	Latin American middle-market private companies
Latin America	20-30	Unlisted private companies undertaking sustainable uses of biological diversity
Thailand	425	Companies and financial institutions that are in need of financial restructuring
Tunisia	25	Unlisted Tunisian companies

AGEN.	FUND	FUND MANAGER	ADDRESS
IFC	Turkish Private Equity Fund	Turk Venture Partners LLC	igen@ifc.org.
IFC	ZN Mexico Capital Growth Fund	ZN Management Ltd	320 Park Avenue New York, NY 10022 Tel: 212-508-9400
IIC	Aureos Central America Fund	AUREOS Capital Limited	Erik Peterson, General Manager Tel: + 506 211 1511 Fax: + 506 211 1525 epeterson@aureos.com
IIC	The Caribbean Investment Fund	ICWI Group Limited	28 Barbados Avenue (5) Jamaica Tel: (876) 926-2925
IIC	CEA Latin American Communications Partners Fund	Communications Equity Associates (CEA)	101 East Kennedy Boulevard Suite 3300 Tampa, FL 33602 Tel: 813-226-8844
IIC	Central American Banking Growth Fund	Darby Overseas Inv. Ltd, The Netherlands Dev. Bank, Central American Bank for Economic Integration	BBVA Bancomer Montes Urales 620, 3 piso Col. Lomas de Chapultepec Mexico, D.F. 11000 Tel. (5255) 5325-8054
IIC	The Central America Growth Fund	Provident Group Limited	45 Broadway, 23rd Floor New York, NY 10006 Tel: 212-742-4900
IIC	The Cori Capital Partners Fund	Violy, Byorum & Partners Holdings; CDPQ Capital International	712 Fifth Avenue New York, NY 10019 Tel: 212-707-1200 contact@vbp.com
IIC	Latin American Private Equity Fund II	Advent International	75 State Street Boston, MA 02109 Tel: 617-951-9788
IIC	Multinational Industrial Fund	Wamex, S.A.	
IIC	Negocios Regionales Fondo de Inversión Privado		

GEOGRAPHY	SIZE (Million USD)	SHORT DESCRIPTION
Turkey	40	A diversified portfolio in industries driven by growth, exports, and deregulation
Mexico	50-75	Mexican SMEs with sales no greater than US$100 million
Central America, Panama, and DR		Later-stage SMEs
Caribbean Region	150	SMEs
Latin America and Caribbean	100	Small and middle-market media and telecommunication companies
Central America and Panama	60	Financial sector
Central America and Panama	50	Retailing, food and beverage processing, manufacturing, media and telecom, tourism, and differentiated export products
Latin America	300	SMEs in industries undergoing regional and/or global consolidation
Brazil, Argentina, and Mexico	500	Middle-market growth-oriented companies
Mexico	80	Mexican companies entering into joint ventures with foreign companies to generate exports
Chile	23.5	SMEs

Appendix L: Selected Export Credit Agencies

OECD COUNTRIES

Country	Name of ECA
Australia	Export Finance and Insurance Corporation (EFIC)
Austria	Oesterreichische Kontrollbank Aktiengesellschaft (OeKB)
Belgium	Office National du Ducroire/National Delcrederendienst (ONDD)
Canada	Export Development Canada (EDC)
Czech Republic	Czech Export Bank
Czech Republic	Exportni garancni a pjist ovaci spolecnost, a.s. (EGAP)
Denmark	Eksport Kredit Fonden (EKF)
Finland	Finnvera plc
France	Compagnie Francaise d. Assurance pour le Commerce Exterieur (Coface)
Germany	Hermes Kreditversicherungs-Aktiengesellschaft AG (Hermes)
Germany	Kreditanstlt für Wiederaufbau (KfW)
Greece	Export Credit Insurance Organization (ECIO)
Hungary	Hungarian Export Credit Insurance Ltd. (MEHIB)
Italy	Instituto per i Servizi Assicurativi del Commercio Estero (SACE)
Japan	Japan Bank For International Cooperation (JBIC)
Korea	Korea Eximbank
Korea	Korea Export Insurance Corporation
Netherlands	Atradius

PE = Preexport

ST = Short-Term Post Export

MLTPE = Medium- to Long-Term Post Export

PF = Project Finance

Internet Address	Programs			
	PE	ST	MLTPE	PF
www.efic.gov.au		X	X	
www.oekb.co.at		X	X	X
www.ducroire.be www.delcredere.be		X	X	X
www.edc.ca		X	X	X
www.ceb.cz			X	
www.egap.cz	X	X	X	
www.ekf.dk			X	X
www.finnvera.fi		X	X	X
www.coface.com www.cofacerating.com			X	X
www.hermes-kredit.com		X	X	X
www.kfw.de			X	X
www.oaep.gr		X		X
www.mehib.hu/english	X	X	X	
www.isace.it		X	X	X
www.jbic.go.jp/english	X	X	X	X
	X	X	X	X
www.keic.or.kr	X	X	X	X
www.atradius.com				

OECD COUNTRIES (continued)

Country	Name of ECA
Norway	The Norwegian Guarantee Institute for Export Credits (GIEK)
Poland	Export Credit Insurance Corporation (KUKE)
Portugal	Companhia de Seguro de Creditos, S.A. (COSEC)
Portugal	Conselho de Garantias Financeiras (CGF)
Spain	Compania Espanola de Seguros de Credito a la Exportacion, S.A. (CESCE) or Spanish Export Credit Insurance Company
Sweden	Exportkreditnämnden (EKN)
Sweden	The Swedish Export Credit Corporation (SEK)
Sweden	The Swedish International Development Co-Operation (Sida)
Switzerland	Investment Risk Guarantee (IRG)
Switzerland	State Secretariat of Economic Affairs (SECO)
Switzerland	Swiss Export Risk Guarantee (ERG)
Turkey	Export Credit Bank of Turkey (Turk Eximbank)
United Kingdom	Export Credits Guarantee Department (ECGD)
United States	Export-Import Bank of the United States

NON OECD COUNTRIES

Country	Name of ECA
Argentina	Banco de Inversion y Comercio Exterior (BICE) or Foreign Commerce and Investment Bank
Brazil	Banco Nacional de Desenvolvimento Economico e Social (BNDES) or Brazilian Development Bank
Colombia	Banco de Comercio Exterior de Colombia (BANCOLDEX)
Colombia	SEGUREXPO
Croatia	HBOR
Cyprus	Export Credit Insurance Service (ECIS)
Ecuador	Corporacion Financiera Nacional (CFN) or

PE = Preexport

MLTPE = Medium- to Long-Term Post Export

ST = Short-Term Post Export

PF = Project Finance

Internet Address	Programs			
	PE	ST	MLTPE	PF
www.giek.no	X	X	X	
www.kuke.com.pl		X	X	X
www.cosec.pt	X	X	X	X
www.cesce.es		X	X	X
www.ekn.se		X	X	X
www.sek.se		X	X	X
www.sida.se				X
www.swiss-irg.com		X	X	X
		X	X	X
www.swiss-erg.com	X	X	X	
www.eximbank.gov.tr	X	X	X	X
www.ecgd.gov.uk		X	X	X
www.exim.gov	X	X	X	X

Internet Address	PE	ST	MLTPE	PF
www.bice.com.ar	X	X	X	X
www.bndes.gov.br/english	X	X	X	X
www.bancoldex.gov.co	X	X	X	X
www.segurexpo.com	X	X		
www.hbor.hr		X	X	X
www.cfn.fin.ec	X	X		X

NON OECD COUNTRIES (continued)

Country	Name of ECA
	National Finance Corporation
Hong Kong	Hong Kong Export Credit Insurance Corporation (HKECIC)
India	Export-Import Bank of India (Ex-Im India)
India	Export Credit Guarantee Corporation of India (ECGC)
Indonesia	Asuransi Ekspor Indonesia (ASEI)
Ireland	Export Credit Division
Israel	The Israel Foreign Trade Risks Insurance Corporation (IFTRIC)
Jamaica	National Export-Import Bank of Jamaica Limited (EXIM Bank)
Luxembourg	Societe Nationale de Credit et d'Investissement (SNCI)
Malaysia	Malaysia Export Credit Insurance Berhad (MECIB)
Mexico	Banco de Comercio Exterior, S.N.C. or Mexican Bank for Foreign Trade
New Zealand	Gerling NCM EXGO
Oman	Export Credit Guarantee Agency (ECGA)
Romania	Eximbank of Romania
Russia	RosEximBank (web site in Russian only)
Singapore	Export Insurance Corporation of Singapore Ltd. (ECICS)
Slovak	Export-Import Bank of Slovakia
Slovenia	Slovene Export Corporation (SEC)
Sri Lanka	Sri Lanka Export Credit Insurance Corporation (SLECIC)
Taiwan	The Export-Import Bank of the Republic of China (Eximbank)
Thailand	Export-Import Bank of Thailand
Trinidad	Trinidad and Tobago Export Credit Insurance Co. (EXCICO)
Uzbekistan	Uzbekinvest National Export-Import Insurance Company (UNIC)
Zimbabwe	Credit Insurance Zimbabwe

PE = Preexport

MLTPE = Medium- to Long-Term Post Export

ST = Short-Term Post Export

PF = Project Finance

Internet Address	Programs			
	PE	ST	MLTPE	PF
www.hkecic.com	X	X	X	
www.eximbankindia.com	X	X	X	X
www.ecgcindia.com	X	X	X	
www.asei.co.id	X	X		
	X	X	X	
www.iftric.co.il	X	X	X	X
www.eximbankja.com	X	X	X	X
www.snci.lu		X	X	X
www.mecib.com.my	X	X	X	X
www.bancomext.gob.mx	X	X	X	X
www.exgo.co.nz	X	X		
www.ecgaoman.com	X	X		
www.eximbank.ro	X	X	X	X
www.rosexim.com				
www.ecics.com.sg	X	X	X	
www.eximbanka.sk		X	X	
www.sid.si	X	X	X	X
www.tradenetsl.lk/slecic/#WAS				
www.eximbank.com.tw		X	X	
www.exim.go.th	X	X	X	X
	X	X		
	X			
www.firstre.com/other/insuranceDirectory /zimbabwe/credit.html				

REGIONAL AGENCIES THAT PROVIDE EXPORT FINANCING PROGRAMS

Country (N/A)	Name of ECA
	African Export-Import Bank (AFREXIM BANK)
	ATFP
	Banco Latinoamericano de Exportaciones (BLADEX)
	Central American Bank for Economic Integration (CABEI)
	Corporacion Andina de Fomento (CAF)
	European Bank for Reconstruction and Development (EBRD)
	Islamic Corporation for Insurance of Investments and Export Credits (ICIEC)
	Inter-American Development Bank (IADB)
	Inter-Arab Investment Guarantee Corporation (IAIGC)
	The Islamic Development Bank Group (ISDB)
	Organization of Eastern Caribbean States (OECS)
	Eastern and Southern African Trade and Development Bank (PTA BANK)

PE = Preexport

MLTPE = Medium- to Long-Term Post Export

ST = Short-Term Post Export

PF = Project Finance

| | Programs | | | |
Internet Address	PE	ST	MLTPE	PF
www.afreximbank.com	X	X	X	X
www.atfp.org.ae	X	X	X	
www.blx.com/eng.html		X		
www.bcie.org		X		X
www.caf.com		X	X	X
www.ebrd.com	X		X	X
www.iciec.com		X	X	
www.iadb.org	X	X	X	X
www.iaigc.org				X
www.isdb.org	X	X	X	X
www.oecs.org	X			X
www.ptabank.co.ke		X		X

Commonly Used Acronyms

DOC	United States Department of Commerce
DOD	Department of Defense
DOE	Department of Energy
EBRD	European Bank for Reconstruction and Development
EDA	Economic Development Agency
EPA	Environmental Protection Agency
EXIM	Export-Import Bank of the United States
FAS	Foreign Agricultural Service
IBRD	International Bank for Reconstruction and Development
IDB	Inter-American Development Bank
IFC	International Finance Corporation
IIC	International Investment Corporation
IMF	International Monetary Fund
ITA	International Trade Administration
MIGA	Multilateral Investment Guarantee Agency
NIST	National Institute of Standards and Technology
NMFS	National Marine Fisheries Service
NOAA	National Oceanic and Atmospheric Administration
NTIS	National Technical Information Service
OPIC	Overseas Private Investment Corporation
SBA	Small Business Administration
USAID	United States Agency for International Development
USDA	United States Department of Agriculture
USTDA	U.S. Trade and Development Agency
USTR	United States Trade Representative
WBG	World Bank Group
WTO	World Trade Organization

Commonly Used Terms

(Italicized terms are also defined in this section)

A/B Loan: A syndicated *loan* where commercial banks and other investors provide their own funds and take commercial risk, while a Multilateral Development Bank (MDB) remains the lender of record. B lenders benefit from implicit *political risk insurance* as host governments are less likely to *expropriate* or limit the foreign currency available to an MDB-supported project. The borrower benefits from the capital-raising efforts of the MDB and from lack of withholding taxes on the entire facility.

Acquisition Financing: Funds obtained for buying existing companies or projects, as opposed to *greenfield* financing. Traditionally government agencies have provided only acquisition financing in the context of a major program of expansion or rehabilitation. In general, privatization projects are likely to be supported more actively than private sector mergers and acquisitions.

Additionality: MDBs often have an explicit prohibition from competing with ("crowding out") private sector financial institutions. The additionality test performed early in the screening of a project is meant to assure the MDB that the private sector is not ready to fund the project on "acceptable terms." For *ECAs*, additionality can be satisfied if there is keen ECA-financed foreign competition for a contract.

Bilateral: Direct assistance from a donor country to a recipient country as opposed to *multilateral* aid. Examples of bilateral agencies include OPIC (US), FMO (Netherlands), and AfD (France).

Bond: A negotiable note or certificate that evidences indebtedness. It is a legal contract sold by one party, the issuer, to another, the investor, promising to repay the holder the face value of the bond plus interest at future dates. Bonds also are referred to as notes or debentures. The term *note* usually implies a shorter maturity than *bond.* Some bond issues are secured by a mortgage on a specific property, plant, or piece of equipment. In an emerging markets context, project finance bonds may carry *PRI* from an MDB or an insurer. Additionally, MDBs may provide parallel lending facilities or liquidity reserves in support of a bond issuance. Finally, MDBs may guarantee specific commercial and political risks; for example, to extend the maturity of the bond beyond what the market can do by itself.

BREACH OF CONTRACT: Default on any term or condition of a contract, such as a power purchase agreement or a concession, without legal excuse or compensation; for example, failure to make a payment when due. This is one of the basic *political risk insurance* coverages provided by insurers such as MIGA and OPIC.

BRETTON WOODS INSTITUTIONS: Founded in 1944 and named after the village of Bretton Woods, New Hampshire, the Bretton Woods Institutions were a culmination of international negotiations among 44 nations. It was here that the World Bank and the International Monetary Fund (IMF) were established to direct and manage the world economy after World War II.

BUYER CREDIT: A financial agreement in which a bank or an *ECA* makes a *loan* directly to an overseas purchaser to import goods and services. Disbursements may be made directly to the exporter or to the buyer as reimbursement for previous payments.

CAPITAL MARKETS: An all-encompassing term to include tradable debt (bonds), other securities, and *equity* (exchange traded shares) as distinct from private markets or bank loans. MDBs have recently become more active in assisting *emerging markets* borrowers and projects to access the international capital markets.

COFINANCING: Two groups of lenders (such as *ECAs* and MDBs) agree to a common legal structure that presents the buyer with one financial package rather than a series of separate loans (e.g., only one loan agreement is backed by *ECA* guarantees in proportion to each country's share of the export).

COMMERCIAL COVER: Applies to the financial loss incurred by an insured party as the result of the insolvency and/or partial or total default on payments by a private partner in a contract. Typically, *ECAs* provide commercial cover, while insurers do not.

COMMERCIAL INTEREST REFERENCE RATES (CIRR): The official lending rates of *ECAs* for *direct loans*. They are calculated monthly and are based on government *bonds* issued in the country's domestic market for the country's currency plus a spread. For example, the USD CIRR for long-term loans over 8.5 years is based on the 7-year U.S. Treasury bond yield plus 1 percent.

COMMERCIAL RISK: Risk of nonpayment by a buyer or borrower due to bankruptcy, insolvency, protracted default, and/or failure to accept goods shipped by the terms of the supply contract.

COMMITMENT FEE: The fee charged by a lender to compensate for committing funds, based on undisbursed balances.

COMMITMENT LETTER: A formal offer by a lender making explicit the terms under which it agrees to lend money to a borrower over a certain period of time.

COMPLETION: The point after which the project's cash flows become the primary method of repayment. It occurs after a series of completion tests (technical, financial, and legal) are satisfied. Usually, completion occurs months or even years after the project is actually built and commissioned. Prior to completion, the primary sources of repayment are sponsor and/or contractor guarantees.

COMPLETION SUPPORT: The contingent *guarantees* provided by the project sponsors and contractors before *completion*. These can take the form of corporate guarantees, surety bonds, and letters of credit. The lenders are entitled to call on these guarantees at any time before completion to cover cost overruns, ramp-up failures, and other defaults.

COMPREHENSIVE COVERAGE: Insurance or *guarantee* cover that combines both commercial risk coverage and *PRI* coverage. Typically provided by ECAs.

CONSULTANT TRUST FUNDS: A financial and administrative arrangement between an MDB and an external donor under which the donor (usually an OECD country) entrusts funds to the MDB to finance a specific development-related activity. Consultant Trust Funds pay for services of consultants engaged by MDBs for assignments in support of operational work. Grant agreements often stipulate use of consultants from the donor country.

CORPORATE FINANCE: The practice and philosophy of the ways firms select and finance their investments, choose between debt and *equity* instruments, and disburse cash back to shareholders. Technically, *project finance* is part of corporate finance. As a short-cut, corporate finance is often used to mean "on-balance sheet," rather than "off-balance sheet," financing of projects.

CURRENCY INCONVERTIBILITY AND TRANSFER COVER: A form of *PRI* that protects investors against possible losses from financial crises, hard currency shortages, or political actions that result in a failure of the host country to allow the conversion or transfer of its own currency into foreign currency. This type of insurance does not cover currency depreciation or devaluation.

DELEGATED AUTHORITY: Authority granted to commercial banks or exporters to approve insurance/guarantees without specific approval from the *ECA*. Typically, the ECA gives this approval based on previous experience with the bank/exporter. For example, U.S. Ex-Im Bank has an active working capital gurantee program with delegated authority lenders.

DEVELOPMENT FINANCE INSTITUTION (DFI): Financial institutions created by governments to stimulate and mobilize private investment in private sector projects in developing and emerging economies. DFIs can be *bilateral* or *multilateral*.

DEVELOPMENT IMPACT: The economic and social consequences of a project supported by a DFI. It is usually measured by incremental GDP growth stimulated, employment, infrastructure improvements, technology transferred, schools and hospitals funded, and so forth.

DIRECT LOAN: A loan from an *ECA* or an MDB to a borrower without the intermediation of another bank. It is the opposite of a *guaranteed loan.*

ELIGIBLE COSTS: The sum total of the bona fide project costs that includes personnel, durable equipment, subcontracting, travel and subsistence, financing costs, allocated overhead costs, and other specific project costs. Costs are eligible only when they are necessary for the project and are provided for in project contracts. For *ECAs,* eligible costs are associated with exported goods and services plus a small (15 percent) component for "local" costs.

EMERGING MARKETS: Less-developed countries experiencing rapid economic growth and liberalization of government restrictions on free commerce. The term has almost completely replaced *developing countries* and the former *Second* and *Third World.*

ENVIRONMENTAL IMPACT ASSESSMENT (EIA): A method of identifying the environmental effects of a project. Most MDBs and *ECAs* follow the World Bank EIA guidelines.

EQUITY: Net worth; assets minus liabilities. The stockholder's residual ownership position in a company or project. Some MDBs are willing to provide equity for projects, but *ECAs* do not.

EXPORT CREDIT AGENCY (ECA): A government-owned or sponsored financial agency offering *loans, guarantees,* credit insurance, or financial *technical assistance* to support exporters.

EXPORT CREDITS: Financing provided to an exporter or a foreign buyer from a commercial bank or *ECA* during pre- or postshipment operations.

EXPOSURE: From the perspective of a lender or an insurer, the potential loss in the event of nonpayment by a borrower or counterparty of the insured entity.

EXPOSURE FEE: A fee that protects lenders against possible defaults by borrowers. Exposure fees are the primary pricing mechanism by *ECAs* for direct and *guaranteed* loans and export credit insurance. Exposure fees are based on several factors, including country risk, tenor of the loan, and type of borrower (sovereign versus private enterprise). Exposure fees are usually considered an eligible project cost.

EXPROPRIATION: The official seizure by a government of private property. Any government maintains this right according to international law as long as prompt and adequate compensation is given. This risk is one of the basic *PRI* coverages. PRI policies also cover "creeping" or de facto expropriation.

FACILITY FEE: Up-front payment made by a borrower to a lender for arranging a *loan*. Usually, it is paid out of the proceeds from the first disbursement of funds.

FEASIBILITY STUDY: A comprehensive assessment of the technical, financial, and legal feasibility of a proposed project. A credible feasibility study is usually required by project finance lenders. The expense associated with preparing a feasibility study is usually borne by the project sponsor, although agencies such as USTDA can help defray some costs.

FINANCIAL GUARANTEE: A commitment or assurance that in the event of nonpayment of an export credit by a foreign borrower, the *ECA* will indemnify the financing bank if the terms and conditions of its *guarantees* are fulfilled.

FOREIGN DIRECT INVESTMENT (FDI): Investment in a foreign company or foreign joint venture. The investment is normally made in cash but sometimes in the form of plant and equipment or know-how. As defined by the OECD for statistical purposes, FDI is investment in at least 10 percent of voting stock of a foreign company. FDI is typically a *long-term* investment in unlisted companies or projects, as opposed to *short-term* portfolio investment in listed securities.

GRACE PERIOD: An interval of time allowed to the borrower by the lender after *loan* proceeds are disbursed and before repayment of principal begins. In *project finance,* the grace period usually covers the construction period plus 6 to 12 months.

GRANT: Financing extended by a government agency to a recipient government or a private enterprise that does not carry interest or the obligation to repay. For example, TDA and USAID have a variety of grant programs to promote international development.

GREENFIELD: A new capital investment as opposed to an acquisition of existing assets. Typically, the *project finance* loans provided by MDBs are for *greenfield* investments or major expansions.

GUARANTEE: Any assurance of payment or compensation given to the entity financing an export credit, which is to be honored in the event of default or nonpayment by the primary obligor.

INSURANCE: Cover that indemnifies the insured from loss due to a specified type of contingency or peril. Insurance in project finance is commercial, political, or comprehensive.

LENDER: An investor who provides (senior) debt to a company or project. Typically, lenders are MDBs and commercial banks, but they also can be institutional investors and corporations.

LETTER OF INTEREST (LI): A preexport marketing tool. An LI is an indication of willingness to consider financing for a given export transaction that can be used to assure counterparties. However, an LI does not imply a commitment to finance.

LIBOR: The London Interbank Offered Rate of interest on deposits traded between major banks. There is a different LIBOR rate for each deposit maturity and currency (e.g., Euro LIBOR).

LIMITED RECOURSE FINANCE: See *Project Financing.*

LOAN: A senior debt instrument that is typically held privately rather than traded on an exchange or over the counter (a *bond*).

LOAN GUARANTEE: A partial or comprehensive assurance of repayment provided by an *ECA,* an MDB, or another entity to a lender.

LONG-TERM: Repayment terms greater than five years. OECD rules limit the tenor that can be offered to borrowers. For *project financing, ECAs* are limited to an average loan life of 7.25 years, which is equal to 14 years of level repayment or 12 years of mortgage-style repayment.

MEDIUM-TERM: Repayment terms usually ranging from one to five years.

MULTILATERAL: Agreements or arrangements that involve more than two countries as opposed to *bilateral.* Multilateral banks include the World Bank, IDB, and EBRD.

OECD ARRANGEMENT: An agreement adopted in 1978 by members of the Paris-based Organization for Economic Cooperation and Development (OECD) to limit credit competition among member governments in officially supported *export credits.* The OECD Arrangement superseded the OECD Consensus.

ORGANIZATION FOR ECONOMIC CO-OPERATION AND DEVELOPMENT (OECD): A group of 30 (mostly wealthy) member countries sharing a commitment to democratic government and the market economy. OECD also produces studies, decisions, and recommendations to promote "rules of the game" in areas where multilateral agreement is necessary for individual countries to make progress in a global economy, such as export credits, foreign investment, and intellectual property.

PARTIAL RISK GUARANTEE: Used typically in the context of a *capital markets* financing. An MDB may issue a *guarantee* that covers specific risks (e.g., devaluation) in support of a locally or internationally placed *project finance bond.*

POLITICAL RISK INSURANCE (PRI): Insurance or *guarantee* cover that protects the exporter or financing bank from nonpayment by the buyer or borrower because of political events in the buyer's country or a third country through which either goods or payment must pass. The four basic PRI covers offered by insurers include inconvertibility and transfer restrictions (but not devaluation); *political violence* and war; *expropriation;* and *breach of government contract.*

POLITICAL VIOLENCE COVER: A form of *PRI* that covers loss of assets or income due to war, revolution, insurrection or politically motivated civil strife, terrorism, or sabotage.

PREMIUM RATE: The cost of insurance per dollar of cover, usually calculated on the gross invoice value for *short-term* sales or on the financed portion for *medium-* and *long-term* sales. PRI providers often distinguish between the current rate and a lower standby rate, which is similar to the commitment fee of a *loan*.

PRIVATE EQUITY: Investment in the unlisted stock of a privately held company or project. *Venture capital* refers to early-stage investments, while mezzanine capital refers to later-stage investments when the company is up and running but not quite ready for a public offering. Private equity is often used to denote later-stage investing in established companies; for example, in the context of management buyouts.

PROJECT FINANCING: A technique for financing the projects of a firm. It is a form of "off-balance sheet" financing from the perspective of the sponsoring entity. The primary source of loan repayment is the individual project rather than the entire asset base of the firm.

QUASI-EQUITY: A type of financing that is usually considered debt for tax purposes but that maintains the characteristics of *equity*, such as flexible repayment, higher rates of return, and lack of a security package. Payments to quasi-equity investors are subordinated to senior lenders.

RECOURSE: The right of a financial institution to demand payment from the guarantor of a *loan* when the primary obligor fails to pay. *Project financing* is often referred to as limited recourse financing because the lender cannot force the sponsor to repay the debt after *completion*.

REFINANCING: Repaying existing debt and entering into a new *loan,* typically to meet some corporate objective, such as lengthening maturity or lowering the interest rate. MDBs typically do not provide refinancing loans, but may include limited refinancing as part of the eligible project costs.

REINSURANCE: One lead insurer (e.g., MIGA) fronts the entire cover, while participating insurers (e.g., private-sector players) provide reinsurance. Reinsurance is used to expand the available capacity for any single project or country.

REPAYMENT STYLE: Level repayment of principal, mortgage-style (equal payments of principal and interest), or tailored.

REPAYMENT TERM: The term (also known as the tenor) of the *loan;* e.g., 20 semiannual installments.

RISK CAPITAL: Usually synonymous with *equity* funding, particularly in early stages.

SECURED DEBT: Senior debt that has first claim on specified assts in the event of default. *Project finance loans* are usually secured with all assets of the project and a pledge of sponsor shares.

SHORT-TERM: Repayment terms generally of up to 180 days. Berne Union *OECD* guidelines for *short-term ECA* insurance refer to repayment terms of up to two years depending on the product and the size of transaction.

SMALL TO MEDIUM-SIZED ENTERPRISES (SMEs): Enterprises with between 10 and 300 employees, with total assets of up to $15 million and total annual sales of up to $15 million.

STRUCTURED FINANCE: Financing arrangements that are customized to the specific needs of a borrower.

SUBORDINATED DEBT: All debt (both *short-* and *long-term*) that, by agreement, is subordinated to senior debt. Often subordinated debt is considered a type of *quasi-equity.* Some MDBs offer this type of debt, but *ECAs* do not.

SUPPLIER CREDIT: A financial arrangement in which the supplier (exporter) extends credit to the buyer to finance the buyer's purchases. Normally the buyer pays a portion of the contract value in cash and issues a promissory note or accepts a draft to evidence the obligation to pay the remainder to the exporter. *ECAs* can then insure or guarantee the draft or promissory note.

TECHNICAL ASSISTANCE: The transfer or adaptation of knowledge, practices, technologies, or skills that foster economic development. Financing for this type of assistance is generally granted in order to contribute to the design and/or implementation of a project or program to increase the physical capital stock of the host country.

TENOR: The total repayment period of a *loan*. Also referred to as the "term." Door-to-door tenor refers to the *grace period* (during construction) plus the repayment period. *OECD* rules limit the tenor of the loans that can be extended by *ECAs*.

TIED AID PROGRAM: Provided by agencies of the rich-country governments, sometimes in conjunction with their national *ECAs*. Tied aid differs from typical *export credit* terms offered by ECAs in that it usually involves concessionary terms: total maturities longer than 20 years, interest rates equal to one-half to two-thirds of market rates in the currency of denomination, or large grants.

VENTURE CAPITAL: Risk capital extended to start-up or small going concerns. Venture capital is a form of private *equity*.

WAITING PERIOD: The period following the occurrence of a loss during which exporters or banks must wait before filing a claim with an export credit insurance agency.

WORKING CAPITAL: Cash required to fund inventories and accounts receivable. The accounting definition is current assets less current liabilities. MDBs can fund start-up working capital as an eligible project cost. ECAs have programs to assist the accumulation of export-related working capital.

Index